# They Thought They Were Free

# They Thought

# They Were Free

## THE GERMANS 1933–45

### MILTON MAYER

THE UNIVERSITY OF CHICAGO PRESS
CHICAGO & LONDON

THE UNIVERSITY OF CHICAGO PRESS, CHICAGO 60637
The University of Chicago Press, Ltd., London

Copyright 1955 by The University of Chicago. All rights reserved
Published 1955. Sixth Impression 1971
Printed in the United States of America

ISBN: 0–226–51190–1 (clothbound); 0–226–51192–8 (paperbound)
Library of Congress Catalog Card Number: 55–5137

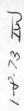

THIS BOOK IS DEDICATED
TO MY TEN NAZI FRIENDS:

Karl-Heinz Schwenke, *tailor*

Gustav Schwenke, *unemployed tailor's apprentice*

Carl Klingelhöfer, *cabinetmaker*

Heinrich Damm, *unemployed salesman*

Horstmar Rupprecht, *high-school student*

Heinrich Wedekind, *baker*

Hans Simon, *bill-collector*

Johann Kessler, *unemployed bank clerk*

Heinrich Hildebrandt, *teacher*

Willy Hofmeister, *policeman*

> The Pharisee stood and prayed thus with himself,
> "God, I thank Thee, that I am not as other men are."

## Foreword to the 1966 Printing

Let a tract for the times be republished after a hundred years or a thousand and there can be no question of its having been timeless from the first. But let it be republished after ten years and the author is lucky if he gets off with no notice at all and an unbloodied head. "Things" have changed in ten years, and they have not changed as he promised (or appeared to promise) that they would. What he would give now if only he hadn't written this line or that one! Let him change them, then, and bring the work up to date —the publisher is generous in these small matters.

In the always admirable hope of playing it safe, I have taken advantage of the publisher's generosity and made all the changes in this edition that I was sure I was safe in making. They were two in number. I inserted the word "late" before a reference to Jawaharlal Nehru and I substituted "Stalin" for "Malenkov" in an abstract reference to modern dictatorship. Otherwise the book stands as it was first published, and if I must eat my words (except for those two), I must eat them.

Every thing changes. Every thing but one. Even the medieval Schoolmen admitted a limitation on God's omnipotence: He cannot change the past. He can, in his own time, disclose it, or let man stumble on it. But he cannot change it. The pre-Nazi and Nazi lives of my ten Nazi friends—and of some millions of other Germans like them—are and ever will be what they were ten years ago and twenty. To the extent that I read them right then, and wrote them right then, the account is long since complete. Nor has anything been revealed in the events of the past ten years (including the trials in Germany compelled by Eichmann's in Israel) to alter the picture that my ten Nazi friends drew of themselves.

When this book was first published it received some attention from the critics but none at all from the public. Nazism was finished in the bunker in Berlin and its death warrant signed on the bench at Nuremberg. It had gone out with a bang. Now there was nothing but rubble between the Americans and the Russians, standing face to face and armed to the teeth. Nobody wanted to hear about what was well gone and well forgotten—least of all to hear that the blood of millions of people had bought nothing definitely durable. Hitler had attacked the civilized world, and the civilized world, including by happiest accident the uncivilized Russians, had destroyed him. *Basta.*

But the civilized world was not, even then, so well satisfied with what it had done and with what, even then, it was doing, as to be able to stop doing what it was doing and take a long thoughtful look at what it had done. Nazism was a drug on the market. This book—and not this one alone— became a collector's item without collectors. But occasionally the publisher got an inquiry from a person (or a school or a college) who wanted it and couldn't get it. The inquiries increased to an interesting trickle. As "things" changed, on the whole for the worse, and the postwar world became the prewar world, and disarmament became rearmament, there arose a modestly circumscribed sentiment that it might be profitable to find out what it was that had made "the Germans" act as badly as they did.

Dreadful deeds like Auschwitz had been done before in human history, though never on so hideously handsome a scale. But they had not been done before in an advanced Christian society like—well, like ours. If we would keep such deeds from ever being done again, at least in advanced Christian societies, it might be worth digging a little deeper than the shallow grave so hurriedly dug at Nuremberg. After the heat of the long moment had gone down, it was equally difficult to cling to the pleasurable doctrine that the Germans were by nature the enemies of mankind and to cling to the still more pleasurable doctrine that it was possible for one (or two or three) madmen to make and unmake the history of the world. These were the things that had met the bloodshot eye. But man has many saving graces, and not the least of them is his impulse to sober up between brawls.

Four wonderful facts of life contributed to the sobriety. First, the Jews of Germany (and of Poland, and of where all else) were dead, and some humanistic men in America and elsewhere had supposed at one time that it was necessary to go to war with Germany to "save the Jews." That, as it turned out, had not been the way (however gratifying its taking may have been to the humanistic impulses). Second, the destruction of Hitler had involved the prior destruction of a whole nation to a degree that was possible to the technology of total war in which battlefields are only incidental areas of operation; and the nation which had been destroyed and revived (by those who had just destroyed it) was now the industrial and military titan of Europe. Third, the Germans were now civilized Christians again and, more than that, good democrats and the front-line defenders of Christian democracy against atheist tyranny. Fourth, after so much blood and wealth invested, and then balm and wealth invested, the suspicion persisted that the "German problem," whatever it was, had not been solved and would not be solved by repeated application of the same dosage.

The "German problem" moves in and out of focus as the twentieth century continues to produce—at an always accelerating tempo—more history than it can consume. Korea is forgotten, and Hungary, Cyprus, and Suez are the new sensations; Hungary, Cyprus, and Suez slide into sudden oblivion, and we are all agog at Tibet and the Congo; Tibet and the Congo vanish before we have time to find them on the map (or to find a map that has them) and Cuba explodes; Cuba subsides to something combining a simmer and a snarl, and Vietnam and Rhodesia (or is it Southern Rhodesia?) seize us. Ghana, Guiana, Guinea. Crisis is our diet, served up as exotic dishes, and dishes ever more exotic, before we are able to swallow (let alone digest) those that were just before us. Remember the "Lebanon crisis" of 1958, in which the United States was deeply involved? Of course not. Who would, these days? Who could? And why?

The "German problem" is different. It is off center stage sometimes, but it is never offstage altogether. Most Americans are inattentive to it—they can't be attentive to *everything*—unless something as pictorial as the Berlin Wall becomes a one-season wonder. (Whatever else it was, the Wall was the worst political *gaffe* since Paris snatched Helen). But to the Europeans—including the Germans—Germany and the Germans are the first order of business every season. The Englishman who remembers the summer of 1940 is dismayed to see the new German *Wehrmacht* conducting exercises on British soil, but he is undismayed to discover that the new *Bürger in Uniform* with the new *innere Führung*—the "civilians in uniform" with "self-leadership"

—were a myth successfully designed to lull the uneasiness of Germany's conquerors.

*Dummer Michel*, the "little man" like my ten Nazis, never accepted the myth. He drags his goose-stepping feet. He may be as provincial as he ever was, as uninformed as he ever was, as sheltered as he ever was by the shabbiest press in the western world. He may not know that the clamor for the "lost lands" beyond the Oder-Neisse has no other purpose than to keep him in line, and that that clamor, like the clamor for reunification, can be satisfied only by a Third World War. But he is not *dumm* clear out to the rind. He knows that, for the first time in his history, he can earn as as worker five times what he can as a soldier. And he knows that the United States is willing to pay him well for the privilege of maintaining its own military establishment in his country—to protect him, of course, from the godless Communist conquest that Goebbels promised.

For five, six, seven years after the Second World War, the German in his ruins wanted only to live. Today he wants to live it up—and why not?—while it lasts. Always while it lasts. The sovietized East German gets out if he can, over or under or through the Wall, to the golden West of West Berlin and then to the still more golden West of the Ruhr; and if he can't, he spends what he has as soon as he has it. *While it lasts.* In the Löwenbräu Keller in Munich the free-enterprising West German sops up the last of the butter-gravy with the last of the bread, pushes his plate away, takes a pull at his stein, lights his cigar, and says, "When I have it here," patting his stomach, "*nobody* can take it away from me."

Full, and more than full, employment is still the fact in the Federal Republic (and in the Democratic Republic, which the "lost land" irridentism of the cynical Western map-makers calls "Middle Germany"). But the bloom is off the *Wirtschaftswunder*—the economic miracle—as, soon or late, it always is. The West German inflation is so spectacular that the budget has to be cut—and the cut is achieved by eliminating the increases promised the civil servants and old-age pensioners to offset the cost of inflation. *Dummer Michel*, whose profit-sharing stocks didn't go up (or actually went down). *Dummer Michel*, who has no expense account and therefore no share in the miracle—unless he compares his condition with that of the ruins twenty years ago. *Dummer Michel*, who was honest, industrious, dependable, and who, in the general moral decline, has become so much less of some of these things that the very face of Germany, so efficiently spick and span before (and in) Hitler's time, is changed by the roadside litter. *Dummer Michel*, the legendary German Worker, whose legend (perhaps for the best) has lost its hold on him.

*While it lasts.* My ten Nazi friends, when I knew them ten years ago, had never believed that "it," the thousand-year Reich, would outlive them—as it didn't. Hitler got them to a pitch and held them there, screaming at them day in and day out for twelve years. They were uneasy through it all. If they believed in Nazism—as all of them did, in substantial part or in all of it—they still got what they could out of it while the getting was good. None of them was astounded when the getting turned bad.

*While it lasts.* The satellite East Germans have the Russians on their backs; my East German friends persuade me that not 30 per cent of them would support the regime there. The satellite West Germans ply their tools and their trades on the backs of the generous Americans whose mercenary "shield" they know themselves to be; my West German friends persuade me that not fewer than 90 per cent of them would support, and, indeed, do support, this thorough-ly cynical pretense of policy. In eastern—Communist—Europe my friends persuade me that Germany, West and East, is the unchanging centerpiece of all policy and all politics in the Soviet Union, Poland and Czechoslovakia.

"The" West Germans want their place in the nuclear sun—the new Lebensraum of mass-murderous power—to erase the last insult they suffered in being demilitarized by the idealistic Americans whose ideals were so sternly pro-nounced and then so sternly reversed. The Russians forbid the Americans to let the Germans have that place. But as I am writing I read a sensational and authoritative headline: *GERMAN MISSILES A-TIPPED BY U.S. SIX YEARS AGO*, followed by the American government's now com-monplace refusal to confirm or deny, followed, a few days later by a dispatch from Washington beginning, "A De-fense Department spokesman acknowledged last night that fighter-bombers of nine North Atlantic Treaty Allies, in-cluding West Germany, were armed with American nuclear warheads." Control of their use was still in American hands—only the evil-minded Bolsheviks could imagine that the Germans could not be relied upon never to get out of control.

When this book was first published ten years ago, it ended, as it still does, with these words: "It is risky to let people alone. But it is riskier still to press my ten Nazi friends—and their seventy million countrymen—to re-embrace mili-tarist anti-Communism as a way of national life." If these words had any validity ten years ago, they have some validity today—and even some small prospective relevance to my own non-Nazi country and my own non-Nazi countrymen. My ten Nazi friends and their seventy million countrymen have been ever more successfully pressed to the national way of life that they so bravely enjoyed and then, at the end, so bravely suffered in Hitler's time. The fact that two-thirds of them embrace militarist anti-Communism and the other third militarist Communism is only a detail—if a historically fatal detail. What is dreadfully, and demonstrably, bad for the Germans, and thus for the rest of the world, is their exposure to a fiery fanaticism that, in a less capable people, would burn itself out with more modest consequences.

The Germans seem to be less frightening now than they were twenty years ago. If they are, it may be because other people are more frightening now than they were then. Of the trillion dollars the world has spent for war since the Second World War ended, only an inconsequential fraction has been spent by the Germans (whose civilian enterprises, including armaments manufacture, have prospered accordingly). Things have happened elsewhere in the past twenty years that have made it impossible to claim that Auschwitz is beyond the moral comprehension of civilized men. A while back the *New York Times'* leading correspondent reported from Saigon that "there comes a time in every war when men tend to become indifferent to human suffering, even to unnecessary brutality, and we may be reaching that point in Vietnam."

The Germans are still the Germans—as aren't we all what we were, or at least no better? Who could have supposed ten years ago that they might have been otherwise? But there were some who so fondly supposed that for the world's good, and therefore for Germany's, a new way would have to be found. To say that instead their conquerors have found an old way—the educators re-educated—would be to say much too much at this date. But to say that the Germans, if a new way can be taught men, would have a harder time finding teachers today than ten years ago is not to say too little.

Where would they have found teachers ten years ago? Where but America? But it was ten years ago, and twenty, that the United States Air Force (in its own words) "produced more casualties than any other military action in the history of the world" in its great fire raid on Tokyo, and Secretary of War Henry L. Stimson, appalled by the absence of public protest in America, thought "there was something wrong with a country where no one questioned" such acts committed in its name (L. Giovannitti and F. Freed, *The Decision to Drop the Bomb* [New York: Coward-McCann, 1965]).

Still and all, I thought (and wrote) ten years ago that it might not be arrogant to assume that the Germans still looked to the Americans for light. I should change those words today if I could. I can't, for I love my country and abide in its hope and the hopes men have had of it. "We had"—always "had"—"such high hopes that the American might do *something*. Nobody else could or would, not our enemies, not our allies, or ourselves." It was not to be. "Something for the Germans," if it could have been devised, had to be abandoned to larger necessities. It is clear that it is not to be now; the time, if there was one, has passed. It passed some time before German missiles were A-tipped by the U.S. and some time after the following notice was nailed to the gate of the American prisoner-of-war camp in Babenhausen/Darmstadt in 1946:

When you, SS-man Willi Schulze, or you, Corporal Rudi Müller, stride out through this gate, your steps will lead you to freedom. Behind you lie months and years of slavish obedience, years of bloodshed, years in which human individuality suffered incredible humiliations, all of which was caused by a criminal regime whose adherents, if they have not already paid the penalty, will not escape due punishment.

You yourself are not to blame. Deluded, you blindly followed the call of a false doctrine. From now on your life in your family circle can unfold free and undisturbed. You have been freed from accursed military service, from guilt-laden German militarism. Never again will a shrill command chase you across the barracks courts or drive you to the battlefield. The ashes of your army ID card have mingled with those of Buchenwald and Dachau.

The victorious United Nations which, through their great sacrifice, have freed you and your descendants forever from military service, have assumed the responsibility of protecting your freedom. But in exchange for that great sacrifice you are duty-bound to make sure that never again in your homeland will a desire for military service arise, that never again will young Germans sacrifice the best years of their lives to the hankerings of the Prussian nobility and their war-thirsty general staff, but that they will, from now on, dedicate their strength and their gifts to peaceful ends.

The notice was signed "U.S. War Department."

# Foreword

As an American, I was repelled by the rise of National Socialism in Germany. As an American of German descent, I was ashamed. As a Jew, I was stricken. As a newspaperman, I was fascinated.

It was the newspaperman's fascination that prevailed—or at least predominated—and left me dissatisfied with every analysis of Nazism. I wanted to see this monstrous man, the Nazi. I wanted to talk to him and to listen to him. I wanted to try to understand him. We were both men, he and I. In rejecting the Nazi doctrine of racial superiority, I had to concede that what he had been I might be; what led him along the course he took might lead me.

Man (says Erasmus) learns at the school of example and will attend no other. If I could find out what the Nazi had been and how he got that way, if I could spread his example before some of my fellow-men and command their attention to it, I might be an instrument of their learning (and my own) in the age of the mass revolutionary dictatorship.

In 1935 I spent a month in Berlin trying to obtain a series of meetings with Adolf Hitler. My friend and teacher, William E. Dodd, then American Ambassador to Germany, did what he could to help me, but without success. Then I traveled in Nazi Germany for an American magazine. I saw the German people, people I had known when I visited Germany as a boy, and for the first time realized that

Nazism was a mass movement and not the tyranny of a diabolical few over helpless millions. Then I wondered if Adolf Hitler was, after all, the Nazi I wanted to see. By the time the war was over I had identified my man: the average German.

I wanted to go to Germany again and get to know this literate, bourgeois, "Western" man like myself to whom something had happened that had not (or at least not yet) happened to me and my fellow-countrymen. It was seven years after the war before I went. Enough time had passed so that an American non-Nazi might talk with a German Nazi, and not so much time that the events of 1933–45, and especially the inner feeling that attended those events, would have been forgotten by the man I sought.

I never found the average German, because there is no average German. But I found ten Germans sufficiently different from one another in background, character, intellect, and temperament to represent, among them, some millions or tens of millions of Germans and sufficiently like unto one another to have been Nazis. It wasn't easy to find them, still less to know them. I brought with me one asset: I really wanted to know them. And another, acquired in my long association with the American Friends Service Committee: I really believed that there was "that of God" in every one of them.

My faith found that of God in my ten Nazi friends. My newspaper training found that of something else in them, too. They were each of them a most marvelous mixture of good and bad impulses, their lives a marvelous mixture of good and bad acts. I *liked* them. I couldn't help it. Again and again, as I sat or walked with one or another of my ten friends, I was overcome by the same sensation that had got in the way of my newspaper reporting in Chicago years before. I *liked* Al Capone. I liked the way he treated his mother. He treated her better than I treated mine.

I found—and find—it hard to judge my Nazi friends. But I confess that I would rather judge them than myself. In my own case I am always aware of the provocations and handicaps that excuse, or at least explain, my own bad acts. I am always aware of my good intentions, my good reasons for doing bad things. I should not like to die tonight, because some of the things that I had to do today, things that look very bad for me, I had to do in order to do something very good tomorrow that would more than compensate for today's bad behavior. But my Nazi friends *did* die tonight; the book of their Nazi lives is closed, without their having been able to do the good they may or may not have meant to do, the good that might have wiped out the bad they did.

By easy extension, I would rather judge Germans than Americans. Now I see a little better how Nazism overcame Germany—not by attack from without or by subversion from within, but with a whoop and a holler. It was what most Germans wanted—or, under pressure of combined reality and illusion, came to want. They wanted it; they got it; and they liked it.

I came back home a little afraid for my country, afraid of what it might want, and get, and like, under pressure of combined reality and illusion. I felt—and feel—that it was not German Man that I had met, but Man. He happened to be in Germany under certain conditions. He might be here, under certain conditions. He might, under certain conditions, be I.

If I—and my countrymen—ever succumbed to that concatenation of conditions, no Constitution, no laws, no police, and certainly no army would be able to protect us from harm. For there is no harm that anyone else can do to a man that he cannot do to himself, no good that he cannot do if he will. And what was said long ago is true: Nations are made not of oak and rock but of men, and, as the men are, so will the nations be.

My compulsion to go to Germany and to live there, in a small town, with my wife and children was spurred by Carl Friedrich von Weizsäcker, of Göttingen University, who, with his wife Gundi, lived in my home while he served as Visiting Professor of Physics at the University of Chicago in 1948–49. I corresponded with an old friend, James M. Read, who was serving as Chief of Educational and Cultural Relations in the United States High Commission for the Occupation of Germany. Messrs. Read and Weizsäcker converged on Max Horkheimer, Dean of the Institute for Social Research, in Frankfurt University, and he arranged my appointment. What I did after I got there (and after I got back) was my own responsibility, but where I went was the responsibility of my three friends. It was they who packed me off to live for a year, as close as possible to the Germans, as far as possible from the conquering "Ami," in the town I call Kronenberg.

MILTON MAYER

CARMEL, CALIFORNIA
December 25, 1954

# Contents

# Contents

## PART III. THEIR CAUSE AND CURE

## PART I

Ten Men

# Kronenberg

November 9, 1638:

## "HEAR, YE TOWNSFOLK, HONEST MEN"

It is ten o'clock at night—give or take ten minutes. The great E-bell of the Katherine Church has begun to strike the hour. Between its seventh and eighth strokes, the Parish bell begins to strike. You would suppose that the sacristan of the Parish Church had been awakened by the Katherine bell, pulled himself out of bed, and got to his bell rope just in time to avoid complete humiliation (like a man running shirtless and shoeless to a wedding to get there before the ceremony is over). But you would probably be wrong, for every night, ever since there have been two bells in Kronenberg, the first stroke from the Parish Church has come just after the seventh from the Katherine; in deference, perhaps, for the Katherine Church was once (up until the Reformation a century ago) a cathedral.

Now Kronenberg has, besides two church bells and two churches, six thousand churched souls; and a university, with a theological faculty and almost a hundred students; and a Castle, which crowns the hill on which the closely packed, semicircular town is built (a hill so steep in places that some of the houses can be entered only from the top floor); and a river at the foot of the hill, the Werne. The Werne isn't navigable this far up from the Rhine, but its course around the flowering hill conspires with the Castle at the top, the massed gables of the timbered old houses that climb to the edge of the Castle park, and the cobblestoned lanes and alleys that gird the hillside like tangled hoops, to make of Kronenberg a picture-book town on a picture-book countryside.

The town has had its troubles, as what town hasn't? In the half-dozen centuries past it has changed hands a dozen times. It has been stormed, taken, liberated, and stormed and taken again. But it has never been burned; its prettiness (for it is small enough to be pretty rather than beautiful) may have shamed off the torches which have gutted so many old towns; and now, in 1638, Kronenberg is always designated as "old Kronenberg," an ancient place.

The Great War of Europe is twenty years old, but maybe it is over; the Prince of Hesse has decided to join the Peace of Prague, to drive the Protestant Swedes out of the Catholic Empire without, it is hoped, incurring submission to the Catholic Emperor in Vienna. True, Catholic France has just attacked Catholic Spain and, in alliance with Protestant Sweden, has just declared war on the Emperor. But Kronenberg has only heard vaguely about these wonderful events, and who knows what they mean? "The King makes war, and the people die"; it's an old, old saying in Kronenberg.

Times have been very hard everywhere these last years, in Kronenberg, too; taxes and tolls always higher, men, animals, and grain taken, always more, for the armies. But the war, moving from north to south, from south to north, and from north to south again, has spared the town, except for a siege which was driven off by the Protestant armies. All in all, the Kronenbergers can't complain. And they don't.

Pestilence and famine recur in Kronenberg—as where don't they?—and, where there are Jews, what is one to expect? After the Black Death of 1348, the Judenschule, or prayer-house, was burned in Kronenberg, and the Jews were driven away. (Everyone knew they had poisoned the wells, all over Europe.) A few years afterward the finances of the Prince of Hesse were so straitened that he had to pawn Kronenberg to the Jews in Frankfurt, but in 1396 Good King Wenceslaus declared void all debts to the Christ-killers. But that wasn't the end of it, because the princes always brought the Jews back, to do the un-Christian business of banking forbidden Christians by canon law. So it was, until 1525, when the Bürgermeister of Kronenberg implored the Prince to drive the Jews out again. "They buy stolen articles," he said. "If they were gone, there would be no more stealing." So the Prince drove them out again; but he exercised the imperial privilege given by Karl V to keep a certain number of Jews in the town on the condition that they pay a protection tax, a Schutzgeld. If they failed to pay the Schutzgeld, the Prince removed his protection.

Those were good times, before the Great War of Europe. Times are hard now; but they might be worse (and nearly everywhere are) than they are in Kronenberg, and tonight the burghers and their manservants and their maidservants are sleeping contented, or as contented as burghers and their manservants and maidservants may reasonably expect to be in this life. So are their summer-fattened cattle and their sheep in the meadows (it is not yet cold in early November), and their pigs and chickens and geese and ducks in the barn at the back of the house; sleeping, all, at ten o'clock.

The two church bells are dissonant, the Parish bell's A-flat ground tone against the Katherine's E; workmanship

5

is not what it was when the Katherine bell was cast three or four centuries ago. But it takes more than the dissonance of the bells to awaken the people of Kronenberg. It takes even more than the rooster on top of the Town Hall to do it.

The Town Hall rooster is a wonderful rooster. It flaps its wings and crows a heroic crow, once for the quarter-hour, twice for the half-hour, three times for the three-quarter-hour, and four times for the hour—and then it crows the hour. If (as it does) it begins its ten o'clock crow when the Katherine bell is finished and the Parish bell has just struck its sixth stroke, the fault cannot be the rooster's, for the bell-ringers are human and fallible, but the rooster is mechanical. To say that the rooster was wrong would be to say that the Town Clock was wrong, and this no one says.

Now the dissonance of the two bells is as nothing to the cacophony of the rooster and the last four strokes of the Parish bell; still the Kronenbergers sleep. They sleep until their own flesh-and-blood roosters respond to the crowing atop the Town Hall. The response begins, naturally, in the barns and dooryards near by and fans out in an epidemic descent down the whole Kronenberg hill. The roosters awaken the ducks and the geese, then the pigs and the sheep; then the cattle stir and low. The house dogs are the last to be heard from, but, once begun barking, they are the last to stop.

All Kronenberg turns over underneath its mountainous feather beds. Everyone half-awakens with the dissymphony, remains half-awake until it is over, and then slips back, but not all the way back, into sleep. The Kronenbergers have yet to have their ten o'clock lullaby, the lullaby they have had, and their ancestors before them, every night of their lives, the Night Watchman's Stundenrufe, or calling of the hours.

Every night the Night Watchman stands in the Market Place until the clatter of the bells and the animals is ended; an old pensioner in the raiment of his office, a long green greatcoat and a high-crowned green hat, his horn slung over his back, his lantern in one hand, his pikestaff in the other. Staff, lantern, and horn, Night Watchman himself, are increasingly ornamental nowadays. As he makes his hourly round, he watches for fires, which are rare in cautious, pinchpenny old Kronenberg, and for a still rarer pig broken out from a barn.

But he has his dignity, this man who, if only symbolically these days, has the community in his care; he will not compete with roosters and geese. When the last echo of the clatter has died—and not before—he puts his horn to his lips and blows it ten times and then begins his descent through the town, clumping heavy-booted on the cobblestones, singing the Kronenbergers back to sleep:

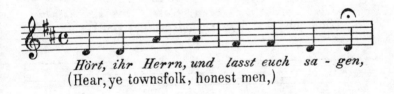

*Hört, ihr Herrn, und lasst euch sa - gen,*
(Hear, ye townsfolk, honest men,)

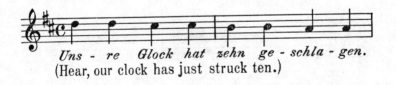

*Uns - re Glock hat zehn ge - schla - gen.*
(Hear, our clock has just struck ten.)

By this time, of course, the Town Hall rooster has long since crowed his one crow for 10:15.

Zehn Ge - bo - te setzt' Gott ein,
(Ten Commandments God has given,)

Gib, dass wir ge - hor - sam sein.
(Who obeys them will be shriven.)

Men - schen-wa - chen kann nichts nüt - zen;
(Watchmen's watching won't protect you;)

Gott muss wa - chen, Gott muss schüt-zen.
(God must watch you, God protect you.)

Herr, durch dei - ne Güt und Macht,
(Lord, by thy e'erlasting might,)

Gib uns ei - ne gu - te Nacht.
(Give us all a quiet night.)

Holding his lantern aloft, the Night Watchman goes through the town, as his counterpart goes through every town in Germany, singing this self-same lullaby from ten o'clock on. A few minutes before eleven (or after; who knows?) he is back at the Market Place, and when the eleven o'clock racket is over, he blows his horn and again makes his round. This time, instead of singing "Zehn Gebote setzt' Gott ein," he sings "Elf der Jünger blieben treu, Hilf dass wir im Tod ohn' Reu" ("Christ's eleven served him true, May we die without one's rue"); at twelve he sings "Zwölf, das ist das Ziel der Zeit; Mensch, bedenk die Ewigkeit" ("Twelve sets men from this day free; Think ye of Eternity"); and at one he sings "Eins ist allein der ew'ge Gott, Der uns trägt aus aller Not" ("One alone is always there, He who lifts us up from care").

From one o'clock on, until dawn, the Night Watchman sings no more. His song has no more stanzas and certainly no more listeners. Each hour, after the bells and the beasts subside, he blows his horn and makes his round, and the Kronenbergers sleep. Should one of them awaken and see a light outside, he knows whose it is and sleeps again. The town will be up at dawn; the day ends at dark. Everyone works, nobody reads, and tallow, except in the university, the hospital, and the Castle, is burned for only an hour or two to feed house stock and mend harness or stockings by.

Just outside the Town Wall, where the toll road along the Werne enters the town at the Frankfurt Gate, stand a half-dozen new houses around a burgeoning square called "Frankfurterplatz." The town is getting bigger, overflowing the new wall of two centuries ago as it has overflowed each successive ring of walls that protected it. The days when the town hugged the Castle for protection are over; this is the middle of the seventeenth century of Christianity, and men may live outside the walls without much danger.

At the corner of Frankfurterplatz, where a wide, un-cobblestoned road runs west outside the wall and along it, a nameless road known as the Mauerweg, is the new inn, the Jägerhof, the Huntsmen's Rest. It is a fine two-storied place with a commodious dormitory above, a public room and a private room (or clubroom) below, and the innkeeper's family quarters in back.

Tonight the lights are burning late in the public room of the Huntsmen's Rest. The old soldiers, the Home Reserve company, are celebrating with a stein of beer or two the fifteenth anniversary of the liberation of the homeland from the shackles of Vienna. The Home Reserve company are patriotic Hessians, of course, but first and last they are Kronenbergers, and it was fifteen years ago tonight that the siege of Kronenberg was lifted. A great event for the old soldiers, and a great anniversary.

It is after midnight when, with two steins of beer or three or four inside them, they leave the Huntsmen's Rest, some of the more patriotic old boys bent on continuing the celebration. The innkeeper does not want to get into trouble with the old soldiers or the authorities, and the instant the soldiers are gone he comes in from the back, snuffs out the lights, and goes to bed.

November 9, 1938:

The public room of the Huntsmen's Rest, at the corner of Frankfurterplatz and the Mauerweg, is alight tonight and crowded with a company of old soldiers celebrating the fifteenth anniversary of the liberation of the homeland from the chains of Versailles. It is the anniversary of the "Bloody Parade" in Munich, in which the Führer was arrested and imprisoned. The old soldiers are the Home Reserve Troop of the Nazi Sturmabteilung, or SA, and the Huntsmen's Rest is their regular meeting place.

Their regular meeting night is Friday, and this is Wednesday. But November 9, whatever the day of the week, is the greatest of all National Socialist Party celebrations. January 30 (the day the Führer came to power) and April 20 (the Führer's birthday) are national celebrations. November 9 is the Party's own.

The formal celebration was at 7:30 P.M. in the Municipal Theater. There were too many speeches, as usual, and one of the Party's poets, Siegfried Ruppel, recited too many of his Party poems. Then the four troops of the SA Kronenberg marched in uniform to their regular meeting places, the Reserve Troop to the upstairs room of the Huntsmen's Rest. Promotions were announced, as they always were on

11

November 9, and then the troop followed Sturmführer Schwenke down to the public room for a glass of beer or two. It is ten o'clock.

## "HEAR, OUR CLOCK HAS JUST STRUCK TEN"

Ten o'clock, precisely, and if you want to check your watch you may get the hourly beep on the National Radio or the half-minute tone signal on Prime Meridian Time by dialing 6 on the telephone. The mechanically operated Parish Church bell begins to strike the hour after the seventh stroke of the Katherine Church bell, which is also mechanically operated. As the sixth stroke of the Parish bell dies away, the mechanical rooster crows atop the Town Hall, a fleshly rooster here and there in the town responds, a few dogs bark, an ox in a far field lows, and the town is quiet. Tradition has it that the two bells and the Town Hall rooster have been dissynchronous for centuries.

Ten o'clock. The policemen on the beat open their corner telephone boxes and report, "Schmidt speaking. All in order," and the sergeant on duty says, "Good." The lights are going out except in the cinemas, the inns and hotels, the university clinics and the students' rooms and professors' studies, in the streetcars and the railroad station and the crossings, and at the street corners dimly lighted by one high-hung bulb.

Kronenberg is a quiet little university town of twenty thousand people—two towns, really, the university and the town, although the university, like all Continental universities, is scattered through the town instead of having a campus.

Everything has always been quiet in Kronenberg. In the

years that led up to National Socialism there was an occasional street fight, and one or two meetings of Nazis or Social Democrats were broken up. (The Communists were too weak to organize meetings.) In 1930, when Party uniforms were forbidden, the Party paraded quietly in white shirts, and, when the Führer spoke in Kronenberg in 1932, forty thousand people crowded quietly into a super–circus tent on the Town Meadow to hear him. (Nazi open-air meetings were forbidden.) That was the day that a Swastika flag was run up on the Castle; in England or France it might have been taken for a college-boy prank, but in Kronenberg the culprit, who proudly admitted his guilt, was heavily fined.

Kronenberg went quietly Nazi, and so it was. In the March, 1933, elections, the NSDAP, the National Socialist German Workers Party, had a two-thirds majority, and the Social Democrats went out of office. Only the university— and not the whole university—and the hard-core Social Democrats held out until the end, and in nonindustrial Kronenberg there were no trade-unions to hold the mass base of the Social Democrats. The town was as safely Nazi now, in 1938, as any town in Germany.

Of course Kronenberg isn't Germany. To begin with, it's in Hesse, and Hesse is conservative, "backward," if you will; when city people elsewhere want to call a man stupid, they call him a blinder Hesse, a "blind Hessian." And Kronenberg, so old and changeless, off the main line and the Autobahn, is conservative even for Hesse. But its very conservatism is a better guaranty of the Party's stability than the radicalism of the cities, where yesterday's howling Communists are today's howling Nazis and nobody knows just how they will howl tomorrow. A quiet town is best.

## "TEN COMMANDMENTS GOD HAS GIVEN"

The talk in the public room of the Huntsmen's Rest is (as might be expected of old soldiers) of old times, and Sturmführer Schwenke does more than his share of talking, as usual. But you have to hand it to him, he knows how to tell a story; when a character in the story roars, Schwenke doesn't say he roared—he roars himself. He tells how the SA Kronenberg got its orders fifteen years ago to assemble on November 9 and await word for the Putsch. There were 185 of them, waiting for trucks to take them to Frankfurt. They waited all day. The word never came, the trucks never came.

"I wasn't too disappointed," says Schwenke. "The time was too soon. I always said so. That's the trouble with the men at the top—they stand between the Führer and men like me who know the people and the conditions. N'ja [which in Hessian dialect means "Yep" or "So"], when the Führer got out of prison and reorganized the Party and accepted only those he knew were faithful to him, that was the right principle. With that principle, selecting the best, nothing could stop us."

The talk turns to another historic November 9, in 1918, and here again the Sturmführer does most of the talking: "I was on duty in Erfurt that night. A Bolshevik in civilian clothes came to the post and wanted to talk to the soldiers. The men chose me to represent them. The Bolshevik said we should join the townspeople and form a Workers and Soldiers Council. I said we would form our own Councils without any Reds. He said they had three cannon trained on the post, and I said we had two machine guns trained on them and we'd take our chances. They didn't have any cannon, and we didn't have any machine guns, but I hollered him down." "I'll bet you did," says one of the younger SA men, who has drifted in from another troop.

Somehow the talk drags this evening. Something is up, no one seems to know what.

Two days ago the German Councilor of Embassy in Paris, vom Rath, was shot by a Polish Jew. Immediately an intense campaign against the Jews began on the German National Radio. Are Germans to be sitting ducks all over the world for Jew murderers? Are the German people to stand helpless while the Führer's representatives are shot down by the Jew swine? Are the Schweinehunde to get off scot free? Is the wrath of the German People against the Israelite scum to be restrained any longer? "If vom Rath dies, the Jews of Germany will answer to the German People, not tomorrow, but today. The German People have suffered long enough from the parasite assassins."

This was the work of Dr. Goebbels, whom most people hated and nobody loved; even in Schwenke's loyal circle the Minister of Propaganda and Public Enlightenment was known, quietly, as Jupp der Stelzfuss, Joey the Crip. The university people didn't listen to this kind of broadcast—or, if they listened, they listened fearfully. The townspeople— the townspeople just listened. They listened as the campaign mounted hourly. Vom Rath's condition grew hourly worse. He was certain to die, and he died, on November 9, on the anniversary of the greatest day in the history of the German People, the day on which the liberators of the Homeland had shed their blood for liberty in Munich fifteen years ago.

All afternoon and evening the pitch has been mounting over the radio, and by now the Daily Kronenberger has joined in. Everywhere there are rumors. "Something will happen." What?

At the celebration in the Municipal Theater, earlier this evening, nothing was said about vom Rath or the Jews; strange. The spirit of repression is infectious; at the Huntsmen's Rest, where, ordinarily, SA men (SA men, particularly) tell stories of Jewish depravity and the SA's leadership in the Judenkampf, nothing is said this evening about the Jews, or even about the murder in Paris. No one knows why. "Something will happen." No one knows what.

## "WHO OBEYS THEM WILL BE SHRIVEN"

The door of the Huntsmen's Rest opens, and the commander of the SA Kronenberg, Standartenführer Kühling, enters, in uniform.

"Attention!" says Sturmführer Schwenke.

The SA men stand.

"Heil Hitler!" says Sturmführer Schwenke, saluting.

"Heil. Be seated," says the Standartenführer, without returning the salute.

The SA men sit.

"Sturmführer, kommen Sie mal her, come here a minute," says the Standartenführer. Schwenke rises and comes to him.

The Standartenführer says, "Heute geht die Synagogue hoch, The synagogue will be burned tonight."

It is almost midnight.

## CHAPTER 1

# Ten Men

### 1. *Karl-Heinz Schwenke, Sturmführer and janitor (formerly tailor), age 54*

It was almost midnight of November 9, 1938, when Standartenführer Kühling of the SA Kronenberg entered the Huntsmen's Rest, at the corner of Frankfurterplatz and the Mauerweg, and said:

"The synagogue will be burned tonight."

As the scene was reconstructed by principals and witnesses fifteen years afterward, there were present in the public room of the inn twenty or twenty-five uniformed members of the SA Reserve Troop, composed of men over fifty, and five or ten members of other SA troops who had dropped in. There were no other customers, and the innkeeper testified in 1948 that he was "in and out" of the public room that evening and did not hear any of the conversation or remember who was present.

After Kühling spoke, Sturmführer Schwenke turned to the men in the public room and said:

"You heard what the Standartenführer said. Those who want to help, come into the private room with me."

The Standartenführer said, "I'll be back," and left the inn.

About half the men present, according to the testimony, followed Schwenke into the private room and closed the door. Schwenke reopened the door from within, said, "No more drinking," and closed it again. Those who were left in the public room sat saying nothing for a few moments and then began talking in low tones. They testified afterward that they could hear the talk, but not the words, from the other room.

Twenty minutes later the Standartenführer re-entered the Huntsmen's Rest. The dozen or so men left in the public room were eating buttered bread and drinking coffee, playing Skat, reading the paper, or just sitting there. They got to their feet and said, "Heil Hit——"

"They still in there?" said the Standartenführer.

"Yes, Herr Standartenführer."

The Standartenführer opened the door to the private room and the talk inside stopped. The dozen or so men within got to their feet and said, "Heil Hit——"

"*Jetzt mal, los! los!* Let's get going, let's get going," said the Standartenführer, standing in the doorway. "You, Sturmführer."

"Yes, Herr Standartenführer," said Schwenke. "I thought I would send two men to reconnoiter."

"You be one of them, Sturmführer."

"Yes, Herr Standartenführer. Here, Kramer, come with me. The rest of you, remain where you are until you get orders."

"I'll be back," said the Standartenführer, leaving again.

Schwenke and Kramer walked west on the Mauerweg. Half a block down, in front of the Café Schuchardt, they stopped and stood in the entrance of the darkened café. Kramer looked up and down the street. "No police," he said. "Not a sign," said Schwenke.

They crossed the street to the synagogue, pushed open the iron fence gate, and went around the building, trying the side and back doors. The furnace-room door was unlocked, and they went in. In a few minutes they left again. As they re-entered the private room of the Huntsmen's Rest, the men stood up and said, "Heil—"

"Pechmann," said Schwenke, "I want you and Heinecke and—let me see—Dowe. Upstairs. Quick. You"—to the others—"remain. This is duty. You hear me?"

The five, including Kramer, went upstairs to the SA meeting room. In a few minutes they came down.

"I don't care," Schwenke was saying, "we can use it. We have to have *something*."

"But it's *floor* oil," said Pechmann, "and it belongs to the Theater."

"I don't care," said Schwenke, "it's *oil*. This is duty. You heard the Standartenführer, Pechmann."

"Yes, Herr Sturmführer," said Pechmann.

Pechmann, Heinecke, and Dowe headed for the Theater, a block west of the Huntsmen's Rest, and Schwenke and Kramer returned to the furnace-room of the synagogue. In a few minutes the other three SA men entered the furnace-room, carrying, among them, four three-gallon canisters. There were footsteps above, in the synagogue.

"Can I go now?" said Pechmann to Schwenke, in a whisper. "I'm on duty at six in the morning."

"Go ahead, you s——t," said Schwenke.

"Thank you, Herr Sturmführer," said Pechmann. Heinecke and Dowe left with him, without even asking permission.

"S——ts," said Schwenke.

Pechmann testified against Schwenke after the war, but he supported Schwenke's claim that there were footsteps heard in the synagogue above when the SA men were in the furnace-room. Schwenke denied having had anything to do with the floor oil taken from the Theater; he had, he said, only reconnoitered. The four canisters were never found.

Schwenke and Kramer returned to the Huntsmen's Rest around 12:50 midnight. The Sturmführer led the way to a table in the corner of the public room. Ten minutes passed. Nobody spoke in the public room; the men in the private room, beyond the door, were still talking in a murmur. The two church bells struck 1 A.M., and the rooster atop the Town Hall crowed. Then it was quiet again. Schwenke said something to Kramer, and Kramer left the inn. None of the men in the private room raised his head. Kramer returned and said something to Schwenke. Then Schwenke left the inn and returned at once.

"SA men!" he called. "The synagogue is on fire! Outside, everybody! Close off the street! It's dangerous!"

A voice said, "Shall we call the Fire Department?"

"I'm in charge!" said Schwenke. "Close off the street! It's dangerous! *Schnell*, hurry!" And he turned and went, followed by all the SA men in the inn.

The instant the last man was out the door, the innkeeper of the Huntsmen's Rest entered the public room from the swinging door behind the bar. He closed the outer door to the street, locked it, turned out the lights, and went right to bed.

## 2. *Gustav Schwenke, soldier (formerly unemployed tailor's apprentice)*, *age 26*

Neuhausen is a little summer resort on the Mariasee, an hour by the Post bus, two hours (and twenty-two cents more expensive) by the Scenic Steamer, from the old mining and textile town of Lich, in southern Austria. The Pension Goldener Engel—the Golden Angel Boarding House—

had no guests the night of November 9, 1938, except Private Gustav Schwenke of the German Military Police and his bride of a month. It was their honeymoon.

It was, as a matter of fact, their first time together since the three terrible days they'd had in Kronenberg when they were married a month before. If Gustav had decided, at the last minute, not to take the Scenic Steamer from Lich but to take the Post bus and save on the fare, it had to be admitted that he had hired a very nice room at the Goldener Engel. He got the military rate, of course, with a seasonal discount and (after hard bargaining with the host, while the bride stood by) the special three-day discount (even though the Schwenkes were going to be there only two days, the duration of Gustav's pass from his post at Lich).

Those three terrible days in Kronenberg, after the wedding in October, they had stayed at the groom's home, with the groom's father and mother and younger sister and very young brother. The groom's father, SA Sturmführer Schwenke, had been against the marriage because the bride's father was not even a Party member, and the bride (for all Sturmführer Schwenke knew; she never said anything) might even be a *Gegner*, an opponent of the regime. Frau Sturmführer Schwenke hated the bride from the first and said that the girl's family had "a history of fits." In those three days in Kronenberg, after the wedding, the bride had cried all the time (and Gustav hated crying), and Frau Sturmführer Schwenke said, "She can't help it, poor girl— it's hereditary."

Sturmführer Schwenke had wanted his oldest son to marry a strong Party woman—any strong Party woman. The boy was not a Party enthusiast, except for anti-Semitism. He was willing to join the Party in '32—glad to—when his father got him the first job he'd ever had, in the SA police.

But that was for the job. A job, any job, was all he cared about. A good boy, but he didn't have his father's spirit.

No wonder. And great wonder that he had any spirit at all.

Gustav Schwenke had wet his bed until he was twenty-two years old.

His mother, whose happiest topic of conversation was sickness (she herself had had plenty of it, but her husband "had never been sick a day in his life," except for his war wounds), told everybody in Kronenberg about her trouble with Gustav, the problem child. Everybody in Kronenberg knew that Gustav Schwenke was a bed-wetter, and Gustav knew that they knew, and he knew how they knew.

Long before he was twelve he hated his mother. One whistle from his father, and he came; a thousand whistles from his mother, and he hid. When he was twelve, his mother was pregnant. She said to him, "What if it's a little brother?" and he said, "If he cries at night, I'll cut his throat." Little Robert, when he came, cried at night, and when he cried Gustav wet his bed. Little Robert wet his, of course. "That's why he cries," his mother told Gustav, "because he's ashamed of wetting his bed." Gustav never cried.

Gustav had to pull his little brother around after school, in the play wagon, and the other kids, besides calling him Bettnässer, called him Kindermädchen, nurse girl. One day, in order to play, Gustav left the wagon, with little Robert in it, at the top of a long flight of stone steps leading down from the Market Place, and somehow the wagon went down the steps. A man stopped it halfway down, and Robert fell out and cried. Robert wasn't hurt, but Gustav got the worst beating of his life.

When Gustav was fifteen and his father's apprentice,

the Schwenke tailor-shop failed, and the whole family went on the dole. It was then that Gustav discovered that his father was more interested in politics than in work and would take bread out of his family's mouth in order to make himself a uniform or take a trip to the Nazi Party Day in Munich or Weimar or Nuremberg. His father a spendthrift, and the family hungry. Gustav had always been stingy, a saver of food, scraps of cloth, nails; now he became a real miser, and a miser he remained, with, unfortunately, nothing to save, even in his young manhood, but food, scraps of cloth, nails.

The room at the Goldener Engel on the Mariasee was nice but expensive. Still, a man wasn't married every day. And when Gustav was away from Kronenberg, he didn't feel so bad about spending something. He didn't feel so bad about anything. Away from Kronenberg your bride didn't cry and your mother didn't talk and your father didn't buy himself uniforms and you didn't wet your bed and the wagon didn't go down the steps and you would never go back to Kronenberg and you didn't care what they were doing there or anywhere else tonight. It was after one o'clock in the morning when Private Gustav Schwenke fell asleep by the side of his bride in the Pension Goldener Engel, three hundred miles from the burning synagogue in Kronenberg.

3. *Carl Klingelhöfer, cabinetmaker (and adjutant to the Chief of the Kronenberg Volunteer Fire Department) , age 36*

The telephone rang by the side of the Klingelhöfers' bed in their house on the Altstrasse, in Kronenberg—the telephone by the bed, not the fire alarm on the wall. It was the cabinetmaker's sister calling, Frau Schuchardt, whose husband Fritz had the Café Schuchardt on the Mauerweg. Her voice was a frightened whisper: "Carl, the synagogue is burning. Inside. *Schwer*, bad." It was 1:25 A.M.

Klingelhöfer got into his clothes, his boots, and his fire coat and onto his bicycle. He could have phoned the night-alarm man or, en route to the Mauerweg, have pulled the alarm in front of the Katherine Church; but he didn't. He had to pedal slowly down the cobbled Altstrasse; but then, on the paved Hermann-Göring-Strasse and the Werneweg to Frankfurterplatz, he went at racing speed, a man who (besides flute-playing and picture-painting) had always done physical work, an old hiking-club man, who at thirty-six had the wind of a boy.

There were no policemen at the scene; the Mauerweg was closed off by SA men. But German firemen at the scene of a fire automatically have the status of uniformed policemen, and Klingelhöfer went through the SA cordon and the gate of the synagogue lawn. Smoke had begun to pour through broken windows, heavy black smoke. "Oil," said the fireman, even before he smelled it. On the side away from the smoke he shone his flashlight into the building. What caught his professional eye was the fact that the fire was burning in several separated spots: arson.

The Sturmführer Schwenke ignored him as he ran across the street to his brother-in-law's café and banged on the door; and when Fritz Schuchardt sleepily (or apparently so) opened the door, Klingelhöfer ran in and phoned the alarm man. "Got it already," said the alarm man. "Your buzzer at home rang at 1:38." Klingelhöfer, hearing the fire bells in the street, broke off.

As the first company pulled up, there was an immense *whoosh*; the rose windows in the synagogue dome had been broken by the updraft, and the sparks flew up in the sky.

The top of the wooden dome was almost as high as the wood-shingled roofs of the timbered old houses on the Adolf-Hitler-Strasse (formerly Hochstrasse), a street built up on the ruins of the old Town Wall in back of the synagogue. If the houses up there caught, the town would go. Adjutant Klingelhöfer advised the Fire Chief to send two of the three Kronenberg companies up to the Hitler-Strasse —in his excitement he called it Hochstrasse—and call the companies from the villages of Kummerfeld and Rickling, eight and eleven miles away, to replace them at the synagogue. The Chief agreed, and Klingelhöfer got a search-light and broke in the front doors of the burning building. The benches and prayer stands had all been piled on and around the wooden stage at the center of the prayer hall, where, at the base of the updraft, the fire was fiercest. The dome was supported by four wooden pillars, issuing from the corners of the stage. The pediments of the four pillars could not be seen in the flame; up above, they were blackened.

A little groggy, the fireman went around the edge of the floor and into a smaller room, the vestry, perhaps. There was a chest. He broke it open and scooped up its contents, some sort of altar cloths and sets of embroidered hangings. He went out through the prayer hall. In front of the gate to the lawn stood a policeman now—one policeman—and Klingelhöfer turned the stuff over to him. It was three o'clock in the morning.

There was no killing the updraft; the dome itself was glowing now. A section of it fell in with a roar; a column of fire shot up in the air. It would be dangerous to enter the prayer hall now, on account of the pillars. Klingelhöfer went back in carefully. Now that the dome was partly gone, the draft was stronger above, and the lower sections of the two front pillars could be seen. One was burned, about four feet up, to a diameter of two-and-a-half inches or so; the other, though burned at the same height, looked as if it would hold. But the two back pillars could not be seen.

The smoke was being carried off faster now and, with his searchlight, Klingelhöfer saw on the east wall of the prayer hall a set of gold-embroidered hangings like those he had got from the chest. They were charred, and he saw that something was built into the wall behind them. When I asked him, many years later, if he knew what it was, he said "No," and when I told him that it was the Ark of the Covenant, he said, "The Ark of the Covenant. . . . Well, well." He himself was a vestryman of the Parish Church.

## 4. *Heinrich Damm, Party headquarters office manager (formerly unemployed salesman), age 28*

Heinrich Damm was a country boy, though he'd been in the town ten years now; he was home from the Party anniversary celebration at 9:15, and at 9:30 he was in bed and asleep in his apartment in the attic of the Kreisleitung, Party headquarters for Kronenberg. But he slept light that night; there had been talk around town, and from SA headquarters in the basement of the Kreisleitung had come rumors of out-of-town visitors and unusual activity. He heard a noise downstairs and went down. It was the Kreisleiter, the County Leader.

"What brings you here, boss?" said Damm. (Like all country people, he had a hard time with new titles like Herr Kreisleiter, but nobody cared in Damm's case; he could deal with country people like nobody else in the organization.)

"Some work to finish up," said the Kreisleiter, without looking up.

Damm went back to bed.

It was three o'clock in the morning when a crash somewhere awakened him. There was a glow in the direction of the Hitler-Strasse and sparks shooting up. In ten minutes—and without awakening his hard-sleeping country-girl wife—he reached the synagogue. SA men and firemen were all over the place. One policeman stood in front of the gate to the lawn. A few spectators (remarkably few, for such a big fire) stood outside the SA cordon. Damm muttered, "*Blödsinn,* idiocy," and went back home. He woke up his wife and told her.

"What do you think, Heinrich?" she said. She always asked Heinrich what he thought about things.

"*Blödsinn,*" he said. "Would they have stopped us by burning our headquarters?"

He was undressing when his phone rang. It was the Kreisleiter, at home. "Can you bring your car, Heinrich? We've got to go out in the country." The Kreisleiter, whose father had been a professor, always took Heinrich Damm with him when he had to go out in the country.

On the way to Spelle, the next big town, they said nothing. As they entered Spelle, the Kreisleiter said, "What do you think, Heinrich?"

"What do you think, boss?"

"It's as if *they* had tried to stop *us* in the old days by burning the Kreisleitung," said the Kreisleiter.

"By golly, boss, you're right," said Damm. "I hadn't thought of it that way. It's *Blödsinn.*"

"We have to cover the county," said the Kreisleiter, as they pulled up in front of the Kreisleitung in Spelle. "The Gauleiter's adjutant called. Order from Reichsmarshal Göring. It's everywhere, all over Germany. It must be stopped at once. Whoever lays a hand on *Volksgut* must be punished." Damm glanced at the Kreisleiter when he said V*olksgut*—the "German People's property"—and said nothing.

It was almost dawn when they got back to Kronenberg.

"Where to, boss?" said Damm.

"Home," said the Kreisleiter.

As he got back into bed, Damm's wife said to him, "What do you think, Heinrich?"

"*Blödsinn*," said Damm, one of the "March violets" who flocked into the Party in 1933. "It's as if *they* had tried to stop *us* in the old days by burning the Kreisleitung."

## 5. *Horstmar Rupprecht, high-school student, age 14*

The crash—of the synagogue dome—that awakened Heinrich Damm awakened the Rupprechts on Klinggasse, three blocks from the fire. They saw the sparks from the second-floor window of their house and went up through the hatch to the roof. There they could see the glowing half-dome. Horst's mother held his hand; he hated having his hand held.

"Papa," said his mother to his father, "It's the synagogue."

The father said nothing.

"Of course it's the synagogue," said Horst, excited. "*Juda verrecke!* May the Jews drop dead!"

"Come down," said his father.

"Golly, not yet, Pa."

His father opened the hatch.

"Can I go to the fire, Pa? They'll all be there. Can I?"

The family—Horst was an only child and the only member of either his father's or mother's family who had ever gone to high school instead of to trade school—went down the hatchway to the attic. It was pitch dark, and Horst, his mother still holding on to his hand, heard his father stop instead of opening the door to the stairs.

"They'll all be there, Pa. Can I?"

"They won't *all* be there, Horstmar. *You* won't be there."

That was a long speech for Emil Rupprecht. A long speech, and it meant that a longer speech would follow. Horst's hand stopped wriggling in his mother's.

"Where did you learn to say '*Juda verrecke*'?" said his father.

"In the *Ha-Jot*, the Hitler Youth," said Horst.

"So," said his father, "in the *Ha-Jot*."

"They don't teach it, Pa, you just hear it there. The other kids say it. They all say it."

"Like 'they'll all be there,'" said his father.

"You just hear it, Pa, don't you understand?"

"No."

Father, mother, and son stood there. At fourteen Horst couldn't stand what, when he was grown, he called his father's *Schweigsamkeit*, his taciturnity, any more than he could stand what he later called his mother's *Kadaverge-horsam*, her unresisting obedience to her husband. Horst was one of those fourteen-year-olds who *can't stand* things. And he was in the *Ha-Jot*.

"Horstmar," said his father (he never called him "Horst," and Horst couldn't stand that, either), "do you know what a synagogue is?"

"Of course," said Horst.

His father was silent.

"Tell Papa what it is, Son," said Frau Rupprecht, who was afraid of both her husband and her son.

"It's the Jews'—the Jews'—church," said Horst.

"And a church?" said his father. "What is a church, Horstmar?"

"A house of God, Pa, golly."

"A house of God, without the 'Pa, golly,'" said his father.

"Yes, Pa, a house of God."

"God's house?" said his father.

"Yes, Pa."

"And you, Horstmar, you want to go and see them burn God's house down?"

"No, Pa, golly, you don't understand. You don't—are you for the Jews, Pa?"

Father, mother, and son stood there.

"No, of course not, Son, of course he's not," said Frau Rupprecht, who was afraid of her husband, of her son, of God, and of Hitler.

Emil Rupprecht opened the attic door, and the family went down and back to bed. But Horst was disturbed—and excited. In a way he felt sorry for his father, in a way he had not felt before: a locomotive engineer all his life, at $144 a month, a little man with a little job and a little wife and a little house, a man who said nothing because, the fact was, he had nothing to say, a man who knew nothing of politics and the world and who *claimed* to be a Nazi. Horst had been eight when his father joined the Party in the fall of '32; now he knew that his father was just a me-tooer.

"You want to go and see them burn God's house down?" Men setting fire to houses at night. God's house. Horst's house, his father's house. Horst rolled around in his sleep and awakened, afraid. Whenever Horst was afraid at night, he looked into his parents' room to see if they were there. Now he crept to the door and opened it. The light had begun. His mother was in bed, but his father was sitting in the rocking chair at the window. It was 5:15 in the morning.

## 6. Heinrich Wedekind, baker, age 51

At 5:15 the *Brötchen*, the little breakfast rolls, had to be in the oven to be out with the boy before six. Baker Wedekind, behind his shop at the far west end of Hitler-Strasse, was at work in his slippers and trousers and apron (which needed changing), his suspenders over his quarter-sleeve heavy gray underwear. He got the *Brötchen* in and stepped to the front of the shop to open the door, have a look at the breaking light, and smoke his cigar. He had been thinking of going down to his garden plot, at the edge of town, and turning it before it got any colder, but the dawn looked like rain. He'd go tomorrow.

As he stood there, two men whom he knew came by, from the direction of Frankfurterplatz. "What's up, at this hour?" he said. They told him that the synagogue had burned down in the night. "So," he said, and went back to his *Brötchen*. The synagogue.

In 1933 Baker Wedekind had been Party manager for his block and, as he himself put it, a *flotter SA Mann*, a jaunty Storm Trooper. One day he'd been sitting in the Felsenkeller having a beer, when somebody threw a rock through the window of the Jew Mannheimer's shoestore. Wedekind rushed into the store and scooped up the money from the cash register—just to protect it—and the police came. The next day the plainclothesman, old Hofmeister, called him in and said that some of the money was missing. That was taken care of by the Party, but there was a rumor around town that Baumert, the Social Democrat Bolshevik, had taken a snapshot of the baker standing in front of the cash register with his hands full of money. It was just a rumor, of course, but Wedekind quit the SA as soon as he had a good excuse, when the Handicrafts and Trades Office of the Party in Kronenberg was opened and he was offered the thankless job of mediator.

As he took his rolls from the fire, Baker Wedekind thought that he would like to see the Jew church burned down, but, on second thought, it might be better to go to the garden and work. No use looking for trouble; the shoe shop affair was enough. He would go by tomorrow, just walk past on his way to Frankfurterplatz and have a good look. That was the way to do it.

So he finished the rolls and went upstairs to eat breakfast with his wife, who was just as thick and strong as he was and did social work for the Party. He never talked to his wife, or to his son, whose wife resented her husband's low pay at the bakery, or to his daughter, who had got into trouble and could not be got rid of. The fact is that Baker Wedekind was not a jaunty man at all. He was a baker, and he baked. Each month he looked through that month's *Master-Baker*. Each day he read the headlines of the *Daily Kronenberger*. He had a copy of *Mein Kampf* (who hadn't?), but he had never opened it (who had?).

If he had been a profoundly reflective man, Baker Wedekind might have said to himself, as he ate his breakfast: This life is work. The next—if only a man knew for sure—will be different. In bad times, in this life, you work without reward. In good times, you work with reward. But in bad times and good, you work. These are good times. The regime?—the regime promised the people bread, and I bake the bread. The "Thousand-Year Reich"?—If it lasts a thousand years, fine; a hundred years, fine; ten years, still fine.

It was 6:15 A.M.

Beginning to rain. Baker Wedekind went down to the garden anyway.

## 7. *Hans Simon, bill-collector, age 42*

Hans Simon got up at 6:15, as he always did, shaved, waxed his little mustache, had his breakfast, in the course of which he reviewed the world situation, as he always did, with his wife, his son, and his daughter as audience, and set out (banging the door behind him) for the municipal electric works to pick up his morning calls. He bicycled firmly along, never swerving, preoccupied with the world situation.

He had a right to be. Cell Leader Simon—cell leader was the very lowest rank in the Party—was one of the first Nazis in Germany and the first in Kronenberg. Sturmführer Schwenke, the bankrupt tailor, always claimed to be the first. He always talked about *wir älte Kämpfer*, we Old Party Fighters, but he never gave his Party Number and no one had ever seen his Gold Party Badge. Simon wore his badge on his jacket, where everyone saw it, and whenever it was the thirteenth of the month he walked under ladders and so on and said, "Thirteen is nothing unlucky for me. My Party Number is 5813, the five thousand eight hundred and thirteenth German to join the Party, and I call that lucky. And, before that, a member of the Führer's Freiheits-bewegung, the Freedom Movement, *before* the Bloody Parade in Munich."

These reflections having taken Hans Simon across the Werne Bridge and into Frankfurterplatz, he saw a fire truck a half-block down on the Mauerweg and a small crowd held back by SA men. It was drizzling, but the bill-collector decided to pedal to the scene; it might be something of great importance.

The building was gone. The outer walls and part of the wooden dome, still smoking, were left. There was one policeman present, in front of the gate of the iron fence around the lawn. A skinny old woman was talking in a cackle to whoever would listen: "A church, a church, a church," she kept saying. SA men answered her; no one else said anything.

"A Jew church," said one SA man.

"It's not even a church," said another.

"Why don't you join, Auntie?"

"Be a Jew girl."

"A church, a church, a church," the old woman kept saying.

Bill-collector Simon, Party Number 5813, Gold Party Badge, rode on in the rain to pick up his morning calls and pondered the world situation. It was 7:30 in the morning.

## 8. *Johann Kessler, Labor Front inspector (formerly unemployed bank clerk), age 46*

At 7:30 Inspektor Kessler got off the local train from Kummerfeld and walked to his office in the Labor Front, in Hermann-Göring-Strasse. He got there at twenty to eight (he wasn't due until eight), and Picht came in and said, "Have you heard? They burned the synagogue last night, here, everywhere."

He and Picht picked up Euler on their way out, and the three men walked down the Werneweg to Frankfurterplatz and the Mauerweg in the drizzle. There it was, still smoking.

None of them said anything until they reached the Werneweg on their way back to the office. Then Kessler, a renegade Catholic who "preached" in the Nazi Faith Movement, said:

"This is a change. A big change."

"Burning property," said Picht, shaking his head, "burning property, whether it's a church or whatever."

"It won't make them love us abroad," said Euler.

"Do they love us now?" said Picht. Euler didn't reply.

"A big change," said Kessler again, "*eine Evolution.*" Kessler liked to use flowery language.

Ahead of them Pastor Tresckow of the Katherine Church was walking slowly away from the scene of the fire, an old man who had always kept out of politics. "*Der Pfarrer guckt auch,* the pastor took a squint at it, too," said Euler. Just then there was a shout behind them:

"*Nächstesmal die Katherinenkirche!* The Katherine Church next!"

Picht and Euler raised their eyes to each other, but Kessler, the renegade Catholic, stopped sharply and looked back. People were hurrying to work on both sides of the street, some of them under umbrellas. Nobody but Kessler had stopped or raised his eyes. Pastor Tresckow was walking slowly on.

## 9. *Heinrich Hildebrandt, high-school teacher, age 34*

"Herr Studienrat, Herr Studienrat!" Studienrat Hildebrandt waited until Pfeffermann caught up with him. Pfeffermann was a student at the university now, but he had been one of Hildebrandt's students in the classical high school. Pfeffermann liked and admired Hildebrandt. Even though Hildebrandt was a Nazi, and an ostentatious one, he was a highly cultivated man who really knew literature and music, a true Continental. It was even said—no one knew—that before coming to Kronenberg he had once been an anti-Nazi and owed his survival to the personal influence of his father, an old Army colonel. How anxious Hildebrandt was to talk with Pfeffermann, who was a *Mischling* (his

35

father was the Jew in the marriage, which made it worse), was another question, although the teacher certainly liked the student.

"Have you heard, Herr Studienrat? They have—the synagogue has been burned."

"The synagogue?"

"Yes."

"Have you been there?"

"No. Have you time to go?"

Herr Hildebrandt had time this morning; his literature class were writing their examination, and he always made a point of arriving late on examination days to show the students that he trusted them. He hesitated a moment, began to blush, and then said, "Yes, I have time."

It was 8:45 or so when they got there. The fire had almost burned itself out, but the smoke still came through the half-fallen dome of the building. The fire trucks, one on the Mauerweg, one up above on Hitler-Strasse, were no longer pumping. It was drizzling.

"The synagogue," said Pfeffermann, shaking his head.

Hildebrandt, blushing, said nothing. The American, Henderson, a buoyant young man who was studying (not very hard) at Kronenberg University and, through Pfeffermann, had met Hildebrandt before, came over to them; he said good morning without shaking hands (American fashion), and asked, in German, "Was ist los, Herr Studienrat?" Hildebrandt shook his head, without answering. He felt himself blushing and, feeling himself blushing, blushed worse.

As he entered his classroom, the class interrupted its writing to stand until he had said good morning and sat down at his desk. He opened his briefcase and took out *Crime and Punishment*, in French, with a plain wrapping-paper cover over the binding, to read while the class continued their examination.

Always fire, always fire. The Reichstag fire. The book-burning in the Paradeplatz in Königsberg. He was an anti-Nazi then, in '33, a man who read the *Baseler Nachrichter* and *Le Temps* every day and even once in a while (with great difficulty, for his English was weak) the *Times* of London. Now he was a Nazi, reading *Crime and Punishment* in French, with a plain wrapping-paper cover over the binding. Now he was a Nazi, and the Nazis were burning synagogues.

The noon bell rang. The students brought their examination books to the desk, and each said, "*Guten Morgen, Herr Studienrat*," but the Studienrat, reading his book in the wrapping-paper cover, did not look up.

## 10. *Willy Hofmeister, policeman, age 57*

It was noon, and Plainclothesman Hofmeister of the Kronenberg detective bureau was pedaling over the Werne Bridge on his way to work. Thursday was his morning to paint, but you can't paint in the rain. Hofmeister had chronic lead poisoning; he was allowed to paint once a week, out of doors. His paintings, in oil, were, like Cabinet-maker Klingelhöfer's, what a critic would call "calendar art" as far as subject, mood, and technique were concerned, but of their kind they were skilled and delicate.

Willy Hofmeister had had to give up his profession of scenery-painting when he was twenty-eight. In 1908 he had become a policeman in Kronenberg, first in the traffic police and then in the criminal division. It had not been a bad life. In thirty years there had been only three killings in Kronenberg, only one of them a murder (the other two were sex-maniac cases). In three more years he would retire on full pension. Not bad; but Willy Hofmeister had wanted to paint.

When his wife (who always made him stay in bed late and rest on Thursdays) told him that there was smoke coming up near Frankfurterplatz, Hofmeister knew right away what it was. The morning before, Oskar Rosenthal, the former Bank Director, had come to his office, stood with his hands at his side, and said, as Nazi protocol required, "*Ich bin der Jude*, Oskar Israel Rosen——"

"*Bitte, bitte*, please, please, Herr Direktor," Hofmeister said to the former Bank Director, "sit down, won't you?" When Rosenthal, the chairman of the board of the Kronenberg synagogue, told him that more windows had been broken the night before and the janitor had reported a smell of gasoline, Hofmeister said to the old man:

"A man will investigate at once, Herr Direktor, especially the gasoline smell. The windows—well, such things are difficult, you know, with, well, with the shooting in Paris yesterday."

"I understand, Herr Kriminalinspektor," said Rosenthal.

"So," said Kriminalinspektor Hofmeister, rising, "if you will excuse me a moment, I'll get the stenographer and you can dictate a report of the gasoline smell and the windows, and then we will register the complaint."

"No, no, Herr Kriminalinspektor," said Rosenthal. "I would rather not make a report, and there is certainly no complaint."

"But," said Hofmeister, "a report must be made."

"No, really," said Rosenthal, rising, "it is not at all necessary from our—from my point of view. I would much prefer not to make a report."

"But there *must* be a report, Herr Direktor," said Hofmeister.

"Only if you insist, Herr Kriminalinspektor," said Rosenthal.

The old policeman twisted his immense white mustache and said, "I shall make the report myself, Herr Direktor, after we have investigated. All possible steps will be taken." He held out his hand to the former Bank Director and said, "*Bitte*, Herr Direktor."

The old Jew took his hand and said, "*Bitte*, Herr Kriminalinspektor," and left.

Hofmeister had sent a policeman to the synagogue to investigate and, before he himself left for home at the end of the day, he wrote the report and placed it in the Kronenberg police files, which were found, incompletely burned, in the alley behind the police station when the American troops entered Kronenberg seven years later. The report, dated November 9, 1938, read:

"Synagogue, Mauerweg, report of broken windows, etc.

"Investigation at the scene established the fact that on the night of November 8, seven windowpanes in the synagogue on the Mauerweg were broken by stones thrown by unknown persons. Some of the stones lay in the prayer hall, some on the lawn. On the southeast gable side of the building, just outside the window leading to the furnace-room, which window was also found to have been broken, were the remnants of two wine bottles. These bottles had obviously been filled with a liquid, the odor of which was still present on the glass particles and in the immediate vicinity, corked with paper and rag bits, and ignited. Indications point to an explosion of small extent, i.e., of limited effect. Damage to the building, apart from a blackening on the wall, was not present.

"Criminologically valuable clues not present.

"Search for perpetrators without result, as of 5:20 P.M. instant date.

"On the side of those whose interests were injured, there was no demand for investigation."

That was the afternoon before, and now, as he pedaled over the Werne Bridge, Policeman Hofmeister was worried. The report had gone down to the chiefs of both the traffic and criminal police before 6 P.M., and Hofmeister was sure that there must have been uniformed police guarding the building during the night. The SA—of course it was the SA —did not like the police, and the police despised the SA. So there must have been trouble. Hofmeister decided to go over to the synagogue.

There were SA men everywhere, and only one uniformed policeman, Baumann, of the traffic division, in front of the synagogue gate. Hofmeister talked to him, Baumann answered, Hofmeister asked him something, and Baumann shrugged his shoulders as he replied. Then Hofmeister walked away.

"Heil Hitler, Herr Kriminalinspektor!"

It was Schwenke, the Sturmführer. "*Morgen*," said Hofmeister, getting on his bicycle. Schwenke, the Sturmführer. In 1931 Hofmeister had been sent to search Schwenke's apartment for evidence of illegal possession of arms by the SA, and Schwenke had said, "You find nothing in my mail, Herr Kriminalinspektor; do you think you will find something in my apartment?" Schwenke, the Nazi. Now it was Hofmeister, the Nazi, Schwenke and Hofmeister. The old policeman had three years to go, and then his pension, and the doctor had said that if he wasn't working he could paint.

At the office Hofmeister was told to report to the Police Chief, the Oberinspektor.

"Herr Kriminalinspektor," said the Police Chief, a young

man, "I have here an order to be executed. I will read it to you, and then I will ask you to read it yourself and sign it."

" 'And sign it,' Herr Oberinspektor?" said Hofmeister.

"And sign it, Herr Kriminalinspektor."

The order said that all male Jews in Kronenberg between the ages of eighteen and sixty-five were to be taken into protective custody at once. The order was to be executed before midnight of the instant date, November 10, 1938, by the Criminal Police (who in Germany could always arrest without a warrant). Kriminalinspektor Hofmeister was to deliver the following persons, whose names began with F through M, to the storerooms of the Town Hall, which would be used for custody because of the shortage of custodial quarters.

"Clear, Herr Kriminalinspektor?"

"Yes, Herr Oberinspektor."

"You will remain on duty until all the persons on your list are in custody, and then you will get your overtime off."

"Yes, Herr Oberinspektor."

Policeman Hofmeister took his list and began his round, without his bicycle. He carried no weapon.

It was a long afternoon. It might have been longer, except that every man on the list was at home; no Jew in Kronenberg had gone out of his house since the night before. Still, it was a long afternoon, and when Policeman Hofmeister rang the apartment bell alongside Salo Marowitz's tailor-shop, it was going on nine o'clock.

Marowitz opened the door and said, "Come in, Herr Kriminalinspektor."

"Thank you, Herr Marowitz."

On the parlor table, under the green glass tulip chandelier, was a suitcase, closed. On the sofa were a man's coat and hat.

"Herr Marowitz—"

"Won't you sit down, Herr Kriminalinspektor?"

"I—. Thank you, a moment only, Herr Marowitz."

"You have come for me, Herr Kriminalinspektor."

"Yes, Herr Marowitz. Just for your own protec——"

"I understand, Herr Kriminalinspektor. Shall we go?"

"Yes, if you don't mind. . . . Herr Marowitz, may I ask if you have blankets and food, and a little money?"

"Money, yes, but not blankets. And my wife will bring me food if it's necessary."

"Why don't you take a blanket, just to have one, and maybe some bread and sausage or something, Herr Marowitz? You understand, I don't—"

"Thank you, Herr Kriminalinspektor. . . . Mama, come in and say good evening to Kriminalinspektor Hofmeister."

"No," from the other room.

"I'm sorry, Herr Kriminalinspektor. Frau Marowitz isn't so well this evening. I'll get the blanket and food."

Hofmeister sat in the room alone, and the apartment door was unlocked from the outside. Samuel, the tailor's 17-year-old *Mischling* son came in.

"Hello, Herr Kriminalinspektor. I saw Georg this afternoon, at the synagogue. They blew it up, as a safety measure."

"I know," said Hofmeister; Georg was his youngest son.

"You don't see something like that every day," said Samuel.

"No, you don't, Samuel," said Hofmeister.

"And Georg says he's sure I can get in the Air Corps;

they take half-Jews. He's going to speak to—hello, Pop, what's the blanket for, where you going?"

"Hello, Schmul. I'm going to spend the night out."

"Where?"

"At the Town Hall. Herr Hofmeister is going with me."

"Oh." The boy paused. "Can I go along?"

"Well—"

"Oh, yes," said Hofmeister, "part way, we'll all walk together."

"Well," said Marowitz, "a glass of wine, Herr Kriminalinspektor?"

"No, thank you, Herr Marowitz, not on duty, you know. Maybe just a—. No. Thank you anyway. I appreciate it."

The son carrying the father's suitcase and walking between the two older men, the three of them climbed up through the streets, around the turns, up the steps, to the Market Place which led to the Town Hall.

"We're traveling at a snail's pace," said the son.

"Herr Hofmeister and I are older than you are, Son, aren't we, Herr Kriminalinspektor?"

"Yes, Herr Marowitz," said Hofmeister, "yes, we are." Then he stopped and said, "I'm a little out of breath, if you don't mind, Herr Marowitz. I'm tired tonight. If you and Samuel care to walk on ahead, I'll catch up with you."

## CHAPTER 2

## The Lives Men Lead

These ten men were "little men"; only Herr Hildebrandt, the teacher, had any substantial status in the community. And when I say "little men," I mean not only the men for whom the mass media and the campaign speeches are everywhere designed but, specifically in sharply stratified societies like Germany, the men who think of themselves in that way. Every one of my ten Nazi friends—including Hildebrandt—spoke again and again during our discussions of "*wir kleine Leute, we little people.*"

This self-consciousness is nonexistent—or repressed—in America. European students of our culture have all cited our egalitarianism as an affectation and an expensive one, producing a national leadership indistinguishable from its constituency. If everybody is little, nobody is little. But the rise of National Socialism involved both the elitist and the servile impulses. When "big men," Hindenburgs, Neuraths, Schachts, and even Hohenzollerns, accepted Nazism, little men had good and sufficient reason to accept it. "*Wenn die 'Ja' sagen,*" said Herr Simon, the bill-collector, "*dann sagen wir auch 'Ja.'* What was good enough for *them* was certainly good enough for us."

Foreigners speaking of the "National Socialist Party" miss the point, said the younger Schwenke; it was the

National Socialist German Workers Party, "the party of the little men like me. The only other was the Communist." Emperor and Führer both required the consciousness of littleness in the Germans, but Führer, bringing bigness down, lifted littleness up. The democratic baby-kisser and backslapper does the same thing, but it is more effective when an absolute ruler does it. My friends were little men—like the Führer himself.

These ten men were not men of distinction. They were not men of influence. They were not opinion-makers. Nobody ever gave them a free sample of anything on the ground that what they thought of it would increase the sales of the product. Their importance lay in the fact that God—as Lincoln said of the common people—had made so many of them. In a nation of seventy million, they were the sixty-nine million plus. They were the Nazis, the little men to whom, if ever they voiced their own views outside their own circles, bigger men politely pretended to listen without ever asking them to elaborate.

A year's conversations, in their own language, under informal conditions involving meals, "a glass of wine," or, more preciously, a cup of coffee, exchange of family visits (including the children), and long, easy evenings, Saturday afternoons, or Sunday walks—these were things that not one of my ten friends had supposed possible with an American. None of them had had any but official American contacts. None had been to America or England or outside Germany as civilians, excepting the teacher, who had spent much time in France. None spoke English.

My relationships with them were, in every case, established with considerable difficulty, through a third (or fourth or fifth) person who could convince them of my good faith and my good intentions. And all ten of them, with the possible exception of Baker Wedekind, seemed sooner or later to have accepted my statement of my mission: I had come to Germany, as a German-descended private person, to bring back to America the life-story of the ordinary German under National Socialism, with the end purpose of establishing better understanding of Germany among my countrymen. The statement was true, and my German academic position gave it weight with them. But my greatest asset was my total ignorance of German—the only language that any of them, except the teacher (who spoke French) could speak. They were my teachers. "Mushi," the old tailor, Schwenke, would call to his wife, "just listen to the way the Herr Professor says 'Auf wiedersehen!'" My friends had ample opportunity to display their pedagogy and their patience with the Herr Professor, who was slow, but good-natured.

I did lie to all ten of them on two points: on the advice of my German colleagues and friends, I did not tell them that I was a Jew; nor did I tell them that I had access to other sources of information about them than my private conversations with them.

I think that I may now call all of them, with the exception of the baker, friends of mine. I think that four of the ten, Tailor Schwenke, his son Gustav, Bank Clerk Kessler, and Teacher Hildebrandt (and, possibly, Policeman Hofmeister) told me their stories as fully as the stories were in them to tell. They were none of them, except the teacher, the student, and the bank clerk, at all fluent by temperament, but none of the ten consciously lied to me (in my opinion) except, possibly, Baker Wedekind and Tailor Schwenke, and the latter only on his role in the arson of the synagogue. I found no intolerable discrepancies or contradictions in their individual accounts over months of discussion; memory lapse, normal reserve, and, above all, the confusion and repression inherent in such cataclysmic experiences as theirs seemed to me to explain the small discrepancies and contradictions I observed. At no point did I try to trap any of them.

Only one of my ten Nazi friends saw Nazism as we—you and I—saw it in any respect. This was Hildebrandt, the teacher. And even he then believed, and still believes, in part of its program and practice, "the democratic part." The other nine, decent, hard-working, ordinarily intelligent and honest men, did not know before 1933 that Nazism was evil. They did not know between 1933 and 1945 that it was evil. And they do not know it now. None of them ever knew, or now knows, Nazism as we knew and know it; and they lived under it, served it, and, indeed, made it.

As we know Nazism, it was a naked, total tyranny which degraded its adherents and enslaved its opponents and adherents alike; terrorism and terror in daily life, private and public; brute personal and mob injustice at every level of association; a flank attack upon God and a frontal attack upon the worth of the human person and the rights which that worth implies. These nine ordinary Germans knew it absolutely otherwise, and they still know it otherwise. If our view of National Socialism is a little simple, so is theirs. An autocracy? Yes, of course, an autocracy, as in the fabled days of "the golden time" our parents knew. But a tyranny, as you Americans use the term? Nonsense.

When I asked Herr Wedekind, the baker, why he had believed in National Socialism, he said, "Because it promised to solve the unemployment problem. And it did. But I never imagined what it would lead to. Nobody did."

I thought I had struck pay dirt, and I said, "What do you mean, 'what it would lead to,' Herr Wedekind?"

"War," he said. "Nobody ever imagined it would lead to war."

The evil of National Socialism began on September 1, 1939; and that was my friend the baker.

Remember—none of these nine Germans had ever traveled abroad (except in war); none had ever known or talked with a foreigner or read the foreign press; none ever wanted to listen to the foreign radio when it was legal to do so, and none (except, oddly enough, the policeman) listened to it when it was illegal. They were as uninterested in the outside world as their contemporaries in France—or America. None of them ever heard anything bad about the Nazi regime except, as they believed, from Germany's enemies, and Germany's enemies were theirs. "Everything the Russians and the Americans said about us," said Cabinetmaker Klingelhöfer, "they now say about each other."

Men think first of the lives they lead and the things they see; and not, among the things they see, of the extraordinary sights, but of the sights which meet them in their daily rounds. The lives of my nine friends—and even of the tenth, the teacher—were lightened and brightened by National Socialism as they knew it. And they look back at it now—nine of them, certainly—as the best time of their lives; for what are men's lives? There were jobs and job security, summer camps for the children and the Hitler Jugend to keep them off the streets. What does a mother want to know? She wants to know where her children are, and with whom, and what they are doing. In those days she knew or thought she did; what difference does it make? So things went better at home, and when things go better at home, and on the job, what more does a husband and father want to know?

The best time of their lives. There were wonderful ten-dollar holiday trips for the family in the "Strength through Joy" program, to Norway in the summer and Spain in the winter, for people who had never dreamed of a real holiday trip at home or abroad. And in Kronenberg "nobody" (nobody my friends knew) went cold, nobody went hungry, nobody went ill and uncared for. For whom do men know? They know people of their own neighborhood, of their own station and occupation, of their own political (or nonpolitical) views, of their own religion and race. All the blessings of the New Order, advertised everywhere, reached "everybody."

There were horrors, too, but these were advertised nowhere, reached "nobody." Once in a while (and only once in a while) a single crusading or sensation-mongering newspaper in America exposes the inhuman conditions of the local county jail; but none of my friends had ever read such a newspaper when there were such in Germany (far fewer there than here), and now there were none. None of the horrors impinged upon the day-to-day lives of my ten friends or was ever called to their attention. There was "some sort of trouble" on the streets of Kronenberg as one or another of my friends was passing by on a couple of occasions, but the police dispersed the crowd and there was nothing in the local paper. You and I leave "some sort of trouble on the streets" to the police; so did my friends in Kronenberg.

The real lives that real people live in a real community have nothing to do with Hitler and Roosevelt or with what Hitler and Roosevelt are doing. Man doesn't meet the State very often. On November 10, 1938, the day after the arson of the synagogues, an American news service reported a trivial incident from a suburb of Berlin. A mob of children were carrying great sacks of candy out of the smashed shop window of a Jewish-owned candy store, while a crowd of adults, including some of the children's parents (including, too, a ring of SA men in Brown Shirt uniform), stood watching. An old man walked up, an "Aryan." He watched the proceedings and then turned to the parents and said to them: "You think you are hurting the Jew. You do not know what you are doing. You are teaching your children to steal." And the old man walked off, and the parents broke out of the crowd, knocked the candy out of their children's hands and dragged them wailing away. Man, in the form of the parents, had met the State, in the form of the SA. But it is doubtful if he knew it; after all, the SA men just stood there, without interfering.

In its issue of November 11, 1938, the *Kronenberger Zeitung* carried the following report, at the bottom of page 4, under a very small headline reading *Schutzhaft*, "Protective Custody": "In the interest of their own security, a number of male Jews were taken into custody yesterday. This morning they were sent away from the city." I showed it to each of my ten friends. None of them —including the teacher—remembered ever having seen it or anything like it.

1933, 1934, 1935, 1936, 1937, 1938, 1939—until September 1, when, as the Head of the Government told them, Poland attacked their country—the little lives of my friends went on, under National Socialism as they had before, altered only for the better, and always for the better, in bread and butter, in housing, health, and hope, wherever the New Order touched them. "No one outside Germany seems to understand this," said an anti-Nazi woman, who had been imprisoned in 1943, ostensibly for listening to the foreign radio but actually for hiding Jews (which was not technically illegal). "I remember standing on a Stuttgart street corner in 1938, during a Nazi festival, and the enthusiasm, the new hope of a good life, after so many years of hopelessness, the new belief, after so many years of disillusion, almost swept me, too, off my feet. Let me try to tell you what that time was like in Germany: I was sitting in a cinema with a Jewish friend and her daughter of thirteen, while a Nazi parade went across the screen, and the girl caught her mother's arm and whispered, 'Oh, Mother, Mother, if I weren't a Jew, I think I'd be a Nazi!' No one outside seems to understand how this was."

The German language, like every other, has some glorious epithets, untranslatable, and *wildgewordene Spiessbürger* is one of them. It means, very roughly, "little men gone wild." Of themselves, such men would perhaps use the borrowed and Germanicized term *Fanatiker*. *Fanatiker* are not to be confused either with *Spitzbuben*, rascals, or with *Bluthunde*, hired hoodlums or goons. When I asked (of anti-Nazis and of Nazis) how many genuine *Fanatiker* there were in the Third Reich, how many little men gone wild, the hazard was never over a million. It must be remembered, especially in connection with Communism in Russia, and even with Fascism in Italy, that the National Socialist movement died young; it never had a chance to rear a whole generation of its own.

And the rest of the seventy million Germans? The rest were not even cogs, in any positive sense at all, in the totalitarian machine. A people like ourselves, who know such systems only by hearsay or by the report of their victims or opponents, tends to exaggerate the actual relationship between man and the State under tyranny. The laws are hateful to those who hate them, but who hates them? It is dangerous, in Nazi Germany, to go to Communist meetings or read the *Manchester Guardian*, but who wants to go to Communist meetings or read the *Manchester Guardian?*

In the America of the 1950's one hears, on the one hand, that the country is overcome by mistrust, suspicion, and dread, and, on the other, that nobody is afraid, nobody defamed, nobody destroyed by defamation. Where is the truth? Where was it in Nazi Germany? None of my ten Nazi friends, with the exception of the cryptodemocrat Hildebrandt, knew any mistrust, suspicion, or dread in his own life or among those with whom he lived and worked; none was defamed or destroyed. Their world was the world of National Socialism; inside it, inside the Nazi community, they knew only good-fellowship and the ordinary concerns of ordinary life. They feared the "Bolsheviks" but not one another, and their fear was the accepted fear of the whole otherwise happy Nazi community that was Germany. Outside that community they never went, or saw, or heard; they had no occasion to.

That Nazism in Germany meant mistrust, suspicion, dread, defamation, and destruction we learned from those who brought us word of it—from its victims and opponents whose world was outside the Nazi community and from journalists and intellectuals, themselves non-Nazi or anti-Nazi, whose sympathies naturally lay with the victims and opponents. These people saw life in Germany in non-Nazi terms. There were two truths, and they were not contradictory: the truth that Nazis were happy and the truth that anti-Nazis were unhappy. And in the America of the 1950's —I do not mean to suggest that the two situations are parallel or even more than very tenuously comparable— those who did not dissent or associate with dissenters saw no mistrust or suspicion beyond the great community's mistrust and suspicion of dissenters, while those who dissented or believed in the right to dissent saw nothing but mistrust and suspicion and felt its devastation. As there were two Americas, so, in a much more sharply drawn division, there were two Germanys. And so, just as there is when one man dreads the policeman on the beat and another waves "Hello" to him, there are two countries in every country.

In Russian-Communized East Germany after the second World War, a worker in a State factory is compelled to attend one meeting a week, of two hours, for purposes of what we should call "indoctrination" or "brain-washing" and what the Communists call "education." Beyond that and paying his taxes, he is compelled to do nothing more; he takes military service, secret police, and rationing for granted (as who doesn't?). Of course, he is blared at, from posters, newspapers, radio, and public address systems (as who isn't, for one purpose or another?), but he is let alone.

Most Germans—nearly all of them, after twelve years of Nazism—see nothing inordinate in this amount of compulsion. Even under Nazism (before the war), Party members were required to give only Friday evenings and Sunday mornings to Party or public work. Beyond this point, service to the tyranny was, naturally, highly advisable for the ambitious and the politically suspect, but it was not required of the man who wanted to hold a job, a home, a family, and an honored place in the *Singverein* or the *Turnverein*. I encountered a few civil servants in Kronenberg who had never joined the Party and had not been bothered; they were the kind that never joined anything, and nobody expected them to—the kind, too, that is never promoted; and I met a pastor who had not been persecuted although he had refused to let his children join the Hitler

53

Youth and the German Maidens until membership became automatic.

It is local conditions, even under totalitarianism, which govern the application of public authority to the individual. These conditions, which vary so much elsewhere, varied much more than I had supposed possible under National Socialism and tended almost always to relax the central controls (just as local courts everywhere tend to relax legal principles), except where the local boss was a *Fanatiker*. And these latter instances were the exceptions; local bosses, in order to function effectively, have to be locally popular.

Pastor Wilhelm Mensching, in the village of Petzen, in Lower Saxony, preached anti-Nazism to his little flock during the whole twelve years that the Nazis were in power in Germany. Every Sunday morning he stood in his pulpit and answered the speech which the Bürgermeister, an "Old Party Fighter," made every Saturday night in the Market Place. Mensching was never touched; when the Gestapo came from Hannover to arrest him, the Bürgermeister went to the Gauleiter to oppose them, and the arrest wasn't made. Wilhelm Mensching had "always" been pastor of Petzen, and to disturb him would have been an intolerable disturbance to the configuration of the village. And both he and the Bürgermeister knew it.

There were not enough thousands of Menschings in Germany, simply because such men are not born every day and the church in Germany (as elsewhere) does not nourish their multiplication. But there were dozens enough of them to make the point. To be sure, National Socialism had only a few years to achieve its great *Gleichschaltung*, its integration of man into the State; still, six of them were war years, in which the tempo could be, and was, stepped up considerably. But modern tyrants all stand above politics and, in doing so, demonstrate that they are all master politicians. They know, without having to read Florentine theorists, that politicians cannot afford to be hated. A Niemöller would have to be silenced, at whatever risk to the tyranny; the best-known of all German pastors, he had said, "God is my Führer." He was a national and an international challenge, and he had to be handled the hard way. But there were easy ways (the easiest being to ignore them) to confine the effectiveness of dozens of Menschings to their separate villages without taking steps which would have rocked any good villager on his heels and made him say, "No, not this, not this."

Ordinary people—and ordinary Germans—cannot be expected to tolerate activities which outrage the ordinary sense of ordinary decency unless the victims are, in advance, successfully stigmatized as enemies of the people, of the nation, the race, the religion. Or, if they are not enemies (that comes later), they must be an element within the community somehow extrinsic to the common bond, a decompositive ferment (be it only by the way they part their hair or tie their necktie) in the uniformity which is everywhere the condition of common quiet. The Germans' innocuous acceptance and practice of social anti-Semitism before Hitlerism had undermined the resistance of their ordinary decency to the stigmatization and persecution to come.

In the pleasant resort towns of New England Americans have seen signs reading "Selected Clientele" or "Restricted." They have grown accustomed to seeing such signs, so accustomed that, unless they are non-Caucasian or, perhaps, non-"Aryan" Americans, they take no notice of them and, in taking no notice, accept them. In the much less pleasant cottonseed-oil towns of the Deep South Americans

55

have grown accustomed to seeing signs reading anything from "White" and "Colored" to "Nigger, Don't Let the Sun Set on You Here," and, unless they are non-Caucasian or, perhaps, northern Americans, they take no notice of them. There were enough such signs (literally and figuratively) in pre-Nazi Germany, and there was enough nonresistance to them, so that, when the countryside bloomed in 1933 with signs reading "*Juden hier unerwünscht*, Jews Not Wanted Here," the Germans took no notice of them. So, in the body politic as in the body personal, nonresistance to the milder indulgences paves the way for nonresistance to the deadlier.

It is actual resistance which worries tyrants, not lack of the few hands required to do the dark work of tyranny. What the Nazis had to gauge was the point at which atrocity would awaken the community to the consciousness of its moral habits. This point may be moved forward as the national emergency, or cold war, is moved forward, and still further forward in hot war. But it remains the point which the tyrant must always approach and never pass. If his calculation is too far behind the people's temper, he faces a palace *Putsch*; if it is too far ahead, a popular revolution.

It is in this nonlitigable sense, at least, that the Germans as a whole were guilty: nothing was done, or attempted, that they would not stand for. The two exceptions were euthanasia, which was abandoned, and the pagan "Faith Movement" of Alfred Rosenberg, which was aborted.

Local hoodlums could beat up Communists or Social Democrats, desecrate Jewish cemeteries or smash Jews' windows by night; the local police, overseen by the Gestapo, would make a routine and invariably unsuccessful investigation of the assault; and the ordinary demands of decency would be satisfied. The Kronenbergers, being decent folk, would, perhaps, turn over in their beds—and sleep on.

The burning of a synagogue was something else; it approached, closely and almost dangerously, the point at which the community might be awakened. If not sacrilege, it was, after all, lawless destruction of valuable goods, an affront to the German property sense (much deeper than ours) and, no less, to the responsibility (much sterner than ours) of the authorities to uphold the law. When the synagogue was burned in Kronenberg, local SA men (including Tailor Schwenke, my friend) were used incidentally; but the arson was planned and directed by outsiders, from a big city forty miles away. In the pattern of American gangsterism's importation of killers from New York to Chicago or vice versa, the local officials were helpless and, by transference, the community, too.

The German community—the rest of the seventy million Germans, apart from the million or so who operated the whole machinery of Nazism—had nothing to do except *not to interfere*. Absolutely nothing was expected of them except to go on as they had, paying their taxes, reading their local paper, and listening to the radio. Everybody attended local celebrations of national occasions—hadn't the schools and the stores always been closed for the Kaiser's birthday?—so you attended, too. Everybody contributed money and time to worthy purposes, so you did, too. In America your wife collects or distributes clothing, gives an afternoon a week to the Red Cross or the orphanage or the hospital; in Germany she did the same thing in the Nazi Frauenbund, and for the same reasons. The Frauenbund, like the Red Cross, was patriotic and humanitarian;

did your wife ask the Red Cross if "Negro" plasma was segregated from "white"?

One minded one's own business in Germany, with or without a dictatorship. The random leisure which leads Americans into all sorts of afterhour byways, constructive, amusing, or ruinous, did not exist for most Germans. One didn't go out of one's way, on a day off, to "look for trouble"—there less than here. Germans were no more given to associating with nonconformist persons or organizations than we are. They engaged themselves in opposing the government much less than we do. Few Americans say "No" to the government—fewer Germans. None of my ten friends said "No" to the Nazi government, and only one of them, Teacher Hildebrandt, thought "No."

Men who are ever going to say "No" to the government are for the most part—not uniformly—men with a prior pattern of politically conscious impulse. But such men were, in Hitler's Germany, either Nazis or anti-Nazis. If they were Nazis, they said "Yes," with a will. If they were anti-Nazis, their past record, like the teacher's, hung over their heads. Far from protesting, these, the only Germans who might have protested in quantity, had the greatest incentive of all to conform. They were like men who, in McCarthy-ridden America, had been Communists in their youth, who hoped that their past was safely buried, and whose sole concern was whether or not *their* names turned up in the day's un-American activities testimony. Of all Americans, they would be the least likely to participate *now* in protest or opposition. "I never got over marveling that I survived," said Herr Hildebrandt. "I couldn't help being glad, when something happened to somebody else, that it hadn't happened to me. It was like later on, when a bomb hit another city, or another house than your own;

you were thankful." "More thankful for yourself than you were sorry for others?" "Yes. The truth is, Yes. It may be different in your case, Herr Professor, but I'm not sure that you will know until you have faced it."

You were sorry for the Jews, who had to identify themselves, every male with "Israel" inserted into his name, every female with "Sarah," on every official occasion; sorrier, later on, that they lost their jobs and their homes and had to report themselves to the police; sorrier still that they had to leave their homeland, that they had to be taken to concentration camps and enslaved and killed. But—*weren't you glad you weren't a Jew?* You were sorry, and more terrified, when it happened, as it did, to thousands, to hundreds of thousands, of non-Jews. But—weren't you glad that it hadn't happened to you, a non-Jew? It might not have been the loftiest type of gladness, but you hugged it to yourself and watched your step, more cautiously than ever.

Those who came back from Buchenwald in the early years had promised—as every inmate of every German prison had always had to promise upon his release—not to discuss his prison experience. You should have broken your promise. You should have told your countrymen about it; you might, though the chances were all against you, have saved your country had you done so. But you didn't. You told your wife, or your father, and swore them to secrecy. And so, although millions guessed, only thousands knew. Did you want to go back to Buchenwald, and to worse treatment this time? Weren't you sorry for those who were left there? And weren't you glad you were out?

"*So war die Sache.* That's the way it was." Where the community feels and thinks—or at least talks and acts—pretty much one way, to say or do differently means a kind of internal exile that most people find unattractive to undertake, even if it involves no legal penalty. Oh, it isn't so bad if you have been a lifelong dissenter or radical, or a known criminal; you're used to it. But you—you and I— you're used to saying "Hello" to everyone and having everyone say "Hello" to you. You look every man in the eye, and, though your eyes may be empty, they are clear. You are respected in the community. Why? Because your attitudes are the same as the community's. But are the community's attitudes respectable? That's not the point.

We—you and I—want the community's approval on the community's basis. We don't want the approval of criminals, but the community decides what is criminal and what isn't. This is the trap. You and I—and my ten Nazi friends —are in the trap. It has nothing to do directly with fear for one's own or his family's safety, or his job, or his property. I may have all these, never lose them, and still be in exile. Somebody somewhere in the community (it doesn't matter who or why) is telling somebody else that I'm a liar or a cheater—or a Red. Tomorrow somebody whose closer acquaintance I should never have cultivated—I have never liked him, never really respected him—will pass me without saying "Hello" to me. I am being exiled at home, isolated. My safety, unless I am accustomed to being a dissenter, or a recluse, or a snob, is in numbers; this man, who will pass me tomorrow and who, though he always said "Hello" to me, would never have lifted a finger for me, will tomorrow reduce my safety by the number of one.

In what you and I call the blessings of life—including uncritical acceptance by the whole of the undifferentiated community—every one of my ten friends, excepting Tailor Schwenke, who had once had his own shop and was now a school janitor, was better off than he had ever been before; and not just they and their families, but all their friends, the "whole" community, the widows and orphans, the aged, the sick, and the poor. Germany had been what many Americans would call a welfare state ever since Bismarck, the reactionary Junker, introduced social legislation to stave off social democracy. In the collapse after the first World War, and again in the collapse at the end of the 1920's, the Weimar Republic could not maintain its social services. Nazism not only restored but extended them; they were much more comprehensive than they had ever been before or, of course, than they have been since. Nor were they restricted to Party members; only "enemies" of the regime were excluded from them.

The war was hard, although not, until the bombing became general, anywhere near as hard as the first war, in which the German government had not anticipated the blockade and the civilian population ate acorns; this time, the conquered countries were starved and the Germans were fed. But my friends do not mean 1939–45 when they speak of "the Nazi time." They mean 1933–39. And the best time of one's life is, in retrospect, all the better when, as in Germany after 1945, one supposed that he would not see its like again.

The best time of their lives.

"Yes," said Herr Klingelhöfer, the cabinetmaker, "it was the best time. After the first war, German families began to have only two children. That was bad, bad for the family, the marriage, the home, the nation. There is where Germany was dying, and that was the kind of strength we believed that Hitler was talking about. And he *was* talking about it. After '33 we had more children. A man saw a future. The difference between rich and poor grew smaller, one saw it everywhere. A man had a chance. In 1935 I took over my father's shop and got a two-thousand-dollar government loan. *Ungeheuer!* Unheard of!

"The good development had nothing to do with whether we had a democracy, or a dictatorship, or what. The form of government had nothing to do with it. A man had a little money, a chance, and he didn't pay any attention to any *system*. Inside the system, you see the benefits. Outside it, when you are not benefited by it, you see the faults, I suppose. I suppose that's the way it is in Russia now. That's the way it is everywhere, always, *nicht wahr*? '*Das danken wir unserm Führer*. For all this we thank our Leader,' the kids all said in school. Now they say, '*Das danken wir den Amerikanern*.' If Communism comes, they'll say, '*Das danken wir dem Stalin*.' That's the way men are. I couldn't do that myself."

But he did it.

Herr Klingelhöfer counted his blessings. Who doesn't?

This might be, I suppose, pro-Nazi propaganda. It is also a fact, in so far as men's attitudes are facts and decisive facts. No Occupation could make—or had made—anti-Nazis out of my friends. The evidence they had before their eyes for rejecting that period of their lives that was spent under National Socialism was wholly inadequate. And it was hard to see how any "recovery" under any German government in any foreseeable future (still less, under any Occupation) could make it adequate. At best, until such time as men (or at least these men) changed the root basis of their values, "things" could only some day be as "good" as they had been under Hitler. What we call freedom is not, even if they had all the freedom we have, an adequate substitute, in my friends' view, for all that they had and have lost. Men who did not know that they were slaves do not know that they have been freed.

## CHAPTER 3

## Hitler and I

None of these nine ordinary Germans (and even the tenth, Herr Hildebrandt, is not completely firm on the point) thought then or thinks now that the rights of man, in his own case, were violated or even more than mildly inhibited for reasons of what they then accepted (and still accept) as the national emergency proclaimed four weeks after Hitler took office as Chancellor. Only two of the ten—Hildebrandt, of course, and Simon, the bill-collector—saw the system as in any way repressive. Herr Simon thinks that it was because of what he calls his "democratic" tendency to argue that he rose only to the lowest rank in the Party, cell leader, in spite of his having been one of the oldest members of the Party in Germany. But he was never alienated from his Party faith or its leadership by what he still regards as the local perversions of its principles by "the little Hitlers."

"The little Hitlers" recurred constantly in my conversations with my friends. It did not derogate Hitler—quite the opposite. "The little Hitlers" were the local or provincial officials, fellows you knew or had heard other fellows talk about familiarly. You knew (or had reason to believe) that they were no bigger or better than you were; you detested their imitation of the Führer, above all, of his certainty and the absoluteness that springs from certainty. But, because of the old military principle of command which obtained

63

throughout the Party, you could do nothing about it but dream at night that Schmidt, the little Hitler, had fallen on his face in public and you were chosen by acclaim to replace him.

None of my ten friends, even today, ascribes moral evil to Hitler, although most of them think (after the fact) that he made fatal strategical mistakes which even they themselves might have made at the time. His worst mistake was his selection of advisers—a backhanded tribute to the Leader's virtues of trustfulness and loyalty, to his very innocence of the knowledge of evil, fully familiar to those who have heard partisans of F. D. R. or Ike explain how things went wrong.

Having fixed our faith in a father-figure—or in a father, or in a mother or a wife—we must keep it fixed until inexcusable fault (and what fault of a father, a mother, a wife, is inexcusable?) crushes it at once and completely. This figure represents our own best selves; it is what we ourselves want to be and, through identification, are. To abandon it for anything less than crushing evidence of inexcusable fault is self-incrimination, and of one's best, unrealized self. Thus Hitler was betrayed by his subordinates, and the little Nazis with him. They may hate Bormann and Goebbels—Bormann because he rose to power at the end, and they are ashamed of the end; Goebbels because he was a runt with a "Jewish mind," that is, a facile and cunning mind unlike theirs. They may hate Himmler, the *Bluthund*, above all, because he killed in cold blood, and they wouldn't do that. But they may not hate Hitler or themselves.

"You see," said Tailor Schwenke, the littlest of my ten little men, "there was always a secret war against Hitler in the regime. They fought him with unfair means. Himmler

I detested. Goebbels, too. If Hitler had been told the truth, things would have been different." For "Hitler" read "I."

"The killing of the Jews?" said the "democratic" bill-collector, der alte Kämpfer, Simon. "Yes, that was wrong, unless they committed treason in wartime. And of course they did. If I had been a Jew, I would have myself. Still, it was wrong, but some say it happened and some say it didn't. You can show me pictures of skulls or shoes, but that doesn't prove it. But I'll tell you this—it was Himmler. Hitler had nothing to do with it."

"Do you think he knew about it?"

"I don't know. We'll never know now."

Hitler died to save my friend's best self.

Apart from the partially and secretly anti-Nazi teacher, only the bank clerk, Kessler, the natively eloquent little man who became an official Party speaker in the county, seems to have had any shadow of doubt about Hitler's personal or public goodness—and even he may be projecting his own experience: "Hitler was a spellbinder, a natural orator. I think he was carried away from truth, even from truth, by his passion. Even so, he always believed what he said." "The schemers, Himmler, Goebbels, Rosenberg, Bormann—they built him up into a man of destiny," said Salesman Damm, the Party office manager in Kronenberg. "They did it so skilfully that he finally believed it himself. From then on, he lived in a world of delusion. And this happened, mind you, to a man who was good and great." It could happen to me, Heinrich Damm, too.

These believers (for believers they certainly were) do not seem to have been worshipers any more than we believers in F. D. R. or Ike are—if anything, less so. Hitler was a man, one like ourselves, a little man, who, by doing what he did, was a testament to the democracy "you Americans" talk about, the ability of us little men to become great and to rule the whole world. *A little man, like ourselves.* Such a man is the modern pattern of the demagogical tyrant, "the people's friend" of Plato's mob democracy. These Hitlers, Stalins, Mussolinis are commoner upstarts, the half-literate Hitler the commonest of the lot.

Kings and kaisers rule by God's grace, Hitlers by their own. God's grace puts a father over his children, to rule them in their interest. He is visibly and incontrovertibly endowed with wisdom appropriate to his function, and his walking stick (or his napkin ring or his rocking chair), like the Kaiser's crown, sets him wholly apart from his children. But these Hitlers wear trench coats. Are they in fact father-figures? Or are Leader and Father two separable subconscious entities?

The newest wrinkle in psychoanalytic lingo is "charismatic leader." It seems to mean (if "charismatic" is derived from the Greek *charisma*) the one to whom it is given to take care of his people. Both the Kaiser and Hitler "took care of" the German people, but the Kaiser was endowed by God. He did not have to kiss babies; he did not have to do anything. The most perfect of fathers, he lived far away, in Potsdam; you might see him once or twice in your life, in a great parade, or never at all. Unlike your own biological father, he never punished you for little things or unjustly. Unlike your biological father, he let you be "bad," in your personal life, beat your wife or get drunk or do shoddy work, without ever whipping you or withdrawing his love.

Seven of my friends (the seven oldest of them) had been brought up in a stable society, with their perfect father in Potsdam and their imperfect father at home. One of the seven, Herr Kessler, the bank clerk, had been orphaned early and was brought up by his mother. At least four of the other six feared or hated their fathers (or both), and of Hildebrandt alone am I able to say with some certainty that he neither feared nor hated his.

The old tailor, Schwenke, *still* hates his father, who is still alive, at ninety-three, in a near-by village; Schwenke has not seen him in years. He hated him always in his heart— "he drank too much," "he was cruel to my blessed mother" —and finally he hated him openly, running away from home to the army after his father ordered him to remain in the service of a master-tailor who mistreated him. Heinrich Damm, the country boy, feared his father, who, besides being an ambitious and avaricious farmer, was the village innkeeper and, after a backbreaking day in the fields, could handle any half-dozen sots who tried to keep him from closing the inn at midnight. Damm remembers that his father compelled his pregnant mother to pile rocks until she dropped; when she died, a few years later, his father said, "I guess I worked her too hard." But the son feared his father too much (and still does) to hate him.

By contrast, the five of my friends who now have children in or approaching their teens all marvel at the sassiness, the independence, of their own children. And "marvel" better describes their attitude than "disapprove" or "resent." The younger Schwenke said, "My father"—the old tailor— "would have killed me if I'd talked to him the way my boy talks to me," and he shakes his head. "It's all different now," said Cabinetmaker Klingelhöfer. "When I was a boy, I spoke when I was spoken to; otherwise, never. Now my children disagree with me about everything, and I can't do a thing. My wife is the boss," and he laughs. The clue to the change (and a radical change it seems to be) may be the emancipation of the German woman and, in particular, of the wife, which Nazism tried to overcome. The German child, today as yesterday, seems to be left almost entirely to the mother; even among my non-Nazi friends, the relationship between father and child was generally much more remote than ours. But, whereas the mother once executed the father's will upon the child, she now seems to execute her own.

My friends' youngsters are, to be sure, being brought up in a disintegrated society, in which not only the Kaiser but also the biological father have been dislodged. My friends have lost their jobs or their homes or their status or their security, and their children know it. And the Kaiser is only a character in history, gone without any supposition that he will ever return.

The true father-figure is a true figure, the representation of an ideal essence. Whether Wilhelm II was, as a ruler or a man, good or bad was irrelevant to his status. The failings of one's biological father could not but affect one's attitude, but the failings of the true father-figure were, like the Emperor's new clothes in the fairy tale, beyond the very presumption of his subjects to observe. There were, in Germany, daring intellectuals who attacked the Kaiser's policies before the first World War, but my friends were not daring intellectuals.

One does not presume to judge the true father-figure. One would not—but cannot help himself—judge his biological father. But one judges a man like himself by his own criteria of success and failure. Hitler was, until 1943 or 1944, a success. He displayed all the way to Stalingrad a genius which only a dozen men in the whole world's history have had, a genius for continuous success in public affairs against the odds which only public affairs present. None of my friends hesitates—every soldier is a military expert, and every German is a soldier—to say that he was wrong to invade Poland (or to invade *when* he did or *how* he did) or, perhaps, to attack Russia, which he had so brilliantly immobilized, or to ally himself with Italy or to take on the world so soon. But these wrongs were strategic mistakes. I might—my friends are talking—have made them myself. Napoleon made them.

My friends do not mourn Hitler any more than we mourn those of our own national leaders whose genius culminates in ruin; such geniuses must build their own sarcophagi with the cynical assistance of the political party hacks who find themselves with bare bones on their hands in the next campaign. My Nazi friends do not deify Hitler or (if the distinction may be made) glorify him. They never questioned his absolute right or absolute power to absolute rule. But they do not think of him—and seem never to have done so—as Führer, the Leader, and not just because the Occupation's re-educators suppressed the use of the very word. They think of him as Hitler, and, whatever they dream of reviving, they do not dream of reviving Hitlerism.

Romantic they are, but this romantic they are not. They do not repress his name; they mention it when there is occasion to mention it. But there is little occasion to do so. Old soldiers in Germany have something else to do these days besides spit on the stove and tell stories; the stove is cold. Nothing surprised my friends so much as to hear that Americans still speculate about Hitler's survival, in the flesh in Argentina or Spain or in personal spirit in Germany. He lived, succeeded, failed, died, and is dead.

Adolf Hitler was good for Germany—in my friends' view —up until 1943, 1941, or 1939, depending upon the indi-

## CHAPTER 4

## "What Would You Have Done?"

None of my ten friends ever encountered anybody connected with the operation of the deportation system or the concentration camps. None of them ever knew, on a personal basis, anybody connected with the Gestapo, the Sicherheitsdienst (Security Service), or the Einsatzgruppen (the Occupation Detachments, which followed the German armies eastward to conduct the mass killing of Jews). None of them ever knew anybody who knew anybody connected with these agencies of atrocity. Even Policeman Hofmeister, who had to arrest Jews for "protective custody" or "resettlement" and who saw nothing wrong in "giving the Jews land, where they could learn to work with their hands instead of with money," never knew anyone whose shame or shamelessness might have reproached him had they stood face to face. The fact that the Police Chief of Kronenberg made him sign the orders to arrest Jews told him only that the Chief himself was afraid of getting into trouble "higher up."

Sixty days before the end of the war, Teacher Hildebrandt, as a first lieutenant in command of a disintegrating Army subpost, was informed by the post doctor that an SS man attached to the post was going crazy because of his memories of shooting down Jews "in the East"; this was the closest any of my friends came to knowing of the systematic butchery of National Socialism.

I say none of these ten men knew; and, if none of them, very few of the seventy million Germans. The proportion, which was none out of ten in Kronenberg, would, certainly, have been higher among more intelligent, or among more sensitive or sophisticated people in, say, Kronenberg University or in the big cities where people circulate more widely and hear more. But I must say what I mean by "know."

By *know* I mean knowledge, binding knowledge. Men who are going to protest or take even stronger forms of action, in a dictatorship more so than in a democracy, want to be sure. When they are sure, they still may not take any form of action (in my ten friends' cases, they would not have, I think); but that is another point. What you hear of individual instances, second- or thirdhand, what you guess as to general conditions, having put half-a-dozen instances together, what someone tells you he believes is the case—these may, all together, be convincing. You may be "morally certain," satisfied in your own mind. But moral certainty and mental satisfaction are less than binding knowledge. What you and your neighbors don't expect you to *know*, your neighbors do not expect you to act on, in matters of this sort, and neither do you.

Men who participated in the operation of the atrocity system—would they or wouldn't they tell their wives? The odds are even in Germany, where husbands don't bother to tell their wives as much as we tell ours. But their wives would not tell other people, and neither would they; their jobs were, to put it mildly, of a confidential character. In such work, men, if they talk, lose their jobs. Under Nazism they lost more than their jobs. I am not saying that the men in question, the men who had firsthand knowledge, opposed the system in any degree or even resented having to play a role in it; I am saying, in the words of Cabinet-maker Klingelhöfer, that that is the way men are; and the more reprehensible the work in which they are voluntarily or involuntarily engaged, the more that way they are.

I pushed this point with Tailor Marowitz in Kronenberg, the one Jew still there who had come back from Buchenwald. On his release, in 1939, he was forbidden to talk of his experience, and, in case he might become thoughtless, he was compelled to report (simply report) to the police every day. Whom did he tell of his Buchenwald experience? His wife and "a couple of my very closest friends—Jews, of course."

"How widely was the whole thing known in Kronenberg by the end of the war?"

"You mean the rumors?"

"No—how widely was the whole thing, or anything, known?"

"Oh. Widely, very widely."

"How?"

"Oh, things seeped through somehow, always quietly, always indirectly. So people heard rumors, and the rest they could guess. Of course, most people did not believe the stories of Jews or other opponents of the regime. It was naturally thought that such persons would all exaggerate."

Rumors, guesses enough to make a man know if he wanted badly to know, or at least to believe, and always involving persons who would be suspected, "naturally," of exaggerating. Goebbels' immediate subordinate in charge of radio in the Propaganda Ministry testified at Nuremberg that he had heard of the gassing of Jews, and went to Goebbels with the report. Goebbels said it was false, "enemy propaganda," and that was the end of it. The Nuremberg tribunal accepted this man's testimony on this point and acquitted him. None of my ten friends in Kronenberg—nor anyone else in Kronenberg—was the immediate subordinate of a cabinet minister. Anti-Nazis no less than Nazis let the rumors pass—if not rejecting them, certainly not accepting them; either they were enemy propaganda or they *sounded* like enemy propaganda, and, with one's country fighting for its life and one's sons and brothers dying in war, who wants to hear, still less repeat, even what *sounds* like enemy propaganda?

Who wants to investigate the reports? Who is "looking for trouble"? Who will be the first to undertake (and how undertake it?) to track down the suspicion of governmental wrongdoing under a governmental dictatorship, to occupy himself, in times of turmoil and in wartime with evils, real or rumored, that are wholly outside his own life, outside his own circle, and, above all, outside his own power? After all, what if one found out?

Suppose that you have heard, secondhand, or even firsthand, of an instance in which a man was abused or tortured by the police in a hypothetical American community. You tell a friend whom you are trying to persuade that the police are rotten. He doesn't believe you. He wants firsthand or, if you got it secondhand, at least secondhand testimony. You go to your original source, who has told you the story only because of his absolute trust in you. You want him now to tell a man he doesn't trust, a friend of the police. He refuses. And he warns you that if you use his name as authority for the story, he will deny it. Then you will be suspect, suspected of spreading false rumors against the police. And, as it happens, the police in this hypothetical American community, are rotten, and they'll "get" you somehow.

So, after all, what if one found out in Nazi Germany

(which was no hypothetical American community)? What if one came to know? What then?

There was *nichts dagegen zu machen*, "nothing to do about it." Again and again my discussions with each of my friends reached this point, one way or another, and this very expression; again and again this question, put to me with the wide-eyed innocence that always characterizes the guilty when they ask it of the inexperienced: "What would you have done?"

What is the proportion of revolutionary heroes, of saints and martyrs, or, if you will, of troublemakers, in Stockholm, Ankara, El Paso? We in America have not had the German experience, where even private protest was dangerous, where even secret knowledge might be extorted; but what did we expect the good citizen of Minneapolis or Charlotte to do when, in the midst of war, he was told, openly and official- ly, that 112,000 of his fellow-Americans, those of Japanese ancestry on the American West Coast, had been seized without warrant and sent without due process of law to re- location centers? There was *nichts dagegen zu machen*—not even by the United States Supreme Court, which found that the action was within the Army's power—and, any- way, the good citizen of Minneapolis or Charlotte had his own troubles.

It was this, I think—they had their own troubles—that in the end explained my friends' failure to "do something" or even to know something. A man can carry only so much responsibility. If he tries to carry more, he collapses; so, to save himself from collapse, he rejects the responsibility that exceeds his capacity. There are responsibilities he must carry, in any case, and these, heavy enough under normal conditions, are intensified, even multiplied, in times of great change, be they bad times or good. My friends carried their normal responsibilities well enough; every one of them was a good householder and, with the possible exception of Tailor Schwenke, a good jobholder. But they were unaccustomed to assume public responsibility.

The public responsibilities which Nazism forced upon them—they didn't choose to assume them when they chose to be Nazis—exceeded their capacities. They didn't know, or think, at the beginning, that they were going to have to carry a guilty knowledge or a guilty conscience. Anti-Nazism of any sort, in thought or in feeling (not to say action), would have required them, as isolated individuals, already more heavily burdened than they were accustomed to being, to choose to burden themselves beyond their limit. And this, I think, is always the case with public responsibilities of a volunteer nature—in Germany, America, anywhere— which promise, at best, a deferred reward and, at worst, an imminent penalty.

The American is much better accustomed than the German to responsibilities of a volunteer character, but the principle of rejection is operative here in the United States, too, although the load limit is greater. The greater the combined load of my private and required public responsibility, the weaker my impulse to take volunteer public responsibility; if I'm building a new house and I have to enrol in Civilian Defense, my work with the Boys' Club will suffer. And anti-Nazism in a Nazi dictatorship was no Boys' Club.

Responsible men never shirk responsibility, and so, when they must reject it, they deny it. They draw the curtain. They detach themselves altogether from the consideration of the evil they ought to, but cannot, contend with. Their denial compels their detachment. A good man—even a good American—running to catch a train on an important assignment has to pass by the beating of a dog on the street and concentrate on catching the train; and, once on the train, he has to consider the assignment about which he must do something, rather than the dog-beating about which he can do nothing. If he is running fast enough and his assignment is mortally important, he will not even notice the dog-beating when he passes it by.

The Federal Bureau of Investigation, with its fantastically rapid development of a central record of an ever increasing number of Americans, law-abiding and lawless, is something new in America. But it is very old in Germany, and it had nothing to do with National Socialism except to make it easier for the Nazi government to locate and trace the whole life-history of any and every German. The German system—it has its counterpart in other European countries, including France—was, being German, extraordinarily efficient. American tourists are familiar with the police identity cards they fill out pro forma at Continental hotel desks. Resident nationals don't fill out a card when they come to live in a German town or leave it; they fill out a life-history for the police.

Policeman Hofmeister explained to me, with enthusiasm, how thoroughly the identity system meshed in Germany, before Nazism, during Nazism, and since Nazism. Every town has a criminal registry which contains, always up to date, the record of every person born in the town (no matter where he now lives) who has ever been in "trouble"; in addition, the registry contains the whole record of any person who has ever committed a crime (or been arrested) in the town, no matter where he was born. "Consider," said Policeman Hofmeister, an unenthusiastic Nazi, "how nearly impossible it is, and always has been, in Germany for anyone to escape or 'lose' himself. In such a country, my friend, law and order rule always."

How nearly impossible it is to escape, once a man has come into conflict with the police. Better, far, if you have ever before come into conflict with them (or if you suspect that you have ever come under their suspicion), to come into contact with them on their side; best of all, never come into contact with them at all. Don't see the dog-beating on the street or the wife-beating or the Jew-beating or anything. You have your own troubles.

Everyone everywhere has his own troubles. Two hundred miles from Kronenberg was the great chemicals plant of Tesch & Stabinow. In 1942, the manager—he is not a "little man," like my friends, but a manager—gets his first government order for Cyclon-B gas, which could be used as an insecticide but wouldn't be likely to be (especially since the order is "classified," secret). Now Tesch & Stabinow has been producing poison gases for the Army's chemical warfare service, which has a colonel of engineers attached to the plant for consultation. But this order is not for the Army, and there has been no consultation. The manager may have heard, or guessed, that the famous "final solution of the Jewish problem" was to be mass death by gas; Cyclon-B would be the most suitable preparation for this limited purpose. We learned at Nuremberg that the entire extermination program was directed without written orders, a remarkable fact in itself; still, a big man whose business is poison gas for the government may have heard, or guessed. Perhaps the manager shows the order to the colonel, who is not a "little" man, either.

What did these two big men—not little men, like the Nazis I knew—do then, at that moment, with the government order on the desk between them?

What did they say?

What *didn't* they say?

That is what we did not find out at Nuremberg. That is what we never find out at Nuremberg. That is what we have to imagine. And how are we to imagine it?—We are not colonels or plant managers or Nazis, big or little, with a government order on the desk between us, are we?

Everyone has his own troubles.

None of my ten Nazi friends ever knew—I say *knew*—of these great governmental systems of crime against humanity. None of them except possibly (quite probably, I believe) Tailor Schwenke, the SA Sturmführer, ever did anything that we should call wrong by the measure we apply to ourselves. These men were, after all, respectable men, like us. The former bank clerk, Kessler, told his Jewish friend, former Bank Director Rosenthal, the day before the synagogue arson in 1938, that "with men like me in the Party," men of moral and religious feeling, "things will be better, you'll see." And Hildebrandt, the teacher, thought that it had to be expected, under the conditions that obtained in Germany just before Nazism, that the movement would be proletarian and radical, with fools and villains in positions of leadership, "but as more and more decent citizens joined it, it would certainly change for the better and become a *bürgerlich*, bourgeois development. After all, the French Revolution had its Robespierres, *nicht wahr?*"

My friends meant what they said; they calculated wrong, but they meant what they said. And the moral and religious bank clerk was, on the basis of that mortally wrong calculation, to preach the most barbarous paganism. And the decent bourgeois teacher was to teach "Nazi literature" from Nazi textbooks provided by the Nazi school board. Teachers teach what they are told to teach or quit, and to quit a public post meant, in the early years of the Third Reich, unemployment; later on, when one had an anti-Nazi political past, it meant concentration camp. "Once you were in the Party," said Baker Wedekind, who doesn't say he ever wanted to get out, "you didn't get out easily." A man who had always been nonpolitical might get away with "dropping out"; a political man, a man who had assumed the political responsibility of citizenship, never. Policeman Hofmeister, who had done his duty in Kronenberg since 1908, did his duty in 1938 when he was ordered to arrest Jews for being Jews. One of those he arrested, the tailor Marowitz, calls him "a decent man"—*anständig* is the word he used.

All this in no degree reduces the number and awfulness of Nazi evils; it reduces the number and awfulness of Nazi evildoers. It took so few to manage it all, in a country fabled for the efficiency and faithfulness of its civil servants. Policeman Hofmeister was sworn to fidelity to the Führer in a mass-loyalty-oath ceremony at the Kronenberg Town Hall early in 1933. The whole civil service participated and heard the message from Field Marshal Göring himself: "The Führer knows that every civil servant is faithful to the oath." And so they were, to the holy oath by which Germans (more so than men of either freer or lighter consciences) bound themselves so mortally that the ultimate resistance to Hitler, which exploded July 20, 1944, lost in advance many bitterly anti-Nazi Army officers who would do anything except violate their sworn word. The decision of the resistance conspiracy to assassinate Hitler, rather than arrest and convict him, was made for this very reason; sworn fealty to the Führer bound hundreds of thousands until he was dead.

With the civil service and the military safely "faithful," it took so few at the administrative level and so few more, a million at most, of a population of seventy million, to carry out the whole program of Nazi persecution; a million ex-convicts, future ex-convicts, poolroom hoodlums, dis-heartened young job-seekers, of whom every large country has its million. And Germany had, especially in the north and east, a whole class of recruits better known in eastern Europe and Asia than elsewhere, the brutally bred young *Bauernknechte*, the quasi-serf farm hands, over whom the landowners up to the end of the first World War had had almost absolute feudal jurisdiction.

The "democratic," that is, argumentative, bill-collector, Herr Simon, was greatly interested in the mass deportation of Americans of Japanese ancestry from our West Coast in 1942. He had not heard of it before, and, when I told him of the West Coast Army Commander's statement that "a Jap is a Jap," he hit the table with his fist and said, "Right you are. A Jap is a Jap, a Jew is a Jew." "A German a Ger-man," I said. "Of course," said the German, proudly. "It's a matter of blood."

He asked me whether I had known anybody connected with the West Coast deportation. When I said "No," he asked me what I had done about it. When I said "Noth-ing," he said, triumphantly, "There. You learned about all these things openly, through your government and your press. We did not learn through ours. As in your case, noth-ing was required of us—in our case, not even knowledge. You *knew* about things you thought were wrong—you did think it was wrong, didn't you, Herr Professor?" "Yes." "So. You did nothing. We *heard*, or *guessed*, and we did nothing. So it is everywhere." When I protested that the Japanese-descended Americans had not been treated like the Jews, he said, "And if they had been—what then? Do you not see that the idea of doing something or doing noth-ing is in either case the same?"

"Very early," he went on, "still in spring, '33, one of our SA leaders protested against the dismissal of the Oberbürgermeister, a Social Democrat, a good, really nonpolitical man. The SA leader was arrested and taken away. And this, mind you, was when the SA still had great power in the regime. He never came back. His family is still here. We heard he was convicted, but we never heard for what. There was no open trial for enemies of the State. It was said it wasn't necessary; they had forfeited their right to it." "And what do you think?" "That's a legal question. If the courts say it's so, it's so, *gell?*" *Gell?* is dialect for the rhetorical "isn't it so?" "nicht wahr?" "n'est-ce pas?" and Hessian townsfolk love to use it.

A few hundred at the top, to plan and direct at every level; a few thousand to supervise and control (without a voice in policy) at every level; a few score thousand specialists (teachers, lawyers, journalists, scientists, artists, actors, athletes, and social workers) eager to serve or at least unwilling to pass up a job or to revolt; a million of the *Pöbel*, which sounds like "people" and means "riffraff," to do what we would call the dirty work, ranging from murder, torture, robbery, and arson to the effort which probably employed more Germans in inhumanity than any other in Nazi history, the standing of "sentry" in front of Jewish shops and offices in the boycott of April, 1933.

And all the other millions?

They had only to go on as they were and keep out of trouble. What could be easier? "Only Communists were in trouble," said Herr Simon.

"And in Russia," I said, "only anti-Communists."

"That's the way it is," said Herr Simon.

"But," said I, "besides the Communists, there were the

Socialists and the Jews and the religious opponents of the regime. They were 'in trouble,' too, weren't they?"

"Oh, yes," said Herr Simon, ingenuously, "but that came later. I meant at first."

*Only Communists were in trouble.* And all the other millions of Germans? The SA and the Hitler Youth and the German Maidens marched up the hill and down again on State occasions, which, in such a State, and especially in Germany, are frequent. The workers were dismissed by the Arbeitsfront, the State employer-employee agency, to watch the SA march, just as the government workers in Washington are given a half-day holiday to swell (or, rather, comprise) the crowd that lines the capital's streets to welcome the President of Turkey or the Emperor of Ethiopia; in Nazi Germany swelling the crowd was compulsory. Those who had uniforms strutted in them on Sundays and came home from their Friday night Storm Troop meeting to tell their wives that they had passed a Jewish acquaintance on the street and only nodded to him. And their wives said, "*Gut,*" which, in German, may mean "Good" and may mean "Yes."

## CHAPTER 5

## The Joiners

Party membership in the NSDAP meant absolutely nothing. Like membership in many organizations, it was restricted for the purpose of whetting the appetite of the nonmembers who, by virtue of the restriction, were now excluded. It's an old come-one, known to every real estate promoter. When Hitler was released from prison in December, 1924, he announced that he would accept only 35 per cent of his previous followers, and that was all it took to bring 100 per cent of them to heel again.

In March, 1933, when membership in the triumphant NSDAP was thrown open, millions joined. These "March violets," as they were contemptuously called by both old Nazis and old anti-Nazis, were band-wagoners. Hitler never trusted them, and few of them ever rose to high rank. Hitler was right; the "March violets" joined for good reasons, bad reasons, Nazi reasons, non-Nazi reasons, and even anti-Nazi reasons; and X-number of them for no reason at all—that is, because "everybody" was doing it.

I do not mean that Party membership was the same as buying a tag on tag day in America, but neither was it without any resemblance. Nor was the Nazi block-manager system the same as the civilian defense organization in America; but neither was it entirely noncomparable. Eager beavers, who constituted a distinctly small minority of the block managers in Kronenberg, rode herd for all (and more than) they were worth, swaggering, bullying, discriminating, threatening to denounce, and occasionally denouncing. But the majority served notices of meetings or canvassed for contributions and did not keep official track of delinquency. In American-occupied Kronenberg, after the war, some of the most enthusiastic organizers of American-supported projects had been among the most enthusiastic organizers of Nazi-supported projects. Some of these people were trying to cover up for past misdeeds or mistakes; but most of them were simply enthusiastic organizers of anybody's-supported project.

Men joined the Party to get a job or to hold a job or to get a better job or to save themselves from getting a worse job, or to get a contract or to hold a contract, a customer, a client, a patient. Every third man, in time, worked for the State. In the Weimar Republic the German tradition of the nonpolitical, nonparty civil servant (always safely conservative) was broken down; the Nazis finished the politicalization of the government workers which the Social Democrats began.

It would not be reckless to estimate that half the civil servants had to join the Party or lose their jobs. The other half were well advised to do likewise, and nearly all of them did. Career men in the central and provincial governments and in the city halls, living only for their pensions, could no more resist Party membership (if they ever thought of doing so) than they can the "kickback" in our own Tammanies. In the United States the ancient, if not honorable, practice of compelling state payrollers to support the party in power with 1 per cent or even 2 per cent of their annual salaries is known colloquially as "swinging the mace." In 1954 the Governor of Pennsylvania, admitting that the system was in operation there, said that there was no "macing" involved; the contributions, he said, were voluntary, and no state employee would be fired for failure to contribute.

"Governor Fine is surely not so naïve as his use of that word 'voluntary' would indicate," said the *Pittsburgh Post-Gazette* editorially. "When your political bosses, the men who got you your public job, ask you to chip in for the welfare of the party, there's very little 'voluntary' about the situation. You don't have to chip in, true enough, but if you have any brains or ambition, you'd better. To be considered uncooperative by the political bosses is not the best way to advance or even hang on in a patronage post." In Germany, where, as everywhere in Europe, party membership is formal and the party is supported by regular dues, you did not have to join the National Socialist Party if you were a government employee, but, if you had any brains or ambition, you'd better have.

The exposure of hundreds of former Nazis in the Foreign Ministry of postwar West Germany, although it revealed in a half-dozen sensational cases a real penetration by Nazism of the Adenauer regime, did not tell us, for the rest, whether they were high officials in the Ministry, stenographers, or messenger boys before, during, or after Nazism; or how many of them (if any) had joined the NSDAP for the purpose of covering their anti-Nazism, alleviating the application of inhuman policies, or even participating from within in a hoped-for (or merely dreamed-of) revolt.

Take the late Ernst von Weizsäcker, promoted by Nazi Foreign Minister Ribbentrop in 1934 from Minister to Switzerland to State Secretary for Foreign Affairs. He not only became a Nazi; he accepted the rank of brigadier general in the black-shirted Nazi SS. As Ribbentrop's State

Secretary, he signed the documents by which thousands of Jews were deported to slavery and death. At Nuremberg the American prosecutor called him "the Devil's State Secretary" and "the executive officer of Murder, Incorporated." An American tribunal convicted him of crimes against humanity.

There, certainly, was a Nazi. But at his trial, the diplomats of all the Allied countries (including the United States of America) testified to his hatred of Nazism; all the surviving leaders of the anti-Nazi resistance in Germany testified to his support and encouragement; distinguished Allied churchmen, scholars, scientists, and International Red Cross executives testified to the relentlessness of his efforts to mitigate or circumvent Nazi directives; a procession of German Jews and Jews of Nazi-occupied countries testified that his illegal assistance to them had saved their lives. Bishop Primate Berggrav, leader of the Norwegian resistance and President of the World Council of Churches, said, "Von Weizsäcker was not a Nazi; he was an anti-Nazi. I know this man in the essential character of his soul. I saw him suffer and serve. If he is condemned, we are all condemned."

Expressions like "Nazi teacher," "Nazi actor," "Nazi journalist," "Nazi lawyer," even "Nazi pastor," are as meaningless as "the Devil's State Secretary." Most teachers teach the three R's under all regimes everywhere. Most actors are looking for jobs anywhere. Most journalists are reporting fires or accidents (with most lawyers hard on their heels) and are writing what the management wants, whoever the management. And most pastors in Germany had always preached Christ crucified without seeing—who does?—that he was being crucified all around them every day.

There are many lawyers in the United States who disagree vehemently with the policies and program of the

American Bar Association; but, if they want to practice law, they had better belong to the constituent societies of the ABA. There are even more physicians in the United States who disagree even more vehemently with the policies of the American Medical Association, but, if they want to practice medicine, they had better belong to the constituent societies of the AMA. They may only pay dues, and that grudgingly; but the record shows that they belong. They are officially "guilty" of the policies of the organization which speaks in their name. In Nazi Germany the professional associations were all "blanketed" into the National Socialist organization.

"So it was," said all of my Nazi (and most, not all, of my anti-Nazi) friends and acquaintances in Germany, and always with a sigh that said, "You don't believe it, do you?"

The anti-Nazi son of a railroad worker told me his father's story. In 1931 the German state railways were letting men go because of the depression. Herr Schäfer, who had no interest in politics, learning that his local boss had joined the National Socialist Party, joined it himself in the hope of hanging on to his job. Long after the war, he learned that the local boss had been an anti-Nazi who had joined the Party in the hope of hanging on to *his* job, because *his* boss, the section superintendent, was an ardent Nazi. And the local boss, assuming that Schäfer had joined the Party from conviction, tried covertly to get him fired —unsuccessfully, because the section superintendent was protecting Nazis. "So it was," in one instance, in Kronenberg—perhaps in more than one, and not only in Kronenberg.

None of this means that there was any mass opposition —if opposition is more than unenthusiasm—to National Socialism in Germany. No attempt has ever been made to discover its genuine extent. Perhaps no attempt would be feasible. But we know how little mass opposition to National Socialism there was prior to 1939 outside Germany, where opposition would have been less dangerous than it was within. Those who, as Cabinetmaker Klingelhöfer said, lived outside the system and were not its beneficiaries could see its evils better. How many of those saw them or, seeing them, raised their voices even to demand that their own governments grant refuge to the system's victims? Some few millions of Germans, at least, listened for foreign voices to hearten their opposition: from America they heard a few; from England and France, where the Germans listened more closely, still fewer. Moral indignation outside Germany was free, but it was scarce.

Nonmembership in the Party meant no more than membership. As some men joined for good, bad, or no reasons, so some men, for good reasons, bad reasons, or no reason at all, did not join. "After the war," said Herr Hildebrandt, the teacher, "every nonmember of the Party was an 'anti-Nazi hero.' Some of these heroes weren't Nazis because of the sixty cents a month dues and for no other reason." "Opposition?" said Herr Simon, the argumentative bill-collecter. "What does 'opposition' mean? Employers opposed the Party because it raised wages, capitalists because it cut profits, loafers because it found jobs; but what do they all say now? They all say, 'The poor Jews.' All the criminals who didn't join because they were 'on the lam' —now they are 'anti-Nazi persecutees.' "

"I was a tobacco salesman," said Herr Damm, who had risen to be office manager of the Party headquarters in Kronenberg, "but I was let out when the state tobacco tax was raised 100 per cent in 1930. I reported to the Labor Office immediately and wrote applications for every job, but

I got no work. At first I drew unemployment compensation, but then, since I was still single, I was told I could go back home to the village and live on my father's farm, which, when my father died, my oldest brother would get. That's the way it was in the spring of 1932, when the National Socialists from Kronenberg held a recruiting evening in the village *Bierstube*. Only one member of each household was allowed to sign up, and my family all agreed that I was the one. I agreed, too. Why not? And, by the way, Herr Professor, it was the *only* political party that had ever held a recruiting meeting in our village as far back as anyone could remember."

Cabinetmaker Klingelhöfer was contemptuous when he spoke of those who did not want to join the Party "lest something happen, some day" but who, while the going was good, wanted it known that they were the truest of the Nazis. "My own brother-in-law was one, Schuchardt, who had the café in the Mauerweg. I used to argue with him—not to join, no, but to be *something*, either for or against. He always said it was for 'business reasons' that he was nonpolitical but, of course, that his heart was with the Party. So he made big contributions to the Winter Relief, always hung out the flag, said 'Heil Hitler' a thousand times a day, and then, when the Americans came, he wasn't a Nazi, he had never been in the Party. Such men play both sides, always. You admire them, their cunning. But you wouldn't want to be like them, would you?" "No," I said.

The notes of my conversations with Herr Klingelhöfer, made during or immediately after our meetings, quote him as saying, again and again, *"Die freiwillige Feuerwehr über alles!* The Volunteer Fire Department above everything!" and *"Mein Leben für die freiwillige Feuerwehr!* My life for the Volunteer Fire Department!" I can scarcely believe my own notes; this earnest, middle-aged German cabinetmaker is as fire-department–crazy as a boy. Kronenberg, like all German cities under one hundred thousand population, had a volunteer fire department. In 1927 the Fire Chief asked my friend Klingelhöfer to join because the department was short a trumpeter. In those days each block had a fire trumpeter. The trumpeter had an alarm in his bedroom, and when the alarm rang he blew his trumpet out the window, awakening the other firemen (and everyone else) in the block. So Klingelhöfer, who was interested in trumpeting but not, in those days, in fire-fighting, joined. "N'ja, that's me. I always joined everything."

Beginning in 1932, under the Republic, Klingelhöfer took two weeks off from his shop every summer, at his own expense, to attend the state training school for firemen. In 1933 he was a squad leader in the *freiwillige Feuerwehr* when, the Nazis having come to power, some of the "fellows" said that Party members would get promotion preference in the department. "You see," he said, "before the Hitler time, the firemen chose their own leaders, but after 1933 promotions were proposed by the company chiefs and had to be approved by the Oberbürgermeister. Of course, the Oberbürgermeister was a Nazi, and, when the old chief, who wasn't, quit in 1934, the man promoted from company chief to take his place was a Nazi, too. So I joined. Besides, I thought the Party was a good thing."

"Would you have joined if it hadn't been for the *Feuerwehr?*"

"Not then. Later, probably; oh, yes, certainly. But not then."

"Why not?"

"Because I was against a one-party State. That was one reason. And I was not a strong nationalist; a Frenchman is a man, just as I am. That was another reason. And the race politics didn't make sense; there is no pure race any more, and inbreeding is bad anyway—we know that from plants and animals and from the insanity and feeble-mindedness in the villages where everyone is related to everyone else. That was another reason. We talked about all these things in the Wandervogel, the Youth Movement, when I was young, and I had gone on hikes across the borders a little way, into both France and Switzerland."

"Well," I said, "you've given me three good reasons for not being a Nazi."

"*Und doch war ich in der Partei!* And *still* I was in the Party!" And he laughed exuberantly, and I with him.

Once he was in the Party, he was asked to join the SA and to be a block manager. "I said 'No.' The Volunteer Fire Department was more important, and I said so. The SA didn't like that, and *they* said so," and he laughed again. "But we were independent until (when was it?) 1934, yes, in the reorganization after the Röhm purge. Then we heard that all the fire departments would become either technical troops of the SA or a branch of the police, and at the firemen's training school that summer we were asked which we preferred. There were fifty men in training, one from each county in Hesse. All fifty of them said the same thing—they wanted neither; they wanted to remain independent.

"That's what we *said*, yes, and that fall we were put under the police, and our name was changed to *Feuerlösch-Polizei*, "fire-fighting police." How is *that* for a name, Herr Professor?" and he laughed again.

"Terrible," I said, and laughed with him.

"*So war die Sache*. That's the way it was. Well, at least it wasn't the SA. I was promoted to adjutant to the new chief. At the end of 1938 the police in the towns like Kronenberg were put under the SS, so we, the *freiwillige Feuerwehr*, were part of the Nazi SS! What do you think of *that*, Herr Professor?"

"What did *you* think of it?"

"*Man macht eine Faust im Sack.* One made a fist in one's pocket." He wasn't laughing now, nor was I. Then he brightened and smiled and said, "*Aber, die freiwillige Feuerwehr über alles!*"

"Opposition?" said Herr Klingelhöfer, on another occasion. "How would anybody know? How would anybody know what somebody else opposes or doesn't oppose? That a man *says* he opposes or doesn't oppose depends upon the circumstances, where, and when, and to whom, and just how he says it. And then you must still guess *why* he says what he says. So, too, even in action. The few who tried to kill Hitler and seize the Government in '44, certainly they 'opposed,' but why? Some hated the dictatorship of National Socialism, some hated its democracy, some were personally ambitious or jealous, some wanted the Army to control the country, maybe some could escape punishment for crimes only by a change of government. Some, I am sure, were pure and noble. But they all acted."

"And here in Kronenberg?"

"Here in Kronenberg? Well, we had twenty thousand people. Of these twenty thousand people, how many opposed? How would you know? How would I know? If you ask me how many *did* something in secret opposition, something that meant great danger to them, I would say, well, twenty. And how many did something like that openly, and from good motives alone? Maybe five, maybe two. That's the way men are."

"You always say, 'That's the way men are,' Herr Klingelhöfer," I said. "Are you sure that that's the way men are?"

"That's the way men are here," he said. "Are they different in America?"

Alibis, alibis, alibis; alibis for the Germans; alibis, too, for man, who, when he was once asked, in olden time, whether he would prefer to do or to suffer injustice, replied, "I would rather neither." The mortal choice which every German had to make—whether or not he knew he was making it—is a choice which we Americans have never had to confront. But personal and professional life confronts us with the same kind of choice, less mortally, to be sure, every day. And the fact that it is a platitude does not keep it from being true that we find it easier, on the whole, to admire Socrates than to envy him; to adore the Cross, especially on cloudy Sundays, than to carry it. A still young man in Berlin, an actor forbidden employment since the war, said to me: "I had my choice of acting for Hitler at home or dying for him in Russia. I preferred not to die for him in Russia, not because I was an anti-Nazi (I wasn't) but because I wasn't a hero. If I had wanted to die for Hitler or my country—and this, you understand, was the same thing in the war—I would not have waited to be conscripted. I would have enlisted, like a patriot. Tell me, Herr Professor"—he was too polite to ask me what *I* had done in *my* circumstances—"what would you have done in *my* circumstances?"

## CHAPTER 6

# The Way To Stop Communism

"It had its beginning in Munich," said my friend Herr Kessler, the one-time Catholic from Bavaria's neighboring state of Württemberg in southern Germany, "in the most artistic, cultivated, and Catholic city in Germany, the city of art and of song and of love and *Gemütlichkeit*, the only city in Germany that all the foreign tourists always insisted on visiting. There it had its beginning, a purely local affair without any *Weltanschauung*, philosophy. Nobody outside paid any attention to it. Only after it spread and took root, Bavarians asked, 'Who is Hitler? What is this Party with the fancy name? What is behind it?'

"Hitler was a simple soldier, like millions of others, only he had a *feeling* for masses of people, and he could speak with passion. The people didn't pay any attention to the Party program as such. They went to the meetings just to hear something new, anything new. They were desperate about the economic situation, 'a new Germany' sounded good to them; but from a deep or broad point of view they saw nothing at all. Hitler talked always against the government, against the lost war, against the peace treaty, against unemployment. All that, people liked. By the time the intellectuals asked, 'What is this?' it had a solid basis in the common people. It was the *Arbeiter*, *Sozialist* Party, the

Party of *workers controlling the social order;* it was not for intellectuals.

"The situation in Germany got worse and worse. What lay underneath people's daily lives, the real root, was gone. Look at the suicides; look at the immorality. People wanted something *radical,* a real change. This want took the form of more and more Communism, especially in middle Germany, in the industrial area, and in the cities of the north. *That* was no invention of Hitler; *that* was real. In countries like America there is no Communism because there is no desire for *radical* change.

"Hitlerism had to answer Communism with something just as radical. Communism always used force; Hitlerism answered it with force. The really absolute enemy of Communism, always clear, always strong in the popular mind, was National Socialism, the *only* enemy that answered Communism in kind. If you wanted to save Germany from Communism—to be *sure* of doing it—you went to National Socialism. The Nazi slogan in 1932 was, 'If you want your country to go Bolshevik, vote Communist; if you want to remain free Germans, vote Nazi.'

"The middle parties, between the two millstones, played no role at all between the two radicalisms. Their adherents were basically the Bürger, the bourgeois, the 'nice' people who decide things by parliamentary procedure; and the politically indifferent; and the people who wanted to keep or, at worst, only modify the status quo.

"I'd like to ask the American Bürger, the middle-class man: What would you have done when your country stood so? A dictatorship, or destruction by Bolshevism? Bolshevism looked like slavery and the death of the soul. It didn't matter if you were in agreement with Nazism. Nazism looked like the only defense. There was your choice."

" 'I would rather neither,' " I said.

"Of course, Herr Professor. You are a bourgeois. I was, too, once. I was a bank clerk, remember."

Of my ten friends, only two, Tailor Schwenke and Bill-collector Simon, the two *alte Kämpfer*, wanted to be Nazis and nothing else. They were both positive—still are—that National Socialism was Germany's and therefore their own, salvation from Communism, which, like the much more sensitive bank clerk, they both called "Bolshevism," "the death of the soul." "Bolshevism" came from outside, from the barbarous world that was Russia; Nazism, its enemy, was German, it was their own; they would rather Nazism.

Did they know what Communism, "Bolshevism," was? They did not; not my friends. Except for Herr Kessler, Teacher Hildebrandt, and young Horstmar Rupprecht (after he entered the university, in 1941), they knew Bolshevism as a specter which, as it took on body in their imaginings, embraced not only the Communists but the Social Democrats, the trade-unions, and, of course, the Jews, the gypsies, the neighbor next door whose dog had bit them, and his dog; the bundled root cause of all their past, present, and possible tribulations. Prior to 1930 or 1931, none of my ten friends, except Tailor Schwenke and Bill-collector Simon, hated any Communist he knew (they were few, in nonindustrial little Kronenberg) or identified him with the specter; *these* were flesh-and-blood neighbors, who would not break into your house and burn it down. After 1933 or 1934 these same neighbors were seen for "what they were"—innocently disguised lackeys of the specter. The Bolshevist specter outraged the property sense of my all but propertyless friends, the class sense of these *déclassé* Bürger, the political sense of these helpless subjects of the former Emperor, the religious sense of

97

these *pro forma* churchgoers, the moral sense of these unex-
ceptional characters. It was "the death of the soul."

The question was not whether Communism threatened
the country, as, with the continuation of deteriorating conditions, it certainly did or soon would; the question was
whether the Germans were convinced that it did. And they
were. They were so well convinced, by such means as the
Reichstag fire of 1933, that the Nazis were able, ultimately,
to establish anti-Communism as a religion, immune from
inquiry and defensible by definition alone. When in 1937
the Pope attacked the "errors" of National Socialism, the
Nazi Government's defense of its policies consisted of a
Note accusing the Pope of "having dealt a dangerous blow
to the defense front against the world menace of Bolshevism."

Those Germans who would do anything, be anything, join
anything to stop Bolshevism had, in the end, to be Nazis.
And Nazism did stop Bolshevism. How it stopped Bolshevism, with what means and what consequences, did not
matter—not enough, at least, to alienate them. None of its
shortcomings, mild or hideous, none of its contradictions,
small or calamitous, ever swayed them. To them, then and
now, Nazism kept its promise.

Three of my ten friends, the bank clerk, Kessler, the
salesman, Damm, and the tailor's apprentice, Herr Schwenke's son Gustav, were unemployed when they joined, and
the first two were family men in middle life at the time. In
all three cases they joined, I think, because they were unemployed—which is not in the least to say that they would
not have joined if they hadn't been. The two Old Fighters,
Tailor Schwenke and Bill-collector Simon, when they
joined in 1925, were both employed (the tailor self-em-
ployed), but the inflation which had just ended had re-

duced them (and nearly all other *petit bourgeois* Germans) to near-starvation.

Willy Hofmeister, the old policeman, joined the Party in 1937 because the new Police Chief said that all the men must join. When I asked him if he could have refused, he said, "*Ein Millionär war ich ja gar nicht*. A millionaire I was not." (The Sicherheitspolizei, or detective force, one of whose five members he was in Kronenberg, was subsequently attached willy-nilly to the Gestapo, just as the Volunteer Fire Department was placed under the SS). Horstmar Rupprecht, the student, had been a Nazi since he was eight years old, in the Jungvolk, the "cub" organization of the Hitler Jugend; his ambition (which he realized) was to be a Hitler Youth leader; in America he would certainly have been a Scoutmaster.

The two most active churchmen of the ten, Herr Klingelhöfer, the cabinetmaker, and Herr Wedekind, the baker, both of them vestrymen of their parish church, were the two who today (and, I think, yesterday) put the most emphasis on the "everybody-was-doing-it" theme. (They were both "March violets.") The fact that they were, of the ten, the two retail tradesmen doubtless contributed to their sensitivity to this urge to go along (*mitschwimmen* was the term each of them used) with the Party as they had with the Church; the cabinetmaker freely admitted that his church activity "didn't hurt" his coffin-making, although neither he nor I would say that he was a churchman *because* it was good business to be one.

Neither Klingelhöfer nor Wedekind read the Party Program, the historic Twenty-five Points, before they joined, while they were members, or afterward. (Only the teacher, of the ten, ever read it.) But they were earnestly impressed, as were most ardent churchgoers in the early years of the movement, by the Program's demand, of which every one of my friends had heard, for "positive Christianity" for Germany. The baker left the vestry board in 1937, when the Church-Party struggle had become intense. He says he left voluntarily, as a "good Nazi," because he felt that his Party loyalty compromised his position on the board; his pastor confirms his assertion. But he did not leave the church. Herr Klingelhöfer—"I always joined everything"— remained a vestryman to the end.

All ten of my friends, including the sophisticated Hildebrandt, were affected by this sense of what the Germans call *Bewegung*, movement, a swelling of the human sea, something supraparty and suprapolitical, a surge of the sort that does not, at the time, evoke analysis or, afterward, yield to it. These men were victims of the "Bolshevik" rabies, to be sure. They were equally victims of economic hardship and, still worse, of economic hopelessness, a hopelessness that they suffered more easily by identifying it with their country's. But they were seekers, too, and affirmers—agents, not just patients.

Their country was torn to pieces from without, of course, but still more cruelly from within. Germans had been at one another's throats since 1918, and dissension grew shriller and more bitter all the time. In the course of the decomposition, the principle of *being German*, so newly won under Bismarck and so preciously held for fear of its slipping away, was indeed being lost. The uniting of the country, of all of its people, was possible only on this one principle of *being German*, and my ten friends, even including the old fanatic Schwenke, onlookers at the disruptive struggles of the old parties and the old party politicians, at the process of shredding the mystical fabric which supported this principle, asked, "Where is Germany?" Nazism—Hitler, rather—knew this and knew that nothing else mattered to my friends so much as this, the identification of this Germany, the community again, in which one might know he belonged and, belonging, identify himself. This was the movement which any non-German might see at once for what it was; and this was the movement which restored my friends as the sight of home restores the lost child; or as the sight of the Lorelei Maiden, seen sitting high above the Rhine, combing her golden hair with a golden comb in the surprising late sunshine, bewitches the sailor, who overlooks the rocks beneath the river.

National Socialism was a revulsion by my friends against parliamentary politics, parliamentary debate, parliamentary government—against all the higgling and the haggling of the parties and the splinter parties, their coalitions, their confusions, and their conniving. It was the final fruit of the common man's repudiation of "the rascals." Its motif was, "Throw them all out." My friends, in the 1920's, were like spectators at a wrestling match who suspect that beneath all the grunts and groans, the struggle and the sweat, the match is "fixed," that the performers are only pretending to put on a fight. The scandals that rocked the country, as one party or cabal "exposed" another, dismayed and then disgusted my friends. (One sensed some of this reaction against the celebrated Army-McCarthy hearing in the United States in 1954—not against one side or another but against "the whole thing" as "disgusting" or "disgraceful.")

While the ship of the German State was being shivered, the officers, who alone had life-preservers, disputed their prerogatives on the bridge. My friends observed that none of the non-Communist, non-Nazi leaders objected to the

35,000 Reichsmark salaries of the cabinet ministers; only the Communists and the Nazis objected. And the bitterest single disappointment of Nazism—both to Simon, the insensitive bill-collector, and to Hofmeister, the sensitive policeman—was the fact that Hitler had promised that no official would get more than 1,000 Reichsmarks a month and did not keep his promise.

My friends wanted Germany purified. They wanted it purified of the politicians, of *all* the politicians. They wanted a representative leader in place of unrepresentative representatives. And Hitler, the pure man, the antipolitician, was the man, untainted by "politics," which was only a cloak for corruption. The "mink coat" scandal in the United States at the beginning of the 1950's had its counterpart in Berlin in the beginning of the 1930's, when the Nazis focused their campaign for the mayoralty on the receipt by the wife of the Social Democratic mayor of a fur coat from a man who did business with the city.

Against "the whole pack," "the whole kaboodle," "the whole business," against *all* the parliamentary politicians and *all* the parliamentary parties, my friends evoked Hitlerism, and Hitlerism overthrew them all. The power struggle within the National Socialist Party, which culminated in the Röhm purge of June 30, 1934, was in essence parliamentary and political, but my friends never knew it. They accepted it as a cleanup of moral degenerates, and if they caught a glimpse of the reality underneath the official propaganda, their nascent concern was dissipated by the fact that the Führer acted with an instant and terrible sword and the "debate" with Röhm was finished; the Führer held the country and the countrymen together.

This was the *Bewegung*, the movement, that restored

my friends and bewitched them. Those Germans who saw it all at the beginning—there were not very many; there never are, I suppose, anywhere—called Hitler the *Rattenfänger*, the "rat-catcher." Every American child has read *The Pied-Piper of Hamlin*. Every German child has read it, too. In German its title is *Der Rattenfänger von Hameln*.

## CHAPTER 7

## "We Think with Our Blood"

Heinrich Hildebrandt joined the Party in 1937. He may not have been the only one of my ten friends who was afraid not to join, but he was the only one of them who knew then and now, and says so, that fear was his reason—fear and advantage. ("But how," he said, "is one to separate them?") He had been an anti-Nazi, an active moderate democrat in East Prussia before he came quietly to Hesse in 1935 and, his past uneasily buried, got a job teaching literature and French in the Kronenberg *Realgymnasium*, the humanistic high school. An anti-Nazi and a cultivated man, more clearly aware than most men of the primitive considerations which directed his course of action—and yet he, too, once he was inside the system he hated, sheep that he was in wolf's clothing, found something profoundly good in it.

"Perhaps," he said, "it was because I wanted, unconsciously, to justify what I had done. If so, I succeeded. But I say it now, too, and I know it now. There were good things, great things, in the system—and the system itself was evil."

"For instance?"

"You mean about the evils?"

"No, I know about those. About 'the good things, the great things.' "

"Perhaps I should make it singular instead of plural, the good *thing*. For the first time in my life I was really the peer of men who, in the Kaiser time and in the Weimar time, had always belonged to classes lower or higher than my own, men whom one had always looked down on or up to, but never *at*. In the Labor Front—I represented the teachers' association—I came to know such people at first hand, to know their lives and to have them know mine. Even in America—perhaps; I have never been there—I suspect that the teacher who talks about 'the common people' has never known one, really known one, not even if he himself came from among them, as I, with an Army officer as a father, did not. National Socialism broke down that separation, that class distinction. Democracy—such democracy as we had had—didn't do it and is not doing it now."

"Wedekind, the baker," I said, "told me how 'we simple working-class men stood side by side with learned men, in the Labor Front.' "

"I remember Wedekind," said the teacher. "I didn't know him before I joined the Party, and I don't know him now. Why? Because he was my inferior. A baker is nothing, a teacher is something; in the Labor Front we belonged to something together, we had something in common. We could know each other in those days. Do you understand that, Herr Professor?"

"I understand it because you call me 'Herr Professor,' " I said, smiling.

"Yes. The baker calls me 'Herr Studienrat'—that was my rank—and I call you 'Herr Professor.' It is for me to accept the baker and for you to accept me."

"Neither the baker nor the teacher would call a professor 'Professor' in America," I said.

"Never?"

"Rarely. I can't remember ever having been called 'Professor,' except by friends, who in an argument might say ironically, 'Professor, you're crazy.'"

"It was never like that in Germany," he said, "or anywhere else in Europe—not even, from what I know, in England. Always in Germany, before Nazism, and again now, the title is a genuine reflection of class distinction."

I told Herr Hildebrandt of an incident a German friend, an eminent physicist, had recently reported to me. He was returning to Germany from a scientific congress in Amsterdam, and an American colleague was traveling with him. At the Netherlands-German border the American discovered he had lost his passport. My friend observed that both the Dutch and the German passport inspectors were elderly men, obviously relics of the Imperial days, and he said to the two of them, "Gentlemen, I am Professor Doktor Karl Otto, Baron von G——, and you have my word that Professor W—— possesses a valid passport properly visaed, which he has mislaid. I take personal responsibility for Professor W——'s transit." "It was a gamble," the physicist said, in reporting the incident to me, "but it succeeded. The obvious duty of the two old inspectors was overridden by the word of a Professor Doktor Baron, and W—— came in with me. He was amazed."

"Why was he amazed?" said the teacher, when I told him the story.

"Because," I said, "every side-show medicine salesman in America calls himself 'Professor,' and a man who calls himself 'Baron' or 'Count' is an obvious fraud. An American passport inspector would have turned to one of his colleagues and said, 'Here's a hot one, Joe. The "Professor" wants in and he hasn't a passport. What're you peddling, "Professor," cocaine?'"

"You exaggerate a little?" said the teacher.

"A little," I said, "but only a little."

"I understand," he said. "This is your American feeling of absolute equality. That we have never had here. But there was a democracy in Nazism, and it was real. My— how shall I say it?—my inferiors accepted me."

*My inferiors accepted me.*

The German schoolteacher found himself, in Nazi Germany, as, I dare say, any schoolteacher finds himself in any emerging totalitarianism, in a unique situation which constituted a compulsion upon him unknown (or less painfully known) to other kinds of workers. The National Socialist development entailed the inexorable displacement of the teaching profession from its position in the German community. The teacher everywhere in Europe is much more highly honored than his American counterpart, and more highly paid. In addition, he has had, in Europe, an education so far beyond the financial ability of nearly all his countrymen that the very fact of his being a teacher is taken as evidence of his family's having been prosperous, and the prosperous, in Europe no less than in America, are highly honored and highly paid.

In the small community, the village, and even the town, the teacher and the pastor stand alone in Germany, the two *Respektpersonen*, far above the mayor or the merchant. And, because of the Church-State identity, they stand together as the arbiters of the community's moral and cultural, as well as its religious and intellectual, life. In the village which has only a visiting pastor who comes every second Sunday, the alternative sermon is "naturally" preached by the teacher. Religious education was officially, until 1918, an element of elementary-school education. And the teacher is like as not the organist in the village church.

The pastor sits in judgment on the old, the teacher on the young and on the young's relations with the old. In the villages the parents are still literally afraid of the teacher. His knock at the door in the evening, when the child has misbehaved at school that day, means that the parents will have to promise, then and there, specific disciplinary action. The call will not be social, and the mother as well as the father will rise when he enters the house. If, on a happier occasion, he is willing to accept an invitation to call socially, the house will be cleaned and warmed, cakes will be baked, and the good wine brought out.

In Tailor Schwenke's childhood, at the end of the Nineteenth Century, the teacher had been there "all his life." He may have come to the village directly from the teachers' college, or he may have made one or two changes in his youth before he settled down to stay. The pastor, with his circuit of two or three villages, was likelier to change his residence or even go up the professional ladder. Young Karl-Heinz Schwenke's teacher had taught Karl-Heinz's father and had even taught the grandparents of some of the village children; these, grown to be parents and grandparents, saw their teacher still when he came to the door. And, where the parents might not have close contact with the pastor, they could not help having it with the teacher, who, besides learning the family secrets from the feckless offspring, had to be called in to help transact such business, especially official business, as transcended the father's grasp or self-confidence.

In the summer, in Karl-Heinz's village, the teacher went through the streets at 9 P.M., in the winter at dark; if he found a child on the street, his knock was heard at the door that same evening. At his own discretion, he himself did the disciplining with his *Rohrstock*. If the *Rohrstock* was a hazel branch, it was possible to cut it part way through when the teacher was out of the room, so that, when applied, it would fly to pieces. But Herr Pietsch, who was wise in the ways of three rising generations, had a bamboo stick, which, besides being harder to cut, had a greater flexibility than hazel, adding injury to insult.

One day when the future Sturmführer Schwenke was eleven, he ditched school in the afternoon to engage in the revolutionary act of stealing cherries. That night Herr Pietsch came by the Schwenkes'. Karl-Heinz was lucky; his father, who, like all very small farmers, was often away from home working for other farmers, was away that night, and Mother Schwenke beat the truant. The boy's luck lay in the fact that his mother's beating him meant that she would not tell his father, who would have beat him much harder. But the luck didn't last, for Herr Pietsch knew that Father Schwenke was away and that mothers' hands are sometimes unconvincingly light. The next morning, at the opening of school, Karl-Heinz received the bamboo treatment. The beating was so fierce that the boy bit the teacher's leg; then the teacher beat him harder. "Much harder?" I said. "So much harder," said the old tailor, "that the whole class howled with pain just to see it. That old man Pietsch," the arsonist of the Kronenberg synagogue went on, "he was a regular devil."

The regular devil showered down favors, too, but never on Karl-Heinz, who was poor in his studies. The favorites, who might be the best students, and who might be the worst students who belonged to the best families, were allowed a half-hour out of school to go, in turn, to the teacher's house each day to shine his shoes. Did the parents know this? Of course. Were the children paid? Of course not. What did the parents and children think about it? They didn't think about it.

The authoritative, not to say authoritarian, role that the teacher played in the German community, a role which declined very little in the "democratic" days between 1918 and 1933, is wholly foreign to the American tradition of that sad sack, the schoolteacher (as witness the life and times of Ichabod Crane in *The Legend of Sleepy Hollow*). The teacher in Germany once was, and often is now, the only person in the community who has attended a nonvocational secondary school; the fact that everyone else can read and write does not mean that the villagers do not come to him with important documents to be read or written properly. He is quite likely to be the only university graduate in the village. And he is certain to be the leading cosmopolitan, in respect not only of learning but also of mobility. Two or three merchants may be richer, the landowner certainly so, but they do not waste their money on travel. No professional in America has the status of the teacher in Germany, and to have achieved, as Herr Hildebrandt did, the rank of Studienrat (which means senior high-school teacher), with its title no less than its tenure and pension, is an eminence which no American teacher dreams of.

As the recognized repository of the community's intellect, the teacher would probably be a political conservative, a man not to be influenced by reformers. As a man who, although decently paid, still had to live on a state salary, he would still more probably want to identify himself with the wealthiest members of the community, who could afford to pay him for special lessons for their children. As a State employee, he would not be likely to disagree with Bismarck. But he would not, for all this, be a political protagonist or even a conscious political partisan. He would be above politics, not merely as the public service is above politics, but as the intellect is above politics. His business, and his alone in the community, is thinking, just as the horseshoer's, and his alone, is horseshoeing. Laymen do not presume to advise, still less to command, experts. And, while the historic sterility of German education may be laid in part to the academic's unaccountability, there was, in the pre-Hitler community, an independent, if a rigid and shallow, mind.

This mind was a bulwark, however fragile, not against National Socialism but against National Socialism's transition from practice to theory; for Nazism, unlike modern Communism, began with practice. Because the mass movement of Nazism was nonintellectual in the beginning, when it was only practice, it had to be anti-intellectual before it could be theoretical. What Mussolini's official philosopher, Giovanni Gentile, said of Fascism could have been better said of Nazi theory: "We think with our blood." Expertness in thinking, exemplified by the professor, by the high-school teacher, and even by the grammar-school teacher in the village, had to deny the Nazi views of history, economics, literature, art, philosophy, politics, biology, and education itself.

Thus Nazism, as it proceeded from practice to theory, had to deny expertness in thinking and then (this second process was never completed), in order to fill the vacuum, had to establish expert thinking of its own—that is, to find men of inferior or irresponsible caliber whose views conformed dishonestly or, worse yet, honestly to the Party line. The nonpolitical pastor satisfied Nazi requirements by

111

being nonpolitical. But the nonpolitical schoolmaster was, by the very virtue of being nonpolitical, a dangerous man from the first. He himself would not rebel, nor would he, if he could help it, teach rebellion; but he could not help being dangerous—not if he went on teaching what was true. In order to be a theory and not just a practice, National Socialism required the destruction of academic independence.

In the years of its rise the movement little by little brought the community's attitude toward the teacher around from respect and envy to resentment, from trust and fear to suspicion. The development seems to have been inherent; it needed no planning and had none. As the Nazi emphasis on nonintellectual virtues (patriotism, loyalty, duty, purity, labor, simplicity, "blood," "folkishness") seeped through Germany, elevating the self-esteem of the "little man," the academic profession was pushed from the very center to the very periphery of society. Germany was preparing to cut its own head off. By 1933 at least five of my ten friends (and I think six or seven) looked upon "intellectuals" as unreliable and, among these unreliables, upon the academics as the most insidiously situated.

Tailor Schwenke, before the first World War, had made suits for some of the prosperous professors of Kronenberg University. If, as of course he did, he resented their superior station, he was nevertheless proud and boastful of being tailor to such a distinguished trade. In 1925, when he was starving and joined the new political movement, they, although they were no longer able to order tailor-made suits, still had their sinecures, and he was no longer able to identify himself with them; they were sinking, as he was, but they had much further to sink. In 1927 he left the Party in the hope of recapturing their custom; he himself says this is why. But what he calls the "boycott" persisted (partly, of course, because the ready-made suit had taken the custom tailor's place).

In 1931, when Tailor Schwenke rejoined the Party, his Nazi indoctrination plus his personal experience had awakened his hostility toward professors in general, many of whom in Kronenberg, he told me, were Communists. (None was.) And in 1933, when the Party came to power, he was given a school janitor's job—with, of course, the title of *Hausmeister*—and the command of the local SA Reserve Troop. From that point on, he had no difficulty in placing academics (who, no doubt, had been patronizing when they were patrons) entirely outside the pale of the great community, the New Germany, which *he* now represented.

He was not, of course, sure of the New Germany or of himself; he was still, after fifty years of being Karl-Heinz Schwenke, Karl-Heinz Schwenke, and the Herr Professor was still the Herr Professor. The New Germany was, of course, Schwenke's, but the Herr Professor had something, and something German, that the New German had not. Tailor Schwenke would not, after 1933, any more than before, have failed to tip his hat to the Herr Professor; all the more joyously he received the revelation that half the academics were traitors and the other half dupes and boobies who might be tolerated—under close surveillance—by the New Germany which Tailor Schwenke, at your service, Sir, represented.

## CHAPTER 8

## The Anti-Semitic Swindle

Gustav Schwenke, the tailor's son, was twenty when he became a Nazi. This was in 1932. His father's business had collapsed; he himself, after his apprenticeship to his father, had never found work. There was simply no work to do for a strong, intelligent, well-trained young man of nineteen, eighteen, seventeen, sixteen. For four years he had gone on foot, like hundreds of thousands of other young men, from village to village, looking for work. Apart from an occasional odd job, he had, during this period, two months of state work relief service on the roads, for food and lodging and two dollars a week. Then his "old sickness," bed-wetting, came on him again and he had to go home and start over. But he never became a bum or a brawler; he slept only in youth hostels or in the fields. And then, in 1932, Gustav Schwenke became an SA policeman, for pocket money and a uniform—and a place in the sun.

What Gustav Schwenke wanted, and the only thing he wanted, was security. The job he wanted, and the only job he ever wanted, was a job with the State, any job with the State, with its tenure, its insurance, and its pension. Gustav was not, I imagine, the only boy born in Germany in 1912 who wanted security and thought, until 1933, that he would never have it. When he got it, when the Party Police were incorporated into the Military Police in 1935, his dream was come true. At last he *belonged*. He was a man at last.

As a boy, Gustav had clung to his father and kept away from his mother. He always did his homework in the afternoons in his father's workshop in the front of the house. There he fed on his father's manhood, which took the form of political power, and starved out his mother's womanhood, which took the form of domestic power. When he was seven he heard his father call the Weimar Constitution *Dreck*, dirt. So Gustav hated the Constitution. (He didn't know what it was.) When he was eleven, a customer came in to call for a suit, which had been ordered eight days before for 8,000 Reichsmarks; now, eight days later, 8,000 Reichsmarks would buy one pound of butter; and, when Gustav asked his father what caused the inflation, his father said, "The Jews." So Gustav hated the Jews. (He didn't know any Jews and wouldn't have bothered them if he had. His father would.)

Old Karl-Heinz Schwenke was a product of "the golden time" before the first World War. Even in the golden time he had, as he said, "only been a tailor." "But I had ten suits of my own when I married," said the iron-faced old dandy. "Twenty-five years later, when their 'democracies' got through with me in 1918, I had none, not one. I had my sweater and my pants. Even my Army uniform was worn out. My medals were sold. I was nothing. Then, suddenly, I was needed. National Socialism had a place for me. I was nothing—and then I was needed."

"And now," I said, "you are down to your sweater and pants again."

"Yes," he said, "now that their 'democracies' are through with me again."

"National Socialism," I said, gently, "didn't leave its enemies that much."

"They had it coming. You see what their 'democracies' did to us."

By "they" Herr Schwenke always meant the Jews. He was the most primitive of my ten friends. He was a very limited man. Facts, although he could apprehend them, had no use he could put them to; he could neither retain nor relate them. He could talk, but he could not listen. I let him talk.

"They say six million Jews were killed"—not that "we" or even "the Nazis" killed them—"but when you see how many there are all over the world today, there are just as many as ever. There are fifteen million in America—"

"Only six or eight, I believe," I said.

"Naturally, that's what they tell you. Do you know how many there are in Russia right now? They control the government, money, everything, everywhere."

I wanted to tell him a story, but I didn't. It's a story about a Jew riding in a streetcar, in Germany during the Third Reich, reading Goebbels' paper, the *Völkische Beobachter*. A non-Jewish acquaintance sits down next to him and says, "Why do you read the *Beobachter*?" "Look," says the Jew, "I work in a factory all day. When I get home, my wife nags me, the children are sick, and there's no money for food. What should I do on my way home, read the Jewish newspaper? 'Pogrom in Roumania.' 'Jews Murdered in Poland.' 'New Laws against Jews.' No, sir, a half-hour a day, on the streetcar, I read the *Beobachter*. 'Jews the World Capitalists.' 'Jews Control Russia.' 'Jews Rule in England.' That's *me* they're talking about. A half-hour a day I'm somebody. Leave me alone, friend."

National Socialism was anti-Semitism. Apart from anti-

Semitism, its character was that of a thousand tyrannies before it, with modern conveniences. Traditional anti-Semitism—what Nietzsche, beloved by the Nazis for his superman, called "the anti-Semitic swindle"—played an important role in softening the Germans as a whole to Nazi doctrine, but it was separation, not prejudice as such, that made Nazism possible, the mere separation of Jews and non-Jews. None of my ten friends except Herr Hildebrandt, the teacher, had ever known a Jew at all intimately in a town of twenty thousand, which included a nine-hundred-year-old Jewish community numbering six or eight hundred persons. The last traces of the ghetto had gone a century and more ago. Generation after generation, these people went on living together, in a small town, with a nonexistent wall between them over which the words "Good morning" and "Good evening" were tossed.

My ten friends had all had business relations with Jews, as both buyers and sellers. Springer, the Jewish jeweler, had even belonged to the town Glee Club, along with the Schwenkes, father and son. "I bought Mushi's wedding ring from Springer," said the tailor, patting his old wife's hand.

"Why from a Jew?" I asked.

"*N' ja*," said the arsonist of the synagogue, "we always traded with Springer. For a Jew, he was decent." I thought of Tacitus' observation on the Hessian tailor's forebears: "The Chatti [Hessians] are intelligent, for Germans."

Seven of my ten friends had known Springer over a period of years, and all seven of them, when I interrupted their animadversions on the Jews to ask them if they had ever known a decent Jew, named Springer first. They had traded with him, sung with him, marched with him (in veterans' organizations), but he had never been in any of their homes nor any of them in his. None of them knew how many children he had or where his ancestors came from.

"What became of him?" I asked the tailor.

"Oh, he went away."

"Where?"

"I don't know. South America, maybe. It was early"—that meant before the synagogue burning of 1938—"and a lot of them went to South America or somewhere."

None of the seven knew what had become of Springer.

I asked Horst Rupprecht, the student and Hitler Youth leader, who had lived around the corner from the synagogue and the Hebrew school, if as a child he had had Jewish friends. "Certainly," he said at once. "I never had a fight with a Jewish boy."

"I don't mean that," I said. "I mean, did you play with any?"

"Oh, no," he said.

"Why not?"

" 'Why not?' I don't know. They played together, and we played together."

In the Dark Ages the Jews had to separate themselves to preserve their communion, just as the Christians (and the Jews) had had to do in pre-Constantine Rome; in the Middle Ages their separation had been recognized and progressively enforced by the non-Jews. But, with the elimination of the formal ghetto in Germany, under Napoleon, the causal conditions of separation had declined. Moses Mendelssohn's translation of the Pentateuch into Luther's High German, at the end of the eighteenth century, had drastically reduced (and was on its way to eliminating) the linguistic separation. In the late nineteenth and early twentieth centuries the formal economic, edu-

cational, and occupational disabilities had all been progressively lifted (the last, in the Army and the higher civil
service, after the first World War).

As the disabilities against them disappeared, the Jews
disappeared. They had never numbered more than 1 per
cent of the German population, and their rate of apostasy
was higher in modern Germany than anywhere else except
Italy. After the first World War, social scientists predicted
that within two generations there would be no more Jews
in Germany. The progression from orthodoxy to agnosti-
cism (via "liberalism") was the largest factor, underlying
the conversion of thousands to nominal Protestantism,
which had economic and, more significantly, social advantages, and even to Catholicism. Conversion tended,
within limits, to remove the "cold" discrimination in the
universities and the professions. Noblemen, Army officers,
and professors married daughters of wealthy Jewish families,
and the motivation was not always money; many Jews of
consequence, having fallen away from their faith, ran as
fast and as far as they could from it, and the distinguished
non-Jew had his pick of not merely wealthy, but cultivated
and beautiful young women. This did not, of course, affect
the "little man" in Germany except, when he heard of it,
to make him hate the "Jew plutocrats" a little more. Nor
was he mollified when he heard that intellectuals, artists,
"bohemians" intermarried without thought of religious
distinction.

Jewish "suicide," by apostasy or conversion, was thus
reducing the Jews without reducing anti-Semitism; on the
contrary. Four years before Hitler was born in Austria, that
country's great anti-Semite, Von Schönerer, said, "*Ob Jud,
ob Christ ist einerlei, in der Rasse liegt die Schweinerei.*
Whether he says he's a Jew or a Christian doesn't matter,

he's depraved by race." Conversion and intermarriage simply shifted the emphasis from the economic and the civil to the racial basis of hatred, and, in doing so, invigorated in new and virulent form the anti-Semitism of the "little man," who, whatever else he was or wasn't, was of German "blood." Long before the first World War, lower-middle-class holiday places, such as the island of Borkum, were beginning to boast of being *judenfrei*.

After all their centuries of exclusion from all the honorable pursuits, the Jews had turned, as their liberation began in the eighteenth and nineteenth centuries, to the "free professions," those which were not organized as guilds or associations excluding them: medicine, law, journalism, teaching, research, and, of course, for the greater part, retail merchandise. (The poorer among them had turned, when they were driven out of the towns in past centuries, to the only possible occupation, the ancestor of retail trade: peddling). Thus the Jews were, on the whole, better off in the years of inflation after the first World War because a smaller proportion of them than of non-Jews were on fixed money incomes of wages, salaries, or pensions; and the "old" Jews of Kronenberg were, before Nazism, nearly all "comfortable." No one in Kronenberg was rich.

Besides the "old" Jews, there were the "new" ones, who had come principally from Poland after the first World War, who spoke Yiddish instead of German and lived as best they could—which might mean peddling and might mean pandering and might mean speculation of the pettiest or the wildest sorts. The Jewish community in Kronenberg had very few "easterners" or, as the "old" Jews called them, "kikes." There were some, of course.

The tailor, Salo Marowitz, had been a Russian soldier,

married to an "Aryan" wife after his release from a German prison camp after the first war. He was honest and respectable, a good man and a good Jew but (as the "old" Kronenberg Jews said) a "kike." There was no doubt that the Marowitzes' older son, Samuel, was born before his parents were married—the kind of scandal that died hard among the "old" German Jews, whose illegitimacy rate, even in the postwar years, was almost nil. Still, he was an honest man.

The three brothers Lipsky, from Poland, were honest, too, but their profession was less creditable. They were notion-peddlers, and they had little dignity. They couldn't afford to have, perhaps; they were none of them very bright. Even though they knew that Tailor Schwenke was a violent anti-Semite, they still came to his house trying to sell him soap. He always called them names and slammed the door on them, but they always came back. The youngest Lipsky, somehow come by the good German name of Bruno, was badly crippled from the waist down. When he walked he had to throw his legs out in front of him, which was enough to make children laugh. Back in the 1920's, when the Reichswehr was supposedly limited to 100,000 men, Kronenberg had a "nonmilitary" battalion which drilled in white shirts, and Bruno insisted on marching beside them, whistling. He would have marched later alongside the SA if they'd let him. He was not very bright.

The Kronenberg Jews were dying out fast enough before Nazism. After 1933 they began moving away from Kronenberg, and from Germany. Most of them stayed on—they didn't believe that "it" would last forever—until the synagogue burning and the pogrom laws of late 1938. But the Jewish community, as a formal organization to which almost every Jew, through choice, heredity, inertia, or social compulsion belonged in a small town, was shrinking steadily *before* 1933.

There was a special reason for the decline of Kronenberg Jewry. The Jewish community, like the town itself, was conservative, old-fashioned, and pietistic. The younger generation, since the first World War, had been turning away from the Tuesday and Thursday prayer service, from the prayer shawl and the white *Kitl* to be worn at the Passover ceremony, even from learning Hebrew. It is true that nearly all of them attended the synagogue school rather than public school; but this was largely a hangover from the days just gone when Christian religious services were part of the public school program. Look at Springer, the jeweler: a member of the community, yes, but when his father died in the 1920's, he had the tombstone inscription carved in German instead of Hebrew!

The Kronenberg synagogue had, under this kind of pressure in the 1920's, inaugurated new, more acceptable "German" customs and abandoned some of the old sacramental and liturgical forms. It had become more liberal. At the time the Nazis came to power, the synagogue's *Shames*, or sexton, a non-Jew, lit fires in only a dozen homes of members who still observed the rigid Saturday Shabbath prohibition against work, and Jewish-owned shops were open on Saturdays and closed on Sundays, just like the Gentiles'.

The concessions to liberalism had not arrested the decline of the Kronenberg congregation. After 1933, however, it began to grow again, in spite of the fact that members were emigrating. Some of those who remained and had fallen away from the faith came back. The Jewish Charity was, of course, more active than it had ever been before, with the demands imposed by the continuing boycott, and the children (who, if they attended a public school and did not belong to the Hitler Youth, had to remain in the schoolroom alone when the rest were dismissed for celebrations) were all back in the synagogue school.

True, the Jews had been disappearing in Germany; and intermingling, at least at the higher levels of culture and society, had been increasing. But the nonexistent wall between the Jews and the "little men" of Germany was as high as ever, and it was a wall with two sides. It was not clearly and simply a matter of exclusion but, rather, of two-way separation, of the independent existence of two communities in one town, a condition which distinguished the small-town situation in Germany from anti-Semitism in, say, the United States.

In this separation the devil slumbered and in slumber built sinew before Hitler was born. "When I was a boy," said the old tailor whom the teacher had caned, "there were maybe half-a-dozen Jew boys in the village. They had their own school and learned Yiddish—"

"Hebrew," I said.

"Hebrew, if that's what it was, and they could talk to each other in it so that the German kids couldn't understand them. They could understand us, but we couldn't understand them. When there was trouble, just kid trouble, they would talk Yiddish to each other. It scared a person; do you know what I mean?" I said I did. And I did.

When my friend Kessler, the former bank clerk, was a child in a Catholic village in Württemberg, a Jewish peddler came to his village once a month. The peddler transacted all the villagers' business for them, including their banking, without charge, and in return he stayed two or three days with the families of the village, in rotation, on his monthly visits. "He was just like a member of the

123

family to us children," said Herr Kessler, "except for one thing. After dinner, when we read from the Lives of the Saints, the peddler went into the corner and stood there facing the wall and put a shawl on and a band around his forehead and said prayers different from ours. It must have frightened us somehow, because I remember my mother's saying not to be frightened—it was because he was a Jew he did that. We did not know what 'Jew' meant.

"I remembered him only many years afterward, after the first war, when I first heard Nazi propaganda in Munich. And I remembered how I had been afraid—perhaps only mystified, but I suppose that with children the two are the same—when the Jew stood in the corner, facing the wall, with that band around his forehead, saying prayers we couldn't understand, in Yiddish."

"In Hebrew," I said.

"Yes, in Hebrew."

"Did your memory of the peddler make you anti-Semitic?"

"No—not until I heard anti-Semitic propaganda. Jews were supposed to do terrible things that the peddler had never done. And still—I had been frightened by him when he prayed, although I think I really loved him otherwise. The propaganda didn't make me think of him as I knew him but of him as a Jew. And it was as a Jew, praying alone, that he frightened us. So I suppose that, in the end, that was part of it, of my anti-Semitism. I can still make myself frightened, put myself back there. I hear my mother saying not to be frightened."

## CHAPTER 9

## *"Everybody Knew." "Nobody Knew."*

When people you don't know, people in whom you have
no interest, people whose affairs you have never discussed,
move away from your community, you don't notice that
they are going or that they are gone. When, in addition,
public opinion (and the government itself) has depreciat-
ed them, it is still likelier that you won't notice their departure or, if you do, that you will forget about it. How
many of us whites, in a white neighborhood, are interested
in the destination of a Negro neighbor whom we know only
by sight and who has moved away? Perhaps he has been
forced to move; at least the possibility occurs to us, and,
if we are particularly sensitive, and we feel that perhaps a
wrong has been done that we can't rectify, it is comforting
to hear that the Negro was also a Communist or that he
will be happier wherever he's gone, "with his own people,"
and was even paid a handsome bonus for moving.

Four of my ten Nazi friends—the tailor and his son, the
baker, and the bill-collecter—said that the only Jews taken
to *Kah-Zed*, concentration camp, were traitors; the 'rest
were allowed to leave with their property, and, when they
had to sell their businesses, "the courts" or "the finance
office" paid them the market value. "I've heard that the
Jews who left late could only take fifty or a hundred Marks
with them," I said to the tailor, who was talking about

125

"the courts." "I don't know about that," he said. "How should I know about that?" He had "known," a moment before, about "the courts," but I didn't remind him. "I've heard," I said to Herr Simon, the bill-collector, who was talking about "the finance office," "that they could only take part of their property with them." "Well, why not?" said Herr Simon. "If they wanted to leave, the State had a right to a share. After all, they had made their money here."

The fact is, I think, that my friends really didn't know. They didn't know because they didn't want to know; but they didn't know. They could have found out, at the time, only if they had wanted to very badly. Who wanted to? We whites—when the Negro moves away—do we want to find out why or where or with what he moved? The teacher, the student, the cabinetmaker, and the bank clerk, these four at least, suspected the truth of the "market value" myth, and the policeman, to whom you or I would intrust our goods and our chattels without hesitation after five minutes of talk, spoke with contempt of the *"weisse Juden,"* the "white Jews," the hawks who fell upon the property that the Jews had to sell in a hurry. Four of my friends suspected the truth, at the time; what should they have done?

"What would you have done, Herr Professor?" Remember: the teacher excepted, nine of my ten friends didn't know any Jews and didn't care what happened to them— all this *before* Nazism. And it was their government, now, which was carrying on this program under law. Merely to inquire meant to attack the government's justice. It meant risk, large or small, political or social, and it meant risk in behalf of people one didn't like anyway. Who but an ardent Christian, of the sort that takes Matthew 5 seriously, would undertake the risk of inquiring; who, if injustice were to be discovered by inquiry, would undertake the penalty of protesting? I am sorry to say that none of my friends was that ardent a Christian.

But Cabinetmaker Klingelhöfer, he who remained a vestryman of the church throughout Nazism, was as ardent a Christian as most vestrymen I have met, and his idea of relaxation, during our conversations, was to turn to religious questions. "I know it's not what you're interested in, Herr Professor, but I'd like your views." One day, by way of relaxation, we went through Matthew 24 together. (I didn't say that I was interested or that I wasn't, but I did say that reading aloud with a German friend improved my German.) I read, from the ninth through the thirteenth verses, to improve my German:

"Then shall they deliver you up to be afflicted, and shall kill you: and ye shall be hated of all nations for my sake.

"And then shall many be offended, and shall betray one another.

"And many false prophets shall rise, and shall deceive many.

"And because iniquity shall abound, the love of many shall wax cold.

"But he that shall endure unto the end, the same shall be saved."

I stopped, looked up, and then looked at Herr Klingelhöfer. His head—this was my ebullient friend, "My life for the Volunteer Fire Department!"—was lowered. I waited. He said, without looking up:

"Das ist schwer, Herr Professor. Das ist kolossal schwer. That's hard. That's terribly hard."

And it is hard. It is said to be hard to be a Christian— or even to want to be—under the most propitious of conditions. The conditions in Nazi Germany were not the most propitious. Just consider:

Jews, because they were in such high proportion in the "free professions," tended to be the people one owed money to for goods or services already delivered, for merchandise, say, or for medical care. Now I, in America, cannot well pay my doctor's bill. My doctor is a nice fellow, but his bills, however low they may be, are too high; I didn't want to be sick in the first place, and, now that I'm well, I wish I hadn't had to buy the medical care I no longer need. I wish my doctor well, believe me, and my dentist and my merchant and my lawyer and the jeweler who repaired my watch; if any of them are Jews, I still wish them well, because I am not anti-Semitic. (Remember, my Nazi friends were.)

Now let us imagine that the Jews are emigrating from America, as fast as they can. They liquidate their assets, at whatever loss, and collect such debts as are collectable in a week or a month. Small debts they don't bother with. They may send out a bill with the word "Please" written on it; but I can't pay it, not this month. What I can't avoid wondering is whether my Jewish dentist or doctor or shopkeeper is thinking of emigrating, winding up his affairs, closing his office or shop, selling out (I may still have to pay my debt some day, if he is able to sell his uncollected bills), taking his whole family with him, losing his citizenship and his power to pursue me with his bills. Of course, I'm a nice fellow, too, so I say, "I'll pay when I can."

But I won't. I won't have to. And I know I won't have to, although in my waking, honorable hours I may not know that I know I won't have to. But—oh, if that doctor and his bills, that dentist and his bills, only didn't exist. A Jewish physician in Kronenberg emigrated in 1936. I was able to talk to him after I got back to America, and, when I had asked him what decided his course in 1936 and he had given me the usual good reasons, he added: "I remember the very occasion which fixed my decision. I was in the public telephone room at the Frankfurt railroad station, and I heard the man in the next booth say, 'Don't pay him. Just don't pay him. Don't argue with him. Don't call him names. Don't waste your breath. Be polite. But don't pay him. Mark my words—in another six months or a year you won't have to pay at all. Hold him off.' It was something like that. 'Jew' wasn't mentioned; I don't know who the man was or even what he was talking about. But that decided me. It took me three, four months, to get a sponsor in America and get everything together. I sent bills out. Some were paid, some in full, some in part. I collected more than half of what was owed me; after all, these people had been my patients, and they were decent people. And 1936 was still early. Later, of course, it was different."

In 1934 I visited a family of remote relatives of mine in a country village outside Hannover. These Jews were small shopkeepers; they had been there for seven centuries, and there were too few of them to constitute a formal Jewish community. There was no anti-Semitism in Eichdorf. (There was no intermarriage, either.) In those first years of Nazism their non-Jewish friends continued to trade with them openly; later, secretly. Little children—it began with little children—who called them names on the street were taken home and spanked. The villagers, except for a few officials and a few young rowdies, simply would not let Nazism have its way, not in Eichdorf.

Nine years later, in 1943, the Jews of Eichdorf were "sent away." In such a small community they could not be "sent" unnoticed. After the war one of their neighbors was telling about it: "Everybody knew, but nobody came out on the street. Some looked from behind their curtains, not many."

"Did you?"

"No."

"Why not?"

"Why? What good is it to look?"

Kronenberg was, of course, bigger. None of my ten friends ever saw any Jews leave in a group. It wasn't required that they see. Only Policeman Hofmeister, of the ten, knew of the details of the departure of the Jews, and he only of their departure, not of their destination. And only Herr Hildebrandt, the teacher, ever corresponded with any Jews afterward or knew what had become of them. Everyone knew that Jews were moving away, from 1933 on. All of my ten friends had heard that these Jews or those were going or gone. A Jewish woman came to Herr Wedekind's bakery to pay her bill and wanted to make sure that there was nothing left owing him. "You're leaving?" he said. "Yes," she said. That was all. Three of my friends heard, during the war, that a bus load of Jews had left the Market Place at dawn one day. That was all.

Shortly after the war began, a group of Jews were seen working on the street, laying blocks in the trolley-car track (Jews were now forbidden any but common labor). Hofmeister waved a greeting to some he knew but didn't talk to them. Cabinetmaker Klingelhöfer spoke to one he knew, a lawyer, who had been a customer of his. "Did you ask him how he happened to be there?" I said.

"No. I knew."

"How?"

"Everybody knew."

"How?"

"Oh—we just knew."

"What did you say to him?"

"I asked him how he was, and he said, 'Fine.' He looked all right."

"Did you shake hands with him?"

"No. . . . One doesn't shake hands with a man who is busy with both hands, *nicht wahr?*"

"No, not in America, but you Germans always shake hands so much, I thought maybe—. By the way, Herr Klingelhöfer, do you think you were brave to talk with him on the street?"

"Brave? No, not brave. Maybe, a little. No, not really. My loyalty was known."

Herr Kessler, the unemployed bank clerk risen to Party speaker and department head in the local Labor Front, saw Stein on the Kronenberg platform waiting, as he himself was, for the northbound train. He had known Stein well, in a business way; Stein, to help him out when he was unemployed, had always hired him to audit the books of his drygoods store. The Jew was an old man. It was—when was it? —early in 1939. "He pretended not to see me. Maybe he thought it would embarrass me, or just that I wouldn't want to talk to him. That was wrong; I wasn't a *Fanatiker.* Finally I went up to him and shook hands and asked him how he was. He said, 'Fine.' I couldn't ask him how his business was, because I knew he had sold out. Then, when the train was coming, I said, 'Are you going away, Herr Stein?' Of course he was going away, or he wouldn't have been waiting for the train, but a man may go away for a day or forever; I didn't ask that. I said, 'Are you going away, Herr Stein?' He said, 'Yes,' and then I said, 'Well, goodbye,' and held out my hand, but he had already turned away."

"Did you both get on the train?"

"Yes."

"Together?"

"No. He got on the nonsmoker end of the car, and I got on the smoker."

"Did you smoke?"

"No."

I did not initiate the discussion of the Jews with any of my ten friends. Somewhere between the beginning of the second conversation and the end of the fourth, each of them introduced the subject, and each of them, except Messrs Hildebrandt, Kessler, and Klingelhöfer, reverted to it continually. I would ask Tailor Schwenke, "Did you like the Program, in '25?" "The Party Program?" he would say. "Yes, it was very good, very. Take the Jewish question, for instance. . . ." (In a subsequent conversation he said he had never seen the Party Program.)

Of the ten men, only the teacher, Hildebrandt, was not anti-Semitic. The policeman, a fine old man, did not want to be; but he was. The student, young Rupprecht, thought he wasn't anti-Semitic, but in his case I am not at all sure; he was glib. Kessler and Klingelhöfer, the two deepest-feeling of my friends (except Hildebrandt), were the mildest; their anti-Semitism was not at all "racial" and almost entirely economic, "rational."

Klingelhöfer's father, from whom the son had taken his trade as cabinetmaker, had told him that Jews were all right: "They were people, like other people, but you couldn't trust them in money matters, that was all. If you went to a Jew to do business, that was one thing, but if a Jew came to you to do business, that was another."

"Why do you suppose that was?" I said.

"I don't know. I don't know. I remember my father telling me about Moses, whose leather-shop was in the Bahnhofstrasse. My father did lots of work for him, and they got along fine. Moses only paid his accounts on Sunday mornings and he always paid a 'round sum,' no *Pfennige*. And he always deducted 3 per cent."

"Why?"

"I don't know. That was his custom, I guess. So my father always arranged *his* accounts so that the 3 per cent was already in. You may say 'cheating the cheater,' but it wasn't like that, exactly. Moses was a nice man. My father liked him. But my father always said that you couldn't trust a Jew in money matters. And he was right."

"Were you ever cheated by a Jew?"

"No, but that was because I was warned and was careful. If you're careful, you have no trouble with them."

"Were you careful with Professor Freudenthal?" (Freudenthal, who committed suicide in 1933, had been a customer of Herr Klingelhöfer's and had sent him a wedding present, a piano shawl of which my friend was proud.)

"No. With him you didn't have to be."

The former bank clerk's thinking was much larger than the cabinetmaker's. The Jews had accumulated too much of the country's economic power; "they should have been reduced economically to their proper proportion in the population."

"How should that have been done?"

"That's what I don't know, but a way should have been found without depriving them of their citizenship or mistreating them."

"Did they exercise this power badly?"

"In a way. I suppose anybody would, especially if he was looked down on, like the Jews. But it seemed to be very bad with the Jews."

"Do you mean that they introduced a 'Jewish spirit' into

economic life? I have heard other National Socialists say that."

"Well, that was the propaganda, of course, part of the whole 'race' thing, but I wouldn't say that. There is and there isn't a 'Jewish spirit,' but certainly the aggressiveness and competitiveness of some Jews led to abuses—for instance, to pornography in the press, just to sell papers and magazines."

" 'Of some Jews,' " I said.

"Oh, yes, of some; not all."

"And of some non-Jews."

"Of course. That's why I don't like to speak of a 'Jewish spirit.' But there were so many more Jews than non-Jews in these things, proportionately. That's what I mean."

Not one of my ten friends had changed his attitude toward the Jews since the downfall of National Socialism. The five (or six, if young Rupprecht is included) who were extreme anti-Semites were, I believe, not a bit more or less so now than before. What surprised me, indeed, was that, with the war lost and their lives ruined, they were not more so. Certainly Nazism's defeat by force would not make Nazis love the Jews more; if anything, less. Nor would their country's destruction. Nor would the three-quarters of a billion dollars their conquerors compelled them to pay, as restitutive damages, to the Jews of Israel. And the five extremists had never seen the inside of the local *Amerika-Haus* or any other agency of "re-education" and never would.

They, and, to a degree, even the bank clerk, the cabinet-maker, and the policeman, took the greatest pains to convince me that the Jews were as bad as the Nazis said they were. I sat passively, every so often asking a question which betrayed my simple-mindedness, while my friends pressed their argument. If I diverted them, they came back to it. The one passion they seemed to have left was anti-Semitism, the one fire that warmed them still. I thought, as they went on, of the customary analysis: We have to justify our having injured those we have injured, or we have to persuade others to our guilty view in order to implicate them in our guilt. I thought a little, but I didn't say much. What could I have said?

## CHAPTER 10

## "We Christians Had the Duty"

Herr Simon, the bill-collector, was visiting me. He had brought tulips to my wife, as, when I went to his house, I took candy to his. We were drinking coffee, he and I, as, at his house, we (or, rather, I; he was a teetotaler, "like Hitler") always drank wine. He was interested in finding out about America, at least in talking about it. I was telling him about the reservation of powers to the states in our federal system—.

"Do you know any Jews over there, Herr Professor?" he said.

"Oh, yes," I said, "many, quite well. They live among us over there, you know, just like other people."

"Not like Negroes," said the "Old Fighter." "But," he went on, "I want to ask you about the Jews. Can you always tell a Jew when you see one, over there? We can, here. Always. They're not like you and me."

"How can you tell?" I said. "They sometimes *look* like you and me."

"Certainly," he said, "sometimes. It isn't by looks, though. A German can tell. Always."

"Well," I said, like a man who is saying to himself, "You learn something new every day."

"Yes," he said.

Then I said, "Could you tell, if you saw Jesus, that he was a Jew, Herr Simon?"

"I think so," he said, "if he *was* a Jew. *But was he a Jew?* If he was, why did the Jews kill him? Can you tell me that?"—He went right on—"I've never heard a pastor say that Jesus was a Jew. Many scientists say he wasn't. I have heard that Hitler himself said that he was the son of a Greek soldier in the Roman Army."

"I never heard that," I said. I was lying; Reinhold Hanisch, in his memoirs, says that Hitler told him that in 1910, when they were living together in a Vienna flophouse.

"Yes," said Herr Simon, "and do you know, Herr Professor, the Jews have a secret Bible, called the Talmud. Maybe you never heard that, either, but it's true. They deny it, of course. You just ask a Jew about it, and watch him when he says it doesn't exist. But every German knows about it; I've seen it myself. It has their ritual murder in it, and everything else. It tells them—mind you, it was written I don't know how many centuries ago—that they must marry German women and weaken the German race. What do you think of that?"

What did I think of that? I thought I would telephone the dean of the theological faculty at Kronenberg University and ask him, even though it was a Sunday night and a blowy one, to bring a German Talmud to my house. That, I said to myself, will do it, much better than my telling him I'm a Jew. If, I said to myself, I tell him I'm a Jew now, he will be so furious at my previous deception of him that I shall have no opportunity to point out to him that he didn't know a Jew when he saw one. I wanted a minute to think it over, first.

"You say," I said idly, "that you have seen this—this—?"

"Talmud," said the bill-collector, a small, spectacled man who needed a strong mustache (he had a weak one). "But watch out, Herr Professor, that they don't fool you.

I've seen the real one. The Jews would show you a fake, if you trapped them, and even in your own universities you will find professors in the pay of the Jews who will tell you that it is genuine. We had such professors here—before. And again now, of course."

What did I think of that? I thought that I would not telephone to the dean, and, later on, as I said, "We'll have to have many more talks, Herr Simon," I thought that we'll have to have many more generations of Herr Simons, emerging, somehow without being led or driven, from the wilderness in which this generation of Simons lived with their "real" Talmud.

I was visiting Tailor Schwenke, my lusty old *Fanatiker* friend. He was in his sweater and pants, and we were having soup and unbuttered bread, a meal which, German country bread being what it is, was not so light as it sounds. His wife had baked a cake, and I had brought tea. "And so," I was saying, "we come to the end of your father's life-story, and that brings us to the end of the story of all your ancestors on both sides, down to you. I marvel, Herr Schwenke, that you know so much about each one of them, for so many generations back."

"That's the way we Germans are," said my friend. "We are proud of our families. The Americans took my Bible— they sent a Jew to do it, naturally—or I could give you all the dates exactly, birth, baptism, marriage, children, death."

"Your family," I said, very carefully, "seems always to have been lucky. Never any great troubles. Never lost their homes or their land. A very unusual family, always to have had such good fortune."

"Always, always," said the tailor. "As far back as we go— up to my own bad fortune—it was always very good, with my father, my grandfathers, my great-grandfathers, all of them."

This exchange occurred in our fourteenth conversation. In the course of the second, long before we had begun the remarkably detailed examination of the lives of his ancestors, he had talked about the Jews, saying, "I had reason enough to hate them, even before, for the way they ruined my ancestors for generations back. Stole everything from them, ruined them," and his face was furious with filial wrath.

I think that my friend believed what he was saying—at the time he was saying it—both in our second conversation and in our fourteenth. I might have shot home the contradiction. It would not have made him any less anti-Semitic, and, besides, men's lives are what they think they are. So I didn't.

I was visiting Herr Damm, the country boy who, his oldest brother being destined to get the family farm under Hessian primogeniture, had come to Kronenberg to get a job. He lost it in the depression and went back home, joined the Party at the "recruiting evening" the Nazis held in the village in 1932, and rose to be office manager of the Kronenberg Party headquarters. It was the twelve hundredth anniversary of the founding of the country village, where the Damms had settled in A.D. 808, and I was attending the celebration.

"Yes," said Herr Damm, "our family were always great anti-Semites. My father and grandfather were followers of Dr. Böckel, who founded the Anti-Semitic Party in Hesse, way back in the eighties. We used to have the Party flag, with the anti-Semitic inscription on it, 'Freedom from Jewry,' but the Americans took it away."

"Did you ever have any dealings with Jews?" I said.

"Always," he said. "We had to, in the country. Before the farmers' credit union was founded by Dr. Böckel—it was anti-Semitic, to save the farmers from the Jews—we were at the mercy of the cattle dealers. They were all Jews, and they all worked together."

"How do you know that they all worked together, Herr Damm?"

"They always do. They held us in the palm of their hand. Do you know what one of them once did? He bought a calf from my father and took it to town and sold it to my father's cousin, *at a profit.*"

"Yes," I said, "but that is just the profit system. You believe in the profit system, don't you? You're certainly no Communist!"

"Of course," he said, "but only think—to my father's own cousin! If my father had known his cousin wanted the calf, he could have sold it to him himself, without the Jew."

"Well—" I said.

"Look, Herr Professor, a Jew buys a cow. When he buys it, it's terrible, everything's wrong with it, he wouldn't have it for a gift. So he pays a few Marks for it. Then he goes to the next farmer with it, to sell it, and it's the most wonderful cow in the world. Do you see what I mean?"

"I think so," I said, wreathed, internally, with a smile as I thought of "the American Way," "but don't Germans," that is, non-Jews, "buy as low and sell as high as possible?"

"Yes, but that's just it. Look, Herr Professor," he went on, patiently, "Germans couldn't trade with one another. There was always a Jew between them. All Jews are *Händler*, traders, never workers or farmers. Every child knows this. All trade was in the hands of the Jews. What could we poor Germans"—he was speaking of what Hitler calls, in *Mein Kampf*, the "genius-race"—"do?"

I liked Herr Damm. He was a professional clodhopper—he had been used for Party work among the farmers, whose "language," that is, whose mind, he spoke—but he was still a clodhopper. On another occasion, he was visiting me in town; or, rather, since it was to be our last talk together, I was his host at a one-dollar de luxe dinner at Kronenberg's best restaurant. I brought the talk back to one of our first conversations, in which he had told me that he was the only Kreisamtsleiter in our whole *Gau* who had refused to leave the Church. "I told them I was born in the Church," he had said, "and I would die in it, and not in the 'German Church,' but the Christian Church."

"Now," I said, as we were lighting up after dinner, "what many Christians in America cannot understand is how you Christians in Germany could accept the persecution of the Jews, no matter how bad they were. How could you accept it *as Christians?*"

It was the first time I had taken the initiative on the subject. "The Jews?"—he said—"but the Jews were the *enemies* of the Christian religion. Others might have other reasons for destroying them, but we Christians had the *Christian duty* to. Surely, Herr Professor, you know how the Jews betrayed our Lord?"

None of my friends was the least interested in Nazi race theory as such, not even the tailor or the bill-collector. Five of the ten of them laughed when they spoke of it, including the cabinetmaker. "That was nonsense," said Herr Klingelhöfer, "for the SS and the universities. Look at the shape of my head: broad as a barnside. Look at my brunette wife. Do you suppose *we're* not Germans? No; that they could teach to the SS and the university students. The

SS *Flott* ["cream," sacastically] would believe anything that made them great, and the university students would believe anything complicated. The professors, too. Have you seen the 'race purity' chart?" "Yes," I said. "Well, then, you know. A whole system. We Germans like systems, you know. It all fitted together, so it was science, system and science, if only you looked at the circles, black, white, and shaded, and not at real people. Such *Dummheit* they couldn't teach to us little men. They didn't even try."

What my friends believed—and believe—is an accumulation of legend, legend which comes to them no more guiltily than the cherry-tree story comes to us. Only in their case, esteeming themselves as they did as "little men," "little people," who did not amount to anything except in so far as they were Germans, the legend of a people among them who were not Germans and who, therefore, were even less than they, was especially precious.

Nobody has proved to my friends that the Nazis were wrong about the Jews. Nobody can. The truth or falsity of what the Nazis said, and of what my extremist friends believed, was immaterial, marvelously so. There simply was no way to reach it, no way, at least, that employed the procedures of logic and evidence. The bill-collector told me that Jews were filthy, that the home of a Jewish woman in his boyhood town was a pigsty; and the baker told me that the Jews' fanaticism about cleanliness was a standing affront to the "Germans," who were clean enough. What difference did the truth, if there were truth, make?

I suggested from time to time, and always in hesitant fashion, that perhaps the medieval exclusion of Jews from citizenship and landholding, their subsequent exclusion, after 1648, from guild apprenticeship, and their confinement for a thousand years to the practice of moneylending, with the attendant risk of the despicable creditor against the knightly debtor, might have required cunning of most of the Jews in most of early Europe as the condition of survival itself; that the consequent sharpening of the intellect under such circumstances would have produced a disproportionate number of unusually noble and unusually ignoble dispositions among any people, their unusualness, in the marginal occupations to which they were driven, disappearing as the great community removed the disadvantagements which produced it. I reminded the bank clerk, Kessler, that the ancestors of the Christians who now forbade Jews to be bank presidents once compelled them to be. He was a Swabian, from Württemberg, and the Swabians are humorous—"for Germans," as Tacitus would say. He appreciated the joke.

None of my ten friends argued with me when I said these things. None of them, except the bank clerk and, of course, the teacher, listened. Everything I said, all of them might have learned long ago. But there are some things that everybody knows and nobody learns. Didn't everybody know, in America, on December 8, 1941, that the Japanese, or Japs, were a treacherous people?

In the American Embassy in Berlin, in 1935, an official of the German Foreign Press Office told me the story of a North Sea town where there had never been a Jew. When Goebbels announced the boycott of the Jews for the month of April, 1933, the Bürgermeister of the town sent him a telegram: "Send us a Jew for our boycott."

## CHAPTER 11

## The Crimes of the Losers

Long before the second World War ended, the Allies decided that, in case they won, they would not again write a "war guilt" clause (which the Germans would again repudiate) into the peace treaty. They would this time, by a great legal proceeding, convict the Germans of their guilt under international law and convince them of it. And this time the guilt, in addition to breach of the peace, would include war crimes and crimes against humanity. The day the International Military Tribunal opened at Nuremberg, the American prosecutor, Justice Jackson of the United States Supreme Court, called the occasion "a rare moment in history," and the day after the Nazi leaders were hanged the New York Times said: "Mankind has entered a new world of international morality."

The Nazi leaders were hanged, but they were not impressed. They pleaded, during the legal proceeding against them, that they had all acted under orders (wasn't Nazi Germany a dictatorship?); that, if anyone were guilty, their judges were as guilty as they themselves were (especially the Russians; why, they asked, wouldn't the Tribunal press the charge it had made that it was the Germans, not the Russians, who had slaughtered the Polish officers in the Katyn Forest?); that international law was law only by analogy, that it wasn't codified, that even if it were codified

144

it would not supersede national law (which, obviously, they had not broken), and that even if it were codified and superseded national law it would not permit one party to a suit to try another or bring only one party, rather than both, to trial.

There were Americans who wondered whether the Nuremberg gallows trap was a wide enough entrance to a new world of international morality for mankind, but such wonderers were not numerous in 1946. Most Americans were satisfied with the operation, even if they did not share the premature ecstasy of Justice Jackson. But the succeeding "international" tribunals at Nuremberg, twelve in all, had to be conducted by the United States without the co-operation of its Allies. Nuremberg, after the "big show" of the IMT trial, lost its interest, not only for the other three European Allied governments, but also for most American citizens. It was water over the dam—spilled milk, at worst.

But it was gall, if not wormwood, for the Germans, and not just for the Nazis among them. As far as my ten friends were concerned, the Nuremberg method of convincing them of their guilt was a failure. It was not that it miscarried; it simply had no fundamental effect on them at all. It was taken as an incidental penalty of losing the war, another turn of the screw.

My friends were, they all said, little men; why should they repent those acts of State (and of a dictatorship State in which they had no controlling voice) which the highest surviving ministers of the State did not repent? Repentance is not of the essence, or even of the atmosphere, of a legal proceeding anyway, still less of a military proceeding. Repentance is effectively urged when the urger stipulates in the indictment that we are all sinners, and the Nuremberg indictments made no such stipulation.

If, after all the wars of history, the losers had not been roughly treated without a formal finding of guilt, the treatment of the Germans after the last war, upon a formal finding, might have impressed my friends. As it was, they were, in their own view, simply paying the usual price of losing. "Why so much money to hang us?" said Göring to his neighbor in the dock when the American prosecutor, complaining at the trial's delays, said that the procedure was costing his government thousands of dollars a day. Five irreparable years later, the man we sent to Germany to re-educate the Germans found himself re-educated: "In looking backward," said former High Commissioner Mc-Cloy, "I wish we had been able to erect tribunals not composed exclusively of the victors." Why weren't we able to?

In 1950, in October, United States General Douglas MacArthur approved a legal procedure, modeled after Nuremberg, for trying North Korean and Chinese war criminals after the war in Korea would be won. Legal teams scoured the Korean peninsula as far north as the Yalu River, accompanied by motion-picture photographers. A year later the United Nations commander in Korea, General Matthew Ridgway, said that there were 400 "active cases and 126 suspects" of war crimes in UN custody. But a year later North Korean and Chinese war criminals went home, untried and unhung; Secretary Dulles, an international lawyer, announced the good news, as he called it, that the North Korean–Chinese command had agreed to release enemy personnel charged with war crimes on the condition that the UN command release enemy personnel so charged. The "rare moment in history" had passed; the war in

Korea had not been won; international law, like international conquest, required losers before it could operate.

Losers are hard to convince of their guilt. The suffering they have undergone in losing constitutes, as they see it, expiation and more for their own offenses, real or alleged. Boys fighting in alleys are that way. The battered and bloody vanquished is seldom magnanimous enough to admit that he got what was coming to him—about all he can be got to say is "uncle"—and more seldom still to admit that he ought to get more. Men should not be that way, but they sometimes are. My friends were.

It is a principle of animal training that, for the punishment to be effective, the offender must associate it with the crime. You must catch him in the act, on the scene, or he will have forgotten what he did and the punishment will appear abusive to him. Men, too, have a way of dating their guilt and innocence from the injuries they suffer, not from those they inflict. No matter how far back in history I went with my National Socialist friends, they would want to begin its writing with their own or their country's agonies. When I spoke of 1939, they spoke of 1945; when I spoke of 1914, they spoke of 1918; when I spoke of 1871, they spoke of 1809. As a university-educated American, I knew that there had been a Dawes Plan for the payment of German reparations after the first World War, and a Young Plan which had liberalized the payments. But seven of my ten friends—five of whom had not gone beyond six years of folk school—knew that the Young Plan payments were to have been continued until 1988, "when," said Policeman Hofmeister, "my son will be eighty years old."

My fellow-Americans in Germany were sick of the Germans' self-pity. "I'll tell you about them," said one of the Occupation officials, "in a nutshell. They're like dogs. If you don't kick them, they bite you; and, when you kick them, they whine." An American Occupation judge was trying to get transferred. "It's got so," he said, "that the minute a German starts whining, I know I'm going to find him guilty. And they all whine. They all have a hard-luck story. Well, they *have* had hard luck. But they gave other people lots harder luck first. Of course, they've forgotten that."

The judge was equating inequivalents. The hard luck the Germans have had *they* have had, while the hard luck they gave, somebody else had, somebody they don't know; and they don't even believe that it was they who gave it. Herr Damm, after losing his career and his home and possessions, was now earning $47 a month as a "black," that is, unauthorized worker; he did not see the equivalence between his boycott of Jews in the past and his own children's undernourishment now. He hadn't seen the Jews who, as the ultimate consequence of *his* legal acts were slain; and, besides, like everyone else except Hitler, who had a mandate from the German people, Herr Damm had a mandate from Hitler, the head of the government, to boycott Jews.

I am sure that the tailor, Schwenke, had a hand, and a ready one, in burning the Kronenberg synagogue. See the way *he* may see the crime (which he denies): He was a man provoked to fury by extreme misfortune, in which "the Jews" played the central role; and he was one of many; and he was a follower, not a leader; and he was being a patriot in Nazi Germany; and the victim was a building; and so on. And the loss to him (which he admits) was three years' imprisonment late in life, his job, his health, his home, his possessions, and a chance to earn a living to keep from starving. Justice has not overtaken the spirit which led to the Nazi enormities—how could it?—but it has overtaken Herr Schwenke, in his view, with a terrible vengeance.

As my ten friends, all ten of them, told me their troubles, whining, whining, whining, I sympathized with the American complaint. One of the shoemakers in Kronenberg, a man who bears the reputation, and justly so, of a philosopher, said, "I was listening to a German-Swiss soccer game at Zürich, just before you came in. The Swiss were being beaten, and it was near the end of the game. There seem to have been several fouls called on the German team in the course of the game, and here was another. The Swiss announcer said, without raising his voice, 'Foul called on the visitors,' and went on. Do you know what a German announcer would have done, if the situation were reversed and the game were in Germany?—He would have cried out, 'Another foul on the Swiss!" and he would have made the word "Swiss," *Schweitzer*, sound like "pig," *Schwein*. He would have named the Swiss player who fouled, and he would have repeated the name, saying, 'This Baltz is the same Baltz who . . .' and so on. You understand? That's our trouble."

War seems to be the German sport—if not exclusively theirs—and the Germans seem to be poor sports. Baker Wedekind, without having read the ancient Romans, who made the same point on the subject of the Germans, said, "Churchill promised the English 'blood and tears,' *and at the very beginning of the war*. That you would never hear in Germany. You might hear it at the very end, and even then you would hear that we were still winning. We won all the battles, you know; we only lost the war. We are not good losers. I don't know about you. You have never lost, have you?"

Americans have not had the Germans' troubles, perhaps by happy accident, perhaps because they have not made such troubles for others as the Germans have. Americans are not injured, and they don't feel injured. And, if they do, they do not characteristically whine. There is an unbecoming childishness in all this whining, a childishness which is not mitigated by one's looking on one's self as "little." An American may be helpless, but he doesn't know it. The stiff upper lip of the Englishman may be a national affectation, but he keeps it. These Germans, hitting out because somebody tells them to (or doesn't tell them not to), are offended when somebody hits them back. Sacrifice and endurance are more arduously cultivated among the Germans than among other peoples, with strangely mixed success.

My Nazi friends were sorry for themselves because they were wrongfully injured. And they were wrongfully injured, you know; everyone is, in this life. And there seems to be a much greater accumulation of wrongful injury—injury suffered, that is, which weighs heavier than injury inflicted —in Germany than in places off the path of the last twenty centuries' wars. So Germans whine. But there was the woman who told me, "It was my own fault. I should have been more courageous"; and the man who said, "I should have been man enough to say 'No' at the very beginning"; and the priest who stood on the scaffold after the unsuccessful *Putsch* of 1944 and said to his confessor, "In a minute, Father, I shall know more than you"—these, too, were Germans.

Being a German may make whining easier, but not inevitable. In October, 1945, the Confessional church of

Germany, the "church within the Church" which had defied Hitler's "German Christians," issued the "Stuttgart Confession": "We know ourselves to be with our people in a great company of suffering, but also in a great solidarity of guilt. With great pain do we say that through us has endless suffering been brought to many peoples and countries. That to which we have often borne witness before our congregations, we declare in the name of the whole church. True, we have struggled for many years in the name of Jesus Christ against a spirit which has found its terrible expression in the National Socialist regime of violence, but we accuse ourselves for not witnessing more courageously. . . ." Those, too, were German words.

The juridical effort at Nuremberg to punish the evildoers without injuring the losers—when punishment and injury came to the same thing and the losers were identical with the evildoers—was unlikely enough to succeed. The effort to convince my ten friends that *they* were evildoers was even unlikelier. In retrospect, there was one extremely remote possibility of its having been done more successfully in Germany than it had ever been done anywhere else: It might have been possible to exploit the Germans' attachment to "the German spirit" and to have convinced them that this spirit, instead of being good, is evil. How to have gone about doing this I do not know. Certainly not by treating them hard; the Nazis used this technique on the Jews without convincing them of anything.

## CHAPTER 12

## "That's the Way We Are"

There was a peculiar disadvantage in trying to convince the Germans generally that they were guilty of the crimes of the Reich. The German people have never, as single individuals, had to assume the responsibility of sovereignty over their government. The self-governing American regards his government as his mere agent, an animated tool in his hand. If it doesn't suit his purposes, he discards it and tries a new one. He, the constituent, constitutes the State; his ministers minister to him. My Nazi—and most of my non-Nazi—friends in Germany simply do not understand this view of government in which the enduring fact of society, the will of the people, is represented by an instrument which is here today and gone tomorrow. The government must be *embodied*. To say that it is embodied in the law is, in their view, so much gobbledygook; laws are enacted by men. (The Nazis did not even bother to repeal the Weimar Constitution.)

The English constitutional monarchy, a monarchy they themselves never had, my friends might comprehend, with the greatest difficulty; our constitutional democracy, not at all. This seems to say that my friends want despotic rule. They do, if by despotism we mean, not the ruler's oppression, but the ruler's independent right to rule.

This does not mean totalitarianism; it does not mean that

there is no opposition. It means that the opposition is limited to matters below the level of general policy; Bismarck did not govern without the *advice* of the Reichstag; he governed without its *consent*, as the Kaiser, when he finally chose, governed without Bismarck's. The story is told of the last emperor of Austria-Hungary, the famous-visaged Franz Josef of the great white burnsides, that, having on one occasion received an Opposition delegation and heard its demands, he turned to his prime minister and said, "This is not opposition—this is *factious* opposition!" My friend Willy Hofmeister, the policeman, who, now that I think of it, looked like Franz Josef, was telling me that a German policeman never used his gun except in cases of extreme personal peril. "Well," I said, "when you order a car to stop and it doesn't, don't you fire?" "We wouldn't," he said, "but when you order a car to stop, it stops." Opposition.

The history of the Social Democratic Party of Germany is suggestive. In 1890 the Kaiser, with Bismarck gone, let the anti-Socialist laws lapse. In a single generation of legal status the Social Democratic Party transformed itself from a revolutionary underground to a governmental party, reformist, to be sure, even radically reformist, but not, as it was in England and even in Austria, an opposition with an independent program of its own for altering the very basis of government.

In 1914 the Socialists, supporting the Kaiser's demand for war credits, proclaimed that Germany was fighting a defensive war—"In the hour of danger, we will not leave our country in the lurch." A generation later, after its country had left it in the lurch, the Party was even more nationalistic than the anti-Socialist coalition of the Adenauer government; "never again," said the Socialist leader Schumacher, "will the Socialists be caught being less nationalistic than their opponents."—Thus they who of yore proclaimed "the commonwealth of man and the parliament of the world."

The formation of Germany's "black" army after 1918 had its sanction and support from the Reich Ministry of War under the Socialist leadership of Severing, and, at the end of Wiemar, only the Prussian Socialist leadership stood firm in resistance. Like all the rest of the pre-Nazi parties in Germany, left, right, and center, the Social Democratic Party as such provided no independent alternative to the Nazis and the Communists, each of which parties was ready to rule with a program of its own uninhibited by any atavistic subservience to the tradition of the suprapolitical Sovereign. "There was one thing you had to say for the Bolsheviks," said the Nazi *Fanatiker* Schwenke. "Their 'No' wasn't a three-quarters 'Yes.'"

It hadn't always been that way. Just before the first World War one-fourth of the deputies in the Reichstag were Social Democrats, at a time when parliamentary government was a rich man's game, with the deputies unsalaried; at a time, too, when to be a Social Democrat in Germany was almost as bad as being a Communist in the United States thirty years later. Regarded still in those days, as they had been under Bismarck, as traitors, the future party of loyal opposition fought to change the character of their country and the basis of its government. Their workingmen's education movement, although (unlike our own adult programs) it was education for specific social purposes, was the most advanced and widespread in Europe. Their trade-unions, and the men in them, were politically conscious and aggressive; unlike American workers, who were born with civil rights, the German and all other European workers had had to fight to win theirs.

Immediately prior to their turning respectable, at the outset of the first war, the German Social Democrats had been a force for fundamental change among perhaps one-third of all the Germans. Respectability, which the Social Democrats finally achieved by supporting the war government in 1914, killed that force and left its vestiges to the Nazis and the Communists.

Twice in our time, at Weimar and at Bonn, Germany's victorious enemies have tried to turn Germany upside down and install government (as my Nazi friends see it) without rule. Hitler turned Germany (as they see it) right side up. He was an independent Sovereign, popularly supported, in part for no other reason than that he was an independent Sovereign. *This* was government.

Were the props to be pulled out from under it, the Bonn Republic would sooner or later fall, as surely as Weimar, not because Germans find it oppressive but because they find it a *nonregnum*. The chancellor is a party politician at the mercy of party politicians who, to the extent that they are responsible to the people, derive their power, and therefore his, from those creatures furthest removed, in their own estimate, from Sovereignty. A fifty-year-old non-Nazi acquaintance of mine remembered that, when she was a teen-ager, not in the feudal east or imperial south of the country but in modern Westphalia, the farmers took off their hats when the Count's carriage went by *empty*, and Policeman Hofmeister told me, "When all is said and done, it is cheaper to pay one man, who knows how to rule, twenty million marks than to pay five thousand men ten thousand marks apiece."

Chancellor Bismarck ruled Germany; he was the Chancellor of Iron. But the King-Emperor could and did dismiss him, could and did use the independence of the

Crown (which Bismarck, in his hatred of parliamentarianism, had fortified) to launch a mad attack upon Europe in what he regarded as the interest of the German people. He may have been wrong and Bismarck right, but the German people, who regarded him as the man whose business it was to rule them, fought when he told them to. Neither Americans unlaureled nor English poets laureate believe (though the latter say) that it is not ours to reason why. But my Nazi, and some of my non-Nazi, friends believe it; "the King makes war, and the people die." They are good soldiers, these Germans; they lack only what Bismarck (of all people) said they lacked, "civilian courage," the courage which enables men neither to be governed by nor to govern others but to govern themselves.

This does not mean that my Nazi—or non-Nazi—friends are bad men. (They may be bad, but, if they are, it is for other reasons.) It means that their political history is different from ours—we should say "behind" ours. I put "behind" in quotation marks because my friends do not see it that way; they are less ready than we are to identify chronological change with progress. Without having read the Greeks, they use all the arguments against democracy that the Greeks used. "In your government," said the argumentative bill-collector, who wanted to talk about America and had read about it in Luckner, "nobody has authority. This is a fine thing, to be sure, in a big, rich, empty land, unless there is an emergency. Then you suddenly establish authority. You boast that you have elections even in wartime, but you never change governments then; *then* you say, 'Don't change horses in the middle of the stream' (we have the same saying in Germany); and you don't. We don't pretend that we can."

Nor does it mean that my Nazi—or non-Nazi—friends

are politically unconscious. Far from it; their conversation is more political than ours, and they take their politics with what Schopenhauer called *tierischer Ernst*, bovine seriousness. The German press devotes much more of its space than ours to politics and more of its political discussion to issues than to personalities. In our first conversations, when I found that my friends preferred talking about Versailles or the Polish Corridor to talking about themselves, I thought that they were running away from their guilt. I was wrong. They did not regard what they themselves did as important, and they were interested in important things like Versailles and the Polish Corridor.

To say that my German friends were nonpolitical, and to say no more, is to libel them. As in nearly all European countries, a very much larger proportion of Germans than Americans turns out for political meetings, political discussions, and local and general elections. Where the German was (in contrast with the American) nonpolitical was at a deeper level. He was habitually deficient in the *sense of political power* that the American possesses (and the Englishman, the Frenchman, the Scandinavian, and the Swiss). He saw the State in such majesty and magnificence, and himself in such insignificance, that he could not relate himself to the actual operation of the State.

One of my non-Nazi friends made a relevant point, however, in defense of his countrymen, at least against the Americans, if not against the rest of the Europeans: "Our situation differs from yours the way city life differs from the country. Ours is intensely complicated and difficult, sophisticated, so to say, while yours (at least until very recently) has been almost pastoral, primitive in its clarity and simplicity. Ours is much less readily intelligible to us than yours is to you, and our 'average citizen,' therefore, feels more inadequate than yours to deal with it." But the nonpolitical, or, more accurately, politically nonconfident, German, who minded his own business and confined his business to his *Fach* (which means both pigeonhole and specialty), was just as prevalent in business, industry, and finance, in education, in the church, and in the press as in tailoring, baking, or cabinetmaking.

The German universities were crawling with experts on the Akka pygmies of the Aruwimi Congo, but they were closed to political thinking except on the level of detached theory; in the whole state of Hesse not a single course in political science was offered. The German universities began their life with theology, and German theology began its life with the great bicker, the Luther-Melanchthon-Zwingli disputation over the Eucharist, which broke up with Luther's adherence to the literality of the words *Hoc est corpus meum*, which he carved in great letters on the table at Marburg. The German church was out of this world; the social gospel did not enter German preaching, and preaching was rigidly separated from theology (and prophecy from them both).

The press, unlike the church and the universities, was not a state institution, but it was characteristically cautious and dull in a nation where the right to suppress had never been overturned. The *Frankfurter Zeitung*, until it was picked up by the I.G. Farben trust in the 1920's, was a very conservative newspaper of great cultural interest, and the provincial press lacked even cultural interest. The fact that the trade-unions were predominantly Social Democratic said nothing of breadth of the German worker; the leadership was as independent of the membership as it was in some of the more notorious unions in the United States; strikes in Germany were called, not voted; and the

Social Democratic workers, "good citizens," were absorbed, with almost no resistance, in the Nazi Labor Front. Outside the great business, industrial, and financial combines, which influenced public policy through court camarillas, the *Kaiserreich* boss was no more politically alive than his worker. A member of the pre-Hitler Prussian cabinet, asked what caused Nazism, said: "What caused Nazism was the clubman in Berlin who, when he was asked about the Nazi menace in 1930, looked up from his after-lunch game of Skat and replied, '*Dafür ist die Regierung da*. That's what the government's there for.'"

Arguing with an American, you may ask him, with propriety, "All right—what would *you* have done if *you* had been President?" You don't ask one of my Nazi friends what *he* would have done if *he* had been Führer—or Emperor. The concept that the citizen might become the actual Head of the State has no reality for my friends. Why not?—Didn't Hitler become the Head of the State? "Not at all," said Herr Simon, the bill-collector, and then he went on to enlighten me on legitimacy. Hitler was *appointed* by the Head of the State. The true German ruler is the monarch. The first President of Germany, Ebert, was not elected by the people at all, and the second (and last), Hindenburg, was not really elected but was *chosen* by the German people as custodian for the monarchy. My friends, like all people to whom the present is unpalatable and the future unpromising, always look back. Looking back, they see themselves ruled, and well ruled, by an independent Sovereign. Their experience with even the outward forms of self-government does not, as yet, incline them to it.

The concept that the citizen actually is, as such, the Head of the State is, in their view, nothing but self-contra-

diction. I read to three of my friends a lecture I had prepared, in which I was going to say that I was the highest
official of the United States, holding the office of citizen.
I had used the word *Staatsbürger*. "But that," said all three,
in identical words, "is no office at all." There we were. "But
it really is the highest office in America," I said; "the citizen
is the Sovereign. If I say 'souveräner Staatsbürger,' will
that be clearer?"

"Clearer, certainly," said Herr Kessler, the bank clerk,
"but wronger, if I may, Herr Professor. Those two words
do not go together. The idea is not a German idea. It
says that the citizen is the ruler, but there are millions of
citizens, so that would be anarchy. There could be no rule.
A State must have a Head, not a million or fifty million
or a hundred million Heads. If one of your 'sovereign citizens' does not like a law, do you allow him to break it?
If not, your 'sovereign citizen' is only a myth, and you are,
like us, ruled by real rulers. But your theory does not admit it."

"We hear a lot about America," said Policeman Hofmeister, "not only now, but all our lives we have heard
a lot, because so many of us have relatives who have gone
there. Now we always say in Germany, 'Monarchie oder
Anarchie'; there is nothing in between, and *Anarchie* is
mob rule. We have heard of your American cities ruled
by gangsters working with dishonest politicians who steal
the people's money and give them poor service, bad roads,
and such, charging them always for good roads or good
sewers. That we have never known here in Germany, not
under the Kaiser, not under Hitler. That is a kind of
*Anarchie*, maybe not mob rule but something like it."

"You think," said Herr Simon, who did not always remember to call me Professor, "that there is one kind of dictatorship, the kind we had here. But you might have a dictatorship not by the best of your people but by all, or a majority, of your people. Isn't that possible, too?"

"I suppose so," I said, "but it is hard to believe. I should say that National Socialism had some of that in it, that dictatorship by the majority."

"Yes," said Herr Simon, "but what about the law against drinking liquor that you had in the United States. Wasn't that a majority dictatorship?"

I explained, and we went on, but my friend was trying to make a point. In Tennessee a kind of legal mob rule forbade the teaching of evolution, in California (long afterward) it forbade the teaching of internationalism as manifested in UNESCO. My Nazi friend Simon had not heard of John Stuart Mill, the philosopher of liberty, who was worried about "the tyranny of the majority," or of Alexander Hamilton's staggering dictum, "Your 'People,' Sir, is a great beast."

I think it is unfair to say that my friends are irresponsible, at least without adding that irresponsibility, which is a moral failure, may be at least in part a consequence of nonresponsibility, which is historical fact. There is a distinction between "unconscionable" and "conscienceless." The model of the conscienceless pattern of German behavior was (and is) the civil service, whose security and status are the dream of the "little man" in a world where, even in good times, to lose a job is a dreadful prospect. The magnificence of the German civil service is one side of the coin; the training and elevation of a whole conscienceless class of citizens, who hear nothing, see nothing, and say nothing undutiful, the other. The apprenticeship of a *Beamte*, a civil servant, is hard and long, and the man who is seen to do his duty reluctantly or squeamishly is never certified; he is kept on as *Angestellte*, employee. German bank employees, who are not *Beamten*, call themselves *Bankbeamten*, simply to swell their little pride.

This immense hierarchism, based upon blind servility in which the man on the third rung would never dare to imagine that the man on the second would order him to do something wrong, since, after all, the man on the second had to answer to the man on the first, nourished the buck-passing instinct to fantastic proportions. "If," said a friend of mine whose sense of humor was surprising ("for a German"), "you ask the postman whether he thinks it will rain tomorrow (and tomorrow is the day of the Communist parade, and the Communists are illegal), he will excuse himself while he gets his immediate superior's permission to answer, and his superior will take the question up through channels until it reaches an official whose sense of independent moral responsibility is so strong that he dares to lose the question rather than send it on higher. By the time the postman is able to tell you that he has no opinion on the matter, it is day after tomorrow."

Men who learn to live this way get used to it and even get to like it. It is workable, too; good discipline produces, at least in limited areas, the same performance as good self-discipline. The only objection to the scheme is that men who always do as they're told do not know what to do when they're not. Without the thoughtful habit of decision, they decide (when they must decide for themselves) thoughtlessly. If they are forbidden to beat Jews, they learn how not to want to, something a free man who wants to beat Jews never learns; then, when they are allowed to, the release of their repressed wish to beat Jews makes maniacs of them.

All Germans are not "authoritarian personalities." I imagine that most are not. But, while there have been intervals in which the German was actually allowed to concern himself with matters of State, the pattern of German life has been such, over the centuries, that free spirits either had to give up or get out. From Goethe, who said he preferred "injustice to disorder," to Thomas Mann, who gloried in being nonpolitical, German intellectuals contrived to live "above it all," in "the land of poets and thinkers," as Mme de Staël described the Germany of 1810. Those who contrived to live *in* it all fared badly.

Other nations sent their worst people away. Germany sent—drove, rather—its best. Between Prince Metternich's Mainz Commission of 1819 (the Un-German Activities Committee of its day) and the last renewal of Bismarck's anti-Socialist laws in 1888, some four and a half million Germans came to the United States alone, 770,000 of them after the suppression of the Revolution of 1848. Wave after wave, after each unsuccessful movement against autocracy, came over to constitute, wherever they went, the finest flower of immigration. Their letters back home brought new and larger waves of their friends and relatives, who were, in large measure, moved more by economic opportunity than by political hope or necessity—who, however, belonged to families or circles in which political liberalism had led to emigration. Left behind were, in the main, those who conformed, willingly or because they saw no way out. Left behind, too, for the next generation, was the dream, always madder as it was frustrated, which produced new outbreaks, new suppressions, new emigrations. National Socialism brought dream and conformism together into something satanic.

Each new generation's leadership was somewhere in Pennsylvania or the Argentine or Wisconsin or China. But millions of liberty-loving Germans remained, and all men, in whatever form they love it, love liberty. Thus throughout Germany, as everywhere where there is oppression among literate peoples, one encountered, and still encounters, more diversity, more individuality, than there is among, say, Americans, who are unoppressed; more variety in entertainment and in the arts, in political partisanship and in the political complexion of the press; all this, more individuality, more independence, stubborn or sublimated, in the land of the goose step than one finds in the land of the free. Free Americans all read the same papers, wear the same clothes, and vote for the same two transposable parties; Germans dress freely, freely read different papers, and vote a dozen different ways, but they are, in their submissiveness, the same.

Of what are these people guilty, who have never known the responsibility of the sovereign citizen? Of not assuming it, all at once, on January 30, 1933? Their offense was their national history. The crime of all but a million or so of them (and, in part, of these, too) had been committed long before National Socialism. All ten of my friends gladly confess this crime of having been Germans in Germany.

"That's the way we Germans are," said Herr Simon, the *alter Kämpfer*.

"But," I said, "is this the *Herrenrasse*, the superior race?"

"Morally and mentally, yes," he said. "We are industrious and orderly, too. But we are unfortunate in this one respect: we cannot rule ourselves; *wir brauchen eine starke Hand,* we require an iron hand."

"Why?"

"I don't know. That's the way we Germans are."

It is partly self-pity again, partly, of course, self-exculpation, the easy way out. My friends may not present an admirable spectacle. But failure to present an admirable spectacle is not a crime against humanity. Maybe it should be.

## CHAPTER 13

# But Then It Was Too Late

"What no one seemed to notice," said a colleague of mine, a philologist, "was the ever widening gap, after 1933, between the government and the people. Just think how very wide this gap was to begin with, here in Germany. And it became always wider. You know, it doesn't make people close to their government to be told that this is a people's government, a true democracy, or to be enrolled in civilian defense, or even to vote. All this has little, really nothing, to do with *knowing* one is governing.

"What happened here was the gradual habituation of the people, little by little, to being governed by surprise; to receiving decisions deliberated in secret; to believing that the situation was so complicated that the government had to act on information which the people could not understand, or so dangerous that, even if the people could understand it, it could not be released because of national security. And their sense of identification with Hitler, their trust in him, made it easier to widen this gap and reassured those who would otherwise have worried about it.

"This separation of government from people, this widening of the gap, took place so gradually and so insensibly, each step disguised (perhaps not even intentionally) as a temporary emergency measure or associated with true patriotic allegiance or with real social purposes. And all the crises and reforms (real reforms, too) so occupied the people that they did not see the slow motion underneath, of the whole process of government growing remoter and remoter.

"You will understand me when I say that my Middle High German was my life. It was all I cared about. I was a scholar, a specialist. Then, suddenly, I was plunged into all the new activity, as the university was drawn into the new situation; meetings, conferences, interviews, ceremonies, and, above all, papers to be filled out, reports, bibliographies, lists, questionnaires. And on top of that were the demands in the community, the things in which one had to, was 'expected to' participate that had not been there or had not been important before. It was all rigmarole, of course, but it consumed all one's energies, coming on top of the work one really wanted to do. You can see how easy it was, then, not to think about fundamental things. One had no time."

"Those," I said, "are the words of my friend the baker. "One had no time to think. There was so much going on."

"Your friend the baker was right," said my colleague. "The dictatorship, and the whole process of its coming into being, was above all *diverting*. It provided an excuse not to think for people who did not want to think anyway. I do not speak of your 'little men,' your baker and so on; I speak of my colleagues and myself, learned men, mind you. Most of us did not want to think about fundamental things and never had. There was no need to. Nazism gave us some dreadful, fundamental things to think about—we were decent people—and kept us so busy with continuous changes and 'crises' and so fascinated, yes, fascinated, by the machinations of the 'national enemies,' without and within, that we had no time to think about these dreadful

167

things that were growing, little by little, all around us. Unconsciously, I suppose, we were grateful. Who wants to think?

"To live in this process is absolutely not to be able to notice it—please try to believe me—unless one has a much greater degree of political awareness, acuity, than most of us had ever had occasion to develop. Each step was so small, so inconsequential, so well explained or, on occasion, 'regretted,' that, unless one were detached from the whole process from the beginning, unless one understood what the whole thing was in principle, what all these 'little measures' that no 'patriotic German' could resent must some day lead to, one no more saw it developing from day to day than a farmer in his field sees the corn growing. One day it is over his head.

"How is this to be avoided, among ordinary men, even highly educated ordinary men? Frankly, I do not know. I do not see, even now. Many, many times since it all happened I have pondered that pair of great maxims, *Principiis obsta* and *Finem respice*—'Resist the beginnings' and 'Consider the end.' But one must foresee the end in order to resist, or even see, the beginnings. One must foresee the end clearly and certainly and how is this to be done, by ordinary men or even by extraordinary men? Things *might* have changed here before they went as far as they did; they didn't, but they *might* have. And everyone counts on that *might*.

"Your 'little men,' your Nazi friends, were not against National Socialism in principle. Men like me, who were, are the greater offenders, not because we *knew* better (that would be too much to say) but because we *sensed* better. Pastor Niemöller spoke for the thousands and thousands of men like me when he spoke (too modestly of himself) and said that, when the Nazis attacked the Communists, he was a little uneasy, but, after all, he was not a Communist, and so he did nothing; and then they attacked the Socialists, and he was a little uneasier, but, still, he was not a Socialist, and he did nothing; and then the schools, the press, the Jews, and so on, and he was always uneasier, but still he did nothing. And then they attacked the Church, and he was a Churchman, and he did something—but then it was too late."

"Yes," I said.

"You see," my colleague went on, "one doesn't see exactly where or how to move. Believe me, this is true. Each act, each occasion, is worse than the last, but only a little worse. You wait for the next and the next. You wait for one great shocking occasion, thinking that others, when such a shock comes, will join with you in resisting somehow. You don't want to act, or even talk, alone; you don't want to 'go out of your way to make trouble.' Why not?— Well, you are not in the habit of doing it. And it is not just fear, fear of standing alone, that restrains you; it is also genuine uncertainty.

"Uncertainty is a very important factor, and, instead of decreasing as time goes on, it grows. Outside, in the streets, in the general community, 'everyone' is happy. One hears no protest, and certainly sees none. You know, in France or Italy there would be slogans against the government painted on walls and fences; in Germany, outside the great cities, perhaps, there is not even this. In the university community, in your own community, you speak privately to your colleagues, some of whom certainly feel as you do; but what do they say? They say, 'It's not so bad' or 'You're seeing things' or 'You're an alarmist.'

"And you are an alarmist. You are saying that this must

lead to *this*, and you can't prove it. These are the beginnings, yes; but how do you know for sure when you don't know the end, and how do you know, or even surmise, the end? On the one hand, your enemies, the law, the regime, the Party, intimidate you. On the other, your colleagues pooh-pooh you as pessimistic or even neurotic. You are left with your close friends, who are, naturally, people who have always thought as you have.

"But your friends are fewer now. Some have drifted off somewhere or submerged themselves in their work. You no longer see as many as you did at meetings or gatherings. Informal groups become smaller; attendance drops off in little organizations, and the organizations themselves wither. Now, in small gatherings of your oldest friends, you feel that you are talking to yourselves, that you are isolated from the reality of things. This weakens your confidence still further and serves as a further deterrent to—to what? It is clearer all the time that, if you are going to do anything, you must make an occasion to do it, and then you are obviously a troublemaker. So you wait, and you wait.

"But the one great shocking occasion, when tens or hundreds or thousands will join with you, never comes. *That's* the difficulty. If the last and worst act of the whole regime had come immediately after the first and smallest, thousands, yes, millions would have been sufficiently shocked —if, let us say, the gassing of the Jews in '43 had come immediately after the 'German Firm' stickers on the windows of non-Jewish shops in '33. But of course this isn't the way it happens. In between come all the hundreds of little steps, some of them imperceptible, each of them preparing you not to be shocked by the next. Step C is not so much worse than Step B, and, if you did not make a stand at Step B, why should you at Step C? And so on to Step D.

"And one day, too late, your principles, if you were ever sensible of them, all rush in upon you. The burden of self-deception has grown too heavy, and some minor incident, in my case my little boy, hardly more than a baby, saying 'Jew swine,' collapses it all at once, and you see that everything, everything, has changed and changed completely under your nose. The world you live in—your nation, your people—is not the world you were born in at all. The forms are all there, all untouched, all reassuring, the houses, the shops, the jobs, the mealtimes, the visits, the concerts, the cinema, the holidays. But the spirit, which you never noticed because you made the lifelong mistake of identifying it with the forms, is changed. Now you live in a world of hate and fear, and the people who hate and fear do not even know it themselves; when everyone is transformed, no one is transformed. Now you live in a system which rules without responsibility even to God. The system itself could not have intended this in the beginning, but in order to sustain itself it was compelled to go all the way.

"You have gone almost all the way yourself. Life is a continuing process, a flow, not a succession of acts and events at all. It has flowed to a new level, carrying you with it, without any effort on your part. On this new level you live, you have been living more comfortably every day, with new morals, new principles. You have accepted things you would not have accepted five years ago, a year ago, things that your father, even in Germany, could not have imagined.

"Suddenly it all comes down, all at once. You see what you are, what you have done, or, more accurately, what you haven't done (for that was all that was required of most of us: that we do nothing). You remember those early meetings of your department in the university when, if one had stood, others would have stood, perhaps, but no one stood. A small matter, a matter of hiring this man or that, and you hired this one rather than that. You remember everything now, and your heart breaks. Too late. You are compromised beyond repair.

"What then? You must then shoot yourself. A few did. Or 'adjust' your principles. Many tried, and some, I suppose, succeeded; not I, however. Or learn to live the rest of your life with your shame. This last is the nearest there is, under the circumstances, to heroism: shame. Many Germans became this poor kind of hero, many more, I think, than the world knows or cares to know."

I said nothing. I thought of nothing to say.

"I can tell you," my colleague went on, "of a man in Leipzig, a judge. He was not a Nazi, except nominally, but he certainly wasn't an anti-Nazi. He was just—a judge. In '42 or '43, early '43, I think it was, a Jew was tried before him in a case involving, but only incidentally, relations with an 'Aryan' woman. This was 'race injury,' something the Party was especially anxious to punish. In the case at bar, however, the judge had the power to convict the man of a 'nonracial' offense and send him to an ordinary prison for a very long term, thus saving him from Party 'processing' which would have meant concentration camp or, more probably, deportation and death. But the man was innocent of the 'nonracial' charge, in the judge's opinion, and so, as an honorable judge, he acquitted him. Of course, the Party seized the Jew as soon as he left the courtroom."

"And the judge?"

"Yes, the judge. He could not get the case off his conscience—a case, mind you, in which he had acquitted an innocent man. He thought that he should have convicted him and saved him from the Party, but how could he have convicted an innocent man? The thing preyed on him more and more, and he had to talk about it, first to his family, then to his friends, and then to acquaintances. (That's how I heard about it.) After the '44 *Putsch* they arrested him. After that, I don't know."

I said nothing.

"Once the war began," my colleague continued, "resistance, protest, criticism, complaint, all carried with them a multiplied likelihood of the greatest punishment. Mere lack of enthusiasm, or failure to show it in public, was 'defeatism.' You assumed that there were lists of those who would be 'dealt with' later, after the victory. Goebbels was very clever here, too. He continually promised a 'victory orgy' to 'take care of' those who thought that their 'treasonable attitude' had escaped notice. And he meant it; *that* was not just propaganda. And that was enough to put an end to all uncertainty.

"Once the war began, the government could do anything 'necessary' to win it; so it was with the 'final solution of the Jewish problem,' which the Nazis always talked about but never dared undertake, not even the Nazis, until war and its 'necessities' gave them the knowledge that they could get away with it. The people abroad who thought that war against Hitler would help the Jews were wrong. And the people in Germany who, once the war had begun, still thought of complaining, protesting, resisting, were betting on Germany's losing the war. It was a long bet. Not many made it."

## CHAPTER 14

## Collective Shame

My colleague came back, one day, to the subject of "this poor kind of heroism: shame." "The trouble with shame," he said, "is that it goes down deep or it doesn't. If it doesn't, one throws it off as soon as he himself is injured (as, of course, in total war, he is likely to be, in his family, his property, his position, his person). If it does, if it goes down deep enough, it is a form of suicide; it was this that led some men I knew to join the Party later on, an act of throwing themselves away. None of your 'little men,' perhaps—"

"No, not shame," I said.

"But one doesn't know this easily," said my colleague, "this deep shame. With many it took the outward form of their saying that, since National Socialist rule was here, and here for a long time to come, they would join it and reform it from within. But to be effective, they would first have to be accepted—"

"Oh, 'effectiveness,' " I said. "That I heard from my friend the teacher. For the sake of being effective he did everything required of him, and of course he wasn't effective. He knows that now. But then he had hopes of being able to oppose the excesses—"

"Yes, it was always the excesses that we wished to oppose, rather than the whole program, the whole spirit that produced the first steps, A, B, C, and D, out of which the excesses were bound to come. It is so much easier to 'oppose the excesses,' about which one can, of course, do nothing, than it is to oppose the whole spirit, about which one can do something every day."

"All of my 'little men' opposed the excesses, at least the worst excesses," I said, "and the two best of them, the teacher and the bank clerk, blamed them on the radicals who had grown up in the movement when it was irresponsible and attracted the most reckless elements—"

"Yes," said my colleague, shaking his head, "the 'excesses' and the 'radicals.' We all opposed them, very quietly. So your two 'little men' thought they must join, as good men, good Germans, even as good Christians, and when enough of them did they would be able to change the Party. They would 'bore from within.' 'Big men' told themselves that, too, in the usual sincerity that required them only to abandon one little principle after another, to throw away, little by little, all that was good. I was one of those men.

"You know," he went on, "when men who understand what is happening—the motion, that is, of history, not the reports of single events or developments—when such men do not object or protest, men who do not understand cannot be expected to. How many men would you say understand—in this sense—in America? And when, as the motion of history accelerates and those who don't understand are crazed by fear, as our people were, and made into a great 'patriotic' mob, will they understand then, when they did not before?

"We learned here—I say this freely—to give up trying to make them understand after, oh, the end of 1938, after the night of the synagogue burning and the things that followed it. Even before the war began, men who were teachers, men whose faith in teaching was their whole faith, gave up, seeing that there was no comprehension, no capacity left for comprehension, and the thing must go its course, taking first its victims, then its architects, and then the rest of us to destruction. This did not mean surrender; it meant conservation of energy, doing what little one could (now that it was too late to do anything!) and consuming one's energy doing it, to relieve the present victim (if only by brazenly saying 'Hello' to him on the street!) and to prevent, or at least postpone, the fate of the next victim (if only by writing a 'nonpolitical' letter abroad asking somebody to take an emigrant!)."

"Yes," I said.

"You say that is not much"—I tried to protest—"but I say that it is more, under the circumstances, than ordinary life, in Germany, in America, anywhere, has prepared ordinary men to do."

His wife was there. "I hope," she said, "that the Anglo-Saxons"—she obviously meant the Anglos and not the Saxons—"have characteristics that will make them less susceptible to the things we Germans could not resist."

"What would such characteristics be?" I said.

"Oh, farsightedness, I think, above all. Maybe a shorter history makes it easier for people to look ahead instead of always behind. And you are under less pressure, somehow, than we are. You are freer—I don't mean legally, of course—to take the long view." It was the first time, in my conversations in Germany, that the focus had been placed on the word *Druck*, "pressure."

Another colleague of mine brought me even closer to the heart of the matter—and closer home. A chemical engineer by profession, he was a man of whom, before I knew him, I had been told, "He is one of those rare birds among Germans—a European." One day, when we had become very friendly, I said to him, "Tell me now—how was the world lost?"

"That," he said, "is easy to tell, much easier than you may suppose. The world was lost one day in 1935, here in Germany. It was I who lost it, and I will tell you how.

"I was employed in a defense plant (a war plant, of course, but they were always called defense plants). That was the year of the National Defense Law, the law of 'total conscription.' Under the law I was required to take the oath of fidelity. I said I would not; I opposed it in conscience. I was given twenty-four hours to 'think it over.' In those twenty-four hours I lost the world."

"Yes?" I said.

"You see, refusal would have meant the loss of my job, of course, not prison or anything like that. (Later on, the penalty was worse, but this was only 1935.) But losing my job would have meant that I could not get another. Wherever I went I should be asked why I left the job I had, and, when I said why, I should certainly have been refused employment. Nobody would hire a 'Bolshevik.' Of course I was not a Bolshevik, but you understand what I mean."

"Yes," I said.

"I tried not to think of myself or my family. We might have got out of the country, in any case, and I could have got a job in industry or education somewhere else.

"What I tried to think of was the people to whom I might be of some help later on, if things got worse (as I believed they would). I had a wide friendship in scientific and academic circles, including many Jews, and 'Aryans,' too, who might be in trouble. If I took the oath and held my job, I might be of help, somehow, as things went on.

If I refused to take the oath, I would certainly be useless to my friends, even if I remained in the country. I myself would be in their situation.

"The next day, after 'thinking it over,' I said I would take the oath with the mental reservation that, by the words with which the oath began, '*Ich schwöre bei Gott*, I swear by God,' I understood that no human being and no government had the right to override my conscience. My mental reservations did not interest the official who administered the oath. He said, 'Do you take the oath?' and I took it. That day the world was lost, and it was I who lost it."

"Do I understand," I said, "that you think that you should not have taken the oath?"

"Yes."

"But," I said, "you did save many lives later on. You were of greater use to your friends than you ever dreamed you might be." (My friend's apartment was, until his arrest and imprisonment in 1943, a hideout for fugitives.)

"For the sake of the argument," he said, "I will agree that I saved many lives later on. Yes."

"Which you could not have done if you had refused to take the oath in 1935."

"Yes."

"And you still think that you should not have taken the oath."

"Yes."

"I don't understand," I said.

"Perhaps not," he said, "but you must not forget that you are an American. I mean that, really. Americans have never known anything like this experience—in its entirety, all the way to the end. That is the point."

"You must explain," I said.

"Of course I must explain. First of all, there is the problem of the lesser evil. Taking the oath was not so evil as being unable to help my friends later on would have been. But the evil of the oath was certain and immediate, and the helping of my friends was in the future and therefore uncertain. I had to commit a positive evil, there and then, in the hope of a possible good later on. The good outweighed the evil; but the good was only a hope, the evil a fact."

"But," I said, "the hope was realized. You were able to help your friends."

"Yes," he said, "but you must concede that the hope might *not* have been realized—either for reasons beyond my control or because I became afraid later on or even because I was afraid all the time and was simply fooling myself when I took the oath in the first place.

"But that is not the important point. The problem of the lesser evil we all know about; in Germany we took Hindenburg as less evil than Hitler, and in the end we got them both. But that is not why I say that Americans cannot understand. No, the important point is—how many innocent people were killed by the Nazis, would you say?"

"Six million Jews alone, we are told."

"Well, that may be an exaggeration. And it does not include non-Jews, of whom there must have been many hundreds of thousands, or even millions. Shall we say, just to be safe, that three million innocent people were killed all together?"

I nodded.

"And how many innocent lives would you like to say I saved?"

"You would know better than I," I said.

"Well," said he, "perhaps five, or ten, one doesn't know. But shall we say a hundred, or a thousand, just to be safe?"

I nodded.

"And it would be better to have saved all three million, instead of only a hundred, or a thousand?"

"Of course."

"There, then, is my point. If I had refused to take the oath of fidelity, I would have saved all three million."

"You are joking," I said.

"No."

"You don't mean to tell me that your refusal would have overthrown the regime in 1935?"

"No."

"Or that others would have followed your example?"

"No."

"I don't understand."

"You are an American," he said again, smiling. "I will explain. There I was, in 1935, a perfect example of the *kind* of person who, with all his advantages in birth, in education, and in position, rules (or might easily rule) in any country. If I had refused to take the oath in 1935, it would have meant that thousands and thousands like me, all over Germany, were refusing to take it. Their refusal would have heartened millions. Thus the regime would have been overthrown, or, indeed, would never have come to power in the first place. The fact that I was not prepared to resist, in 1935, meant that all the thousands, hundreds of thousands, like me in Germany were also unprepared, and each one of these hundreds of thousands was, like me, a man of great influence or of great potential influence. Thus the world was lost."

"You are serious?" I said.

"Completely," he said. "These hundred lives I saved—

or a thousand or ten as you will—what do they represent? A little something out of the whole terrible evil, when, if my faith had been strong enough in 1935, I could have prevented the whole evil."

"Your faith?"

"My faith. I did not believe that I could 'remove mountains.' The day I said 'No,' I had faith. In the process of 'thinking it over,' in the next twenty-four hours, my faith failed me. So, in the next ten years, I was able to remove only anthills, not mountains."

"How might your faith of that first day have been sustained?"

"I don't know, I don't know," he said. "Do you?"

"I am an American," I said.

My friend smiled. "Therefore you believe in education."

"Yes," I said.

"My education did not help me," he said, "and I had a broader and better education than most men have had or ever will have. All it did, in the end, was to enable me to rationalize my failure of faith more easily than I might have done if I had been ignorant. And so it was, I think, among educated men generally, in that time in Germany. Their resistance was no greater than other men's."

As I thought of my ten Nazi friends in the light of my talks with the philologist and the engineer, it occurred to me that the concept of collective guilt is at bottom a semantic failure. What is really involved is collective shame. Collective shame may be possible, but it cannot be compelled. Shame is a state of being, guilt a juridical fact. A passer-by cannot be guilty of failure to try to prevent a lynching. He can only be ashamed of not having done so.

Even a sovereign, self-governing citizen, such as an American, cannot be guilty of failure to try to prevent an act of State. It would be Nazism itself to take Americans off the street and charge them, in connection with, say, the bombing of Hiroshima, with having violated the Hague Regulations, to which their government, whose sovereign citizens they are, was signatory. Still less than a sovereign citizen can the subject of a dictatorship be guilty of an act of State. And, when the State requires him, personally and individually, to commit what he regards as a crime, and the penalty for his refusal to do so is very heavy, the common law acquits him on the ground of duress. "I was lucky," said Herr Klingelhöfer, the cabinetmaker. "I didn't have to do anything wrong."

Collective shame is something else, but it requires not merely the fact of sovereign citizenship but the most delicate sense of it. I did not discover much collective shame among my ten friends. The President of the West German Federal Republic had called upon them to feel it and had used that very expression, "collective shame." But how does one call, effectively, upon people to feel ashamed?

In the case of Horst Rupprecht, the university student and Hitler Youth leader, who blamed himself for the sins of Nazism, the sins of Germany, the sins of the whole German people, his *mea culpa* was just a little unconvincing: he was eight years old in 1933. I think his testimony is what many non-Germans wanted to hear from the lips of every German: "No, no, it wasn't Hitler and Göring and the rest, it was we Germans, every one of us, I more than any of the rest, who did it"; but I think they would have been disappointed when they heard it, as I was.

At his trial at Nuremberg, young Rupprecht's highest superior, Baldur von Schirach, the Nazi Youth Leader, said: "It is my guilt, and I must bear it before God and the German nation, that I educated German youth for a man whom I thought irreproachable, but who was a murderer millions of times over." Was this the same Baldur von Schirach who had called Hitler "Germany's greatest son," "this genius grazing the stars," who had said that the altar was not in the Church but on the steps of the Feldherrn Hall, where Hitler's *Putsch* had ended in 1923? It was. When, where, and how does one discover that an irreproachable man is a murderer millions of times over? Does it take the hangman's hood on his eyes to open them?

What I found, among my ten friends, was something like regret, regret that things, which they had not done, had been done or had had to be done. All ten of them, even the tailor, I think, *felt bad*, now, about the torture and slaughter of innocent people—not, however, about the deportation, "resettlement, relocation," or even about the expropriation. (My friends had all lost their own possessions, hadn't they, and who but they themselves felt sorry for them?) The six extremists all said of the extermination of Jews, "That was wrong" or "That was going too far," as if to say, "The gas oven was somewhat too great a punishment for people who, after all, deserved very great punishment."

My ten friends had been told, not since 1939 but since 1933, that their nation was fighting for its life. They believed that self-preservation is the first law of nature, of the nature of nations as well as of herd brutes. Were they wrong in this principle? If they were, they saw nothing in the history of nations (their own or any other) that said so. And, once there was shooting war, their situation was like that of the secret opponents of the regime whom my colleague described: there was no further need for the nation, or anyone in it, to be justified. The nation was literally fighting for its literal life—"they or we." Anything went, and what "anything" was, what enormities it embraced, depended entirely on the turn of the battle.

Even Herr Schwenke, the tailor, proud of his having refused a Jew of old acquaintance a light for his cigarette, frankly glad that the synagogue had been burned, said of the gas ovens, "If it happened, it was wrong. But I don't believe it happened." And, if he were ever able to admit that it *did* happen, he would have to admit that it was right and, to prove it, cry out, with his wound rubbed raw, in still greater anguish against the victims and ascribe to them sins even he had not yet been able to dream of.

What we don't like, what *I* don't like, is the hypocrisy of these people. I want to hear them confess. That they, or some of their countrymen and their country's government, violated the precepts of Christian, civilized, lawful life was bad enough; that they won't see it, or say it, is what really rowels. I want them to plead no extenuation. I want them to say, "I knew and I know that it was all un-Christian, uncivilized, unlawful, and in my love of evil I pretended it wasn't. I plead every German guilty of a life of hypocrisy, above all, myself. I am rotten."

I don't like the dolorous mask my friend Klingelhöfer wears when he says, "I always said no good would come of it, and no good *did* come of it." His *freiwillige Feuerwehr* ebullience is suddenly gone, and now he emerges from the wings, like a one-man troupe playing Molière, in judicious melancholy. I want to say to him, "You *Schweinehund*, what you said, and you said it to yourself, was that no good would come of it *if it lost*. And it did lose. If it had won, you'd be drinking blood with the rest of them." But what's the use?

I want my friends not just to feel bad and confess it, but to have been bad and to be bad now and confess it. I want them to constitute themselves an inferior race, self-abased, so that I, in the magnanimity becoming to the superior, having sat in calumnious judgment on them, may choose to let them live on in public shame and in private torment. I want to be God, not alone in power but in righteousness and in mercy; and Nazism crushed is my chance.

But I am not God. I myself am a national, myself guilty of many national hypocrisies whose only justification is that the Germans' were so much worse. My being less bestial, in my laws and practices, than they were does not make me more Godly than they, for difference in degree is not difference in kind. My own country's racist legislation and practices, against both foreigners and citizens, is a whole web of hypocrisies. And, if I plead that racism has been wonderfully reduced in America in the past century, that the forces of good have been growing ever more powerful, how shall I answer my friends Hildebrandt and Kessler, who believed, or affected to believe, that the infiltration of National Socialism by decent men like themselves would, in time, reduce and even eliminate the evils?

The trouble is that these national hypocrisies, which I myself am not called upon to practice in person, with my own hands, are all acts of the State or its culture. I feel bad about them, to be sure; very bad. But I do not in the least feel like a bad man, and I do not want to be punished for them. And, if I beat my breast, like my Nazi friend, young Rupprecht, and say, "It is I, I, I, who did it," I am afraid that I shall sound just as pretentious as he sounded to me. The confession that I want to hear or that I ought to make does not ring real.

What I really want, since (while I want to let my friends

off in my magnanimity) I do not want to have to reproach myself some time later with having let them escape the consequences of their unheroism, is for each of them to have cared enough at the time to have thrown himself under the iron chariot of the State, with its wheels rimmed with spikes. This none of my friends did, and this I cannot forgive them. They did not care enough.

## CHAPTER 15

## The Furies: Heinrich Hildebrandt

How was I to know, or to find out, how much my friends had suffered (if they had suffered at all) or whether they had suffered enough? If, as doctrine has it, man is perfected by suffering, none of my friends had suffered enough, for none of them, I could see, even in my imperfect knowledge of them, was perfect.

Seven of them ducked my question. My question, which I framed very carefully and put to them in a variety of ways in the last weeks of our conversations, was, "What did you do that was wrong, as you understand right and wrong, and what *didn't* you do that was right?" The instinct that throws instant ramparts around the self-love of all of us came into immediate operation; my friends, in response, spoke of what was legal or illegal, or what was popular or unpopular, or what others did or didn't do, or what was provoked or unprovoked. But I was interested, at this point, in none of these things. "Who knows the secret heart?" I was trying to know the secret heart; I knew all about Versailles and the Polish Corridor and the inflation, the unemployment, the Communists, the Jews, and the Talmud.

The eighth of my friends, young Rupprecht, the Hitler Youth leader, having taken upon himself (or having affected to take) sovereign responsibility for every first and last injustice of the whole Hitler regime, was no better able to enlighten me than Herr Schwenke, the old *Fanatiker*, who, when I was at last able to divert him, with my insistent last question, from Versailles, the Polish Corridor, etc., said, "I have never done anything wrong to any man." "Never?" said I, just to hear myself say it. "*Never*," said he, just to hear himself say it. But two of my friends, Herr Hildebrandt, the teacher, and Herr Kessler, the bank clerk, enlightened me, in their own time, in their own ways, without my having asked them my question.

Fear and advantage, Hildebrandt had said, were his reasons for becoming a National Socialist in 1937, a late "March violet" indeed. "Were there," I said, on another occasion, "any other reasons you joined?" He said nothing and then began to blush. "I—," he began, blushing fully, and then he said, "No, no others." It was a long time before I learned all Herr Hildebrandt's reasons for being a Nazi.

"I might have got by without joining," he said more than once. "I don't know. I might have taken my chances. Others did, I mean other teachers in the high school."

"How many?"

"Let me see. We had thirty-five teachers. Only four, well, five, were fully convinced Nazis. But, of these five, one could be argued with openly, in the teachers' conference room; and only one was a real fanatic, who might denounce a colleague to the authorities."

"Did he?"

"There was never any evidence that he did, but we had to be careful around him."

"How many of the thirty-five never joined the Party?"

"Five, but not all for the same reason. Three of the five were very religious. The teachers were all Protestants, of course, but only half a dozen, at most, were really religious; these were all anti-Nazi, these half-dozen, but only three of them held out. One of the three was the history teacher (now the director of the school), very nationalistic, very Prussian, but a strong churchman. He stood near the anti-Nazi Confessional Church, but he couldn't join it, of course, or he'd have lost his job. Then there was the theology teacher, who also taught modern languages; he was the best teacher in the school; apart from his religious opposition, his knowledge of foreign cultures made him anti-Nazi. The third was the mathematics teacher, absolutely unworldly but profoundly pietistic, a member of the Moravian sect."

"And the two who were nonreligious and didn't join?"

"One was a historian. He was not an atheist, you understand, just a historian. He was a nonjoiner, of anything. He was nonpolitical. He was strongly critical of Nazism, but always on a detached, theoretical basis. Nobody bothered him; nobody paid any attention to him. And vice versa. The other nonbeliever was really the truest believer of them all. He was a biologist and a rebel against a religious background. He had no trouble perverting Darwin's 'survival of the fittest' into Nazi racism—he was the only teacher in the whole school who believed it."

"Why didn't he join the Party?"

"He hated the local Kreisleiter, the County Leader of the Party, whose father had been a theologian and who himself never left the Church. The hatred was mutual. That's why the biologist never joined. Now he's an 'anti-Nazi.' "

"And you?"

"Yes," he said, blushing a little again. "I joined. I had my past, of course, in East Prussia. All sorts of care had been taken to bury it, but—one never knew. I had been active in the old Staatspartei, the successor of the Democratic Party in 1930. After 1930 I had lectured regularly at the local folk high school, the adult education program, which was promoted and largely attended by Social Democrats and Communists. In my book program, on the radio, I had praised the works of 'treasonable' writers after the Nazis took power.

"For eight years I held the rank of Studienassessor. It carries no tenure with it. After 1933 my name was not even included in the list of candidates for Studienrat, the rank which is usually given after five years of high-school teaching. The spring the Nazis took power, I was dismissed from my radio program and from my adult-school lectureship. Then I was transferred from the city to one small school after another. So I resigned, very quietly, and came here, to Hesse. My father, through an old Army friend of his here, got me the appointment in Kronenberg. But still I was not promoted, and I was afraid that something was suspected. I waited two years, and then I joined the Party. I was promoted to Studienrat and got married."

"And Frau Hildebrandt?" I said. I watched for the blush, but there was none; it (whatever *it* was) wasn't Frau Hildebrandt.

"Eva went just the other way from me. In 1933 she was for Hitler. Of course, she was much younger than I and her family was petty nobility, who were all in the old Nationalist Party, which threw its weight, at the end, to the Nazis. But she adored the Jewish Professor Neumann at Kiel—who didn't?—and the day of the book-burning there he instructed the secretary of his philosophy seminar to give his books to the students. Eva got three of Neumann's own books, her proudest possession—and still she believed in Nazism. She was what we call *begeistert*, bewitched.

"We first met in 1938, at the Casino, in Kassel, for officers and their families. The young men—we weren't so young any more—all went there with their parents. I was with my parents, she with hers; our fathers were both retired officers and old acquaintances. It happened to be on

January 30, the anniversary of Hitler's coming to power, but that was only an accident; the Casino society was by no means Nazi. We danced, which I was not very good at"— he blushed, just a little—"but a month later I gave a talk there and she came, and 'fell for me.'

"I was already a Party member. She was really nonpolitical, at heart. It's funny; I, with my knowledge of politics, I became more and more Nazi, and she became less and less. After the synagogue burning, at the end of '38, she was strongly anti-Nazi. She got out Neumann's books and cried. I told her she didn't understand these things. She didn't, either, but she knew them, sensed them, better than I did— or than I was willing to. From then on, until I went into the Army in '39, we quarreled all the time. But now it's all right." (It was, too. I had met the Hildebrandt family frequently.)

"She never quit the Party, of course. She had joined in '37, too, not until then; she was a teacher, and she did it to hold her job. But women are braver than men, don't you think?"

"Yes," I said (still wondering what *it* was, besides "fear and advantage," that had made a Nazi of Herr Hildebrandt).

"It's because—well, they don't face things the same way men do. They assume that the man will find a way to support the family. They could be stronger Nazis or stronger anti-Nazis than men, without thinking too much about it. Most of them." I thought I saw a faint blush, at this last, but it was late afternoon in the winter. I turned the lights on.

Hildebrandt had no guilt about his "Nazi" teaching of literature. "One could talk about other things, outside the textbooks, and there was 'un-German' literature that had been overlooked, such as Lessing's *Nathan the Wise*, which we read openly in class. *The Buddenbrooks*, too; it was not specifically forbidden, but everybody knew that the Nazis hated Thomas Mann.

"Privately, certain students read Jewish authors—it went without saying that they were not to be read—like Wassermann, Werfel, Zweig, and wrote papers on them, brought them to me, and I accepted them for credit, although they were not discussed in class. And I gave them French and English literature, more so than before, although to do so was one of those vague betrayals of the 'new spirit'; still, it had not been specifically forbidden. Of course, I always said, to protect myself (but I said it in such a way that I hoped the students would see through it), that the foreign works we read were only a reflection of German literature. So, you see, Herr Professor, a man could show some—some independence, even, so to say, secretly."

"I understand," I said.

"Many of the students—the best of them—understood what was going on in all this. It was a sort of dumb-show game that we were all playing, I with them. The worst effect, I think, was that it made them cynical, the best ones. But, then, it made the teachers cynical, too. I think the classroom in those years was one of the causes of the cynicism you see in the best young men and women in Germany today."

"In the best?"

"Yes. The others, the great majority, are disillusioned now, but that is something else. You see, the young people, and, yes, the old, too, were drawn to opposite extremes in those years. People outside Germany seem to think that 'the Germans' came to believe everything they were told, all the dreadful nonsense that passed for truth. It is a very bad mistake, a very dangerous mistake, to think this. The fact, I think, is that most Germans came to believe everything, absolutely everything; but the rest, those who saw through the nonsense, came to believe nothing, absolutely nothing. These last, the best, are the cynics now, young and old."

"And the others, the believers?"

"Well, the old among them are, I suppose you would say, the hopeless now. The younger, those who were teen-agers then—I don't know what to say about them except that they have lost their old illusions and see nothing new to turn to. This is dangerous, both for them and for the world ten or twenty years from now. They need, well, to be born again, somehow."

I asked Herr Hildebrandt if he could recollect specific instances of his own "dumb-show game," and the next time we met he spoke of them. "In Shakespeare, for instance, only *Macbeth* and, of course, *The Merchant of Venice*, which I never assigned, were recommended. But, again, nothing was forbidden, although *Hamlet* was denounced as embodying the 'flabbiness of soul' that the Nazis condemned in Russian writers like Dostoevski and Tolstoi, the 'soft Slavic soul' that in Tolstoi even went so far as pacifism. So in Shakespeare I could assign *A Midsummer Night's Dream*, which in normal times I should not have bothered with, just so that I could say to the students, 'The music for this was written by Mendelssohn. Your parents all know the music. Mendelssohn was a Jew. We don't play his music any more.' Perhaps that was not much to say, but it was something, don't you think?"

"Yes," I said, "certainly. . . . Tell me, Herr Hildebrandt, what about *Julius Caesar?*"

He smiled very, very wryly. "*Julius Caesar?* No . . . no."

"Was it forbidden?"

"Not that I remember. But that is not the way it was. Everything was not regulated specifically, ever. It was not like that at all. Choices were left to the teacher's discretion, within the 'German spirit.' That was all that was necessary; the teacher had only to be discreet. If he himself wondered at all whether anyone would object to a given book, he would be wise not to use it. This was a much more powerful form of intimidation, you see, than any fixed list of acceptable or unacceptable writings. The way it was done was, from the point of view of the regime, remarkably clever and effective. The teacher had to make the choices and risk the consequences; this made him all the more cautious."

"You spoke of giving certain students books by Jewish authors," I said, on another occasion. "How did you know which students you could trust not to denounce you?"

"Oh, one judges, from person to person. I may say generally that one would be safe in giving such books to *Mischlinge* [mongrels, half-Jews] and those from known liberal families. People who were so far under suspicion would never denounce one, because they would not be believed—people, that is, who were clearly beyond currying favor with the authorities. It was like complaining to Jews about the regime; it was safe."

"I can imagine," I said, "that some Jews would have resented being a sort of secret wailing wall for people who had something on their minds that they did not dare to say openly." I knew he would blush a little, and he did. "Yes. I think most Jews resented it, very deeply. That was why some people didn't do it."

"Yes," I said.

"In those times," he went on, "a student could have denounced me, but it would have been hard to make a case against me, because I was, well, clever in the way I did these things. But, even if I had been denounced, I could have got off, almost certainly, if my past were not revealed, because I was a Party member. You may say that it is a rationalization —I know it is, myself—but a Party member could get away with something, not much, but something. A non-Nazi would not dare to violate the rules. At least none in our school did."

"Were there any spies in the classes?" I said.

"No, unless students volunteered to be informers. The regime regarded informers as patriots, of course, but you know how students would feel; young people despise that kind of thing. There certainly were no spies, or even regular informers, that I heard of in our school. Not before the war, anyway. And certainly not during the war (although I was away in the Army except for my furlough in '40, after the fall of France). During the war even anti-Nazi teachers would not criticize the regime. Once the war began, all this ended. We were 'one folk.' We could not separate the regime from our country then."

"The July 20 conspirators did."

"Yes . . . yes, they did. They did."

I knew he was blushing, as he did so easily, but I did not look up. I was waiting—perhaps I only imagine it now, long afterward—for something that would bring his blush to a boil. I had a long time to wait.

He showed me the government manual for upper-school teaching, issued in 1938. Under *Literatur* there was this: "Of course, only such selections should be chosen as point in the direction of the New Germany, help prepare the new world outlook [*Weltanschauung*], or give instances of its innermost will. As we recognize only the vigorous as educationally valuable, everything must be avoided that weakens or discourages manliness. The thought of race will stand out strongest with a vivid knowledge of Teutonism." And then, apparently as subjects for study: "The nation as a community of fate and struggle. The struggle for living space. Soldiery (Army, Navy, Air Corps). Heroism. War poetry. The soldier of the World War as a legendary figure and a moral force. Woman in the World War. The community of National Socialist struggle. Leadership, comradeship. The fight of the German nation on our frontiers and abroad. Colonies."

"That was all," said Herr Hildebrandt, "although, of course, all these things would be explicated, but still not in detail, in the publications or meetings of the Lehrerbund, the Nazi teacher organization. But it was all very sloppy and vague. Under those headings one could teach almost anything—except, maybe, *All Quiet on the Western Front!*"

"Why was it so sloppy?" I said.

"Partly because the Nazification of the secondary schools was known to be difficult. They were stronger and better organized professionally than the primary schools. There the teachers were much more insecure, and also more susceptible, because, having to teach everything, they had been trained thoroughly in nothing. This half-educated condition made them excellent Nazi material; they could be 'taught' anything fast. We had a joke in those days: 'What is speed?'—'Speed is an instant so short that a grade-school teacher hasn't time to change his politics.'

"Then, too, the primary schools were more important to the regime. There they could reach all the children of the country, while we, in the high schools, had only one-fourth of them. So the primary schools had to be brought into line first, the secondary schools later. They never finished the job, but in another ten years, maybe even five, they would have."

"So soon?"

"So soon. One may say overnight. Resistance is low in a dictatorship. And this was, or would have become, an efficient dictatorship, even in cultural matters. There it was weakest, at the beginning, because the oldest and most trusted Nazis were uncultivated men, except for a few freaks like Rosenberg. And wherever there was a 'deserving' Party member and no other place could be found for him, he would be dumped into education. The Nazi 'educators' were illiterate, from Rust, the Minister of Education, on down. They did not know what they wanted or where to find it. Putting ignorant 'reliables,' from politics or business, over the educators was also part of the Nazi way of humiliating education and bringing it into popular contempt.

"Then, too, the Party education bosses did not know themselves when the Party line would change, and they were afraid of being caught on the wrong side when it did. Any author might suddenly prove to be 'decadent,' although, incidentally, when one hears so much of Goethe now as an anti-Nazi symbol, one recalls that all (almost all, certainly) of Goethe was recommended. His universalism was not so powerful or direct as to embarrass National Socialism. I do not mean to make light of the greatest genius of all, but if he had lived a century longer he might have wished to rewrite every word so that he could not be used by the Nazis."

"It might have ruined his poetry, Herr Studienrat."

He smiled at my form of address, and emphasized his: "Yes, *Herr Professor*, but now we sound like the classroom. I was speaking, oh, yes, of the sudden changes in the Party line. There were not so many, except the great ones, which you know of, like the Russian pact of '39, and these did not immediately affect us. The difficulty was that changes could not be predicted. Living writers, unless they were Party hacks, could not be recommended at all, because they might turn anti-Nazi or be found to have been anti-Nazi or Communistic.

"It was not what a man wrote, but what his politics were (or were accused of being) that counted with the Nazis. Hans Grimm, for instance, was a great Party favorite because of his story, *Volk ohne Raum*, 'A People without Living Space'; then he became critical of the Nazis and had to be anathematized and his books forbidden—no matter what they contained. By the way, even *Wilhelm Tell* was suddenly forbidden during the war, at the time when it was thought that Switzerland might be attacked.

"In history, in biology, and in economics the teaching program was much more elaborate than it was in literature, and much stricter. These subjects were really rewritten. They had to be. But literature could not so easily be rewritten to order. The rewritten subjects were the worst nonsense, and, of course, the cynicism of the teachers and the better students was worst there. Every student had to take a biology examination to be graduated, and the biology course was a complete distortion of Mendelianism to prove that heredity was everything; such technical materials were most effective, of course, because the student had never met them before.

"But mathematics was the most interesting case. You would think that nothing could be done with such a 'pure' subject, but just this subject was handled very cleverly, and I often wondered who in the Party was so clever. I remember well, because Eva, my wife, taught mathematics. The problems to be assigned were all given, but they would almost all be taken from such subjects as ballistics or military deployment, or from architecture, with Nazi memorials or monuments as examples, or from interest rates—'A Jew lent RM 500 @ 12% interest. . . . '—or from population ratios. The students would be given the problem of projecting population curves of the 'Teutonic,' 'Roman,' and 'Slavic' peoples of Europe, with the question: 'What would be their relative sizes in 1960? What danger do you recognize for the Teutonic peoples in this?'

"Everything depended, actually, on the director of the school, everything, that is, outside the textbooks. The director of ours was a Nazi, of course, but not a real one, not a *Fanatiker*. He would tell the district superintendent, when he came for an inspection, that everything was all right, and the superintendent was too busy, and too unsure of himself academically, to look closer. And everything was all right, if what is meant is the absence of talk or teaching against the government. That's the same in America, I think—everywhere."

Herr Hildebrandt's hardest experience was, I felt, somewhere outside his school work. He told me, fairly freely, how hard it was to sit with fellow-members of the Party in a café and hear them vituperate Jews in ignorant passion. "I would sit there," he said, "and say nothing. This was not heroic, and yet it was something, a little something. A wild *Fanatiker* like your friend Schwenke, seeing that I never said anything in agreement, might have taken it into his head to denounce me, and my past, which would have been fatal, might have come out."

Once, in 1938 in a café in Baden-Baden, he saw a family of Jews from Kronenberg. "I was wearing my Party insignia and sitting with some Party men. Understand, I was proud to be wearing the insignia. It showed I belonged,' and the pleasure of 'belonging,' so soon after feeling excluded, isolated, is very great. Maybe in America you don't have these feelings; in that case you are very lucky, but also, in that case, you may have difficulty in understanding what it was like for men like me here.

"Still—I didn't want those Jews from our town to see me wearing my insignia. I never wore it at home, except for special events, where there were no Jews. The uniform and insignia were a sort of anti-Semitism in themselves, and I was not an—an anti-Semite. It hurt me to have Jews see me wearing them. So, when I saw these Jews in the café, I tried to sit so that they wouldn't see me. When I think of that now, I still blush."

"Did they see you?"

"I don't think so," he said, blushing.

Prompted by the blush this time, I thought that I might hit upon Herr Hildebrandt's secret, if he had one. But the tack I took turned out to be empty.

"When were you *really* disillusioned with National Socialism?" I said in a later conversation.

The blush again; deeper, this time. "Only after the war —*really.*"

"That discourages me," I said, "because you are so much more sensitive than most people, and this makes me realize how hard it must be, under such conditions, for people, even sensitive people, to see what is going on around them." He continued to blush, but my blush-detector told me that this was not *it.*

"It's all so well masqueraded," he said, "the bad always mixed up with the good and the harmless, and you tell yourself that you are making up for the bad by doing a few little things like speaking of Mendelssohn in class."

"And so you were," I said.

"No. No," he said, shaking his head, "but that is very kind of you to say. No, I would not be honest with you if I told you that I was always an anti-Nazi, that I always thought and felt like an anti-Nazi. It is so easy these days to say 'anti-Nazi' and even to believe it. Before 1933 I certainly was, but then—only again after the war.

"I fooled myself. I had to. Everybody has to. If the good had been twice as good and the bad only half as bad, I still ought to have seen it, all through as I did in the beginning, because I am, as you say, sensitive. But I didn't want to see it, because I would then have had to think about the consequences of seeing it, what followed from seeing it, what I must do to be decent. I wanted my home and family, my job, my career, a place in the community. I wanted to be able to sleep nights—"

"Weren't you?" I said.

"Not in the period when I was deciding whether to join; but after the decision it was better, always better. I enjoyed doing those little things at school, 'defying' the Party, not because what I did was right (that, too, of course) but because I showed I was clever and, above all, because I 'belonged.' I belonged to the new 'nobility,' and the nobility can get away with certain things just because they are the nobility; merely getting away with them proves that they are the nobility, even to themselves. So I slept."

It was near the end of our many, many conversations that I said, "Those Jews you saw in the café, in Baden-Baden that time, when you tried not to have them see you; who were they, Herr Hildebrandt, do you remember?"

The needle on my blush-detector jumped. "Yes. Yes, of course, I remember. They were friends of the Wolff family, my—my relatives."

"Wolff?"

"Yes."

"Here in Kronenberg?"

"Yes. At the University."

"Professor Wolff? Eberhard Wolff?"

"Yes."

"But he was a Jew."

"Yes."

"How were they related to you, Herr Hildebrandt?"

"Oh, not by blood. Professor Wolff was Jewish, his wife three-quarters Jewish. Their son Erich married my cousin Sibylle."

"Sibylle," I said. "That's a very pretty—"

My two small boys broke into the room, to get their afternoon cake. Being small American boys, they did not say, "*Guten Tag*, Herr Studienrat," they said, '*Tag*'; but, being small boys in Germany, they did have the decency to shake hands all around before grabbing for the cake.

A few visits later I reverted to the Wolff family, and again the needle jumped. The Wolffs were closely related to the most illustrious Jewish name in Germany, and intermarriage between Jews and non-Jews in this great family had been common. The Wolff home in Kronenberg was a great, ancient pile on the Schlossweg, the beautiful wooded area of old mansions on the hill, beyond the Castle. I knew that the aged Frau Professor Wolff (Frau Geheimrat Wolff, her eminent husband having borne the additional eminence of "Geheimrat," or distinguished professor) still lived, alone with a servant, in the family home.

What I learned, without much difficulty (indeed, he spoke with understandable pride, although the blush remained), was that Herr Hildebrandt had saved the Wolffs' home during the Third Reich by arranging for the transfer of its ownership to another "Aryan" in-law in a pretended sale. Hildebrandt had been a frequent visitor at the Wolffs' before he joined the Party; then his visits dropped off and, finally, when the ownership of the home was transferred, although the family still lived there, stopped altogether. Why?

"I felt uncomfortable," said the teacher. "You may well believe that. I wanted to talk about the current situation and to try to explain my position, but Professor Wolff, who was quite old, would never let me talk about such things. He would not tolerate talk about National Socialism, against it or for it.

"I had always felt very much at home there. Everyone did who came. It was like the old times of books, music, poetry, art; another age. And it never changed. But after I joined the Party I felt out of place. When other people were there—it was a great house, with many friends—I knew that I was always the only Nazi. The others were not open anti-Nazis, of course, but the fact that they were there spoke for itself. And the talk always avoided politics. It did everywhere, in those days. It was—well, at the worst, it was simply that, if you had not been present when somebody said something against the regime, there was no danger of anything's being forced out of you later on. So nobody talked politics, not among non-Nazis.

"When I was there alone, after I joined the Party, it was still worse. I played chess with the Professor, or we listened to music, and he never spoke, except politely. And I knew I couldn't speak, to say (at least to try to say) how I felt. So the visits became formal, and then stopped."

"But you saved his home."

"Yes."

"Didn't that make you feel better?"

"No."

"Why not?"

"Because with him I wanted to say how I felt, and he wouldn't let me."

On one of our last visits—Herr Hildebrandt was at my house—he said, "Herr Mayer" (he had, with my help, got over calling me "Herr Professor"), "there is something else I should like to tell you about."

"Please," I said. The blush was coming up again.

"It was at the end of 1940, when I came back on leave. My wife was almost eight months pregnant, and we were living in two furnished rooms. Housing was very short. We heard an apartment was available, but only on the way there did we learn that it was the apartment of the lawyer, Dr. Stern. Have you heard of him?"

"Yes," I said. "Herr Damm, the Kreisamtsleiter, told me he once saved the Sterns' apartment for them, when an SA leader tried to get it. And Policeman Hofmeister mentioned them, too."

The blush mounted sharply. "Did Hofmeister tell you about the—the deportation of the Sterns?"

"No, except to say that they were deported and how bad he felt about it." The blush subsided a little, I thought.

"Well," said Hildebrandt, "it was a lovely apartment. We spoke in a very friendly way with the Sterns (his wife and daughter were there) and they with us. We said that we had not come as Nazis, and we explained our situation. They believed us, obviously, and Dr. Stern said he wanted to move anyway to be nearer their friends and relatives. (Most of the Jews in Kronenberg had moved into the old Bertholdstrasse; I forget what new name the Nazis gave it, but it was not a formal, compulsory ghetto.)

"We assumed that, now that Dr. Stern could have only

Jews for clients, and the Jews were becoming so poor, he could no longer afford the apartment. I felt bad, very bad, and Eva felt worse; she was already so strongly anti-Nazi, and here she felt that her condition was responsible for driving these people from their home, for our wanting an apartment so badly. It was very embarrassing. 'Still,' I said to myself, 'if we don't take it, someone else will,' and just then Dr. Stern said: 'If you don't take it, Herr Studienrat, someone else will.' So we—we took it."

The blush remained level.

It was getting on for evening again, and the room was growing dark. I was fumbling around, in my memory, and in my imagination. There was something connected with Jews, with the Wolffs, possibly with the Sterns, that Herr Hildebrandt wanted (or didn't want) to tell me.

"The Wolffs," I said, groping. "How was it you said you were related to them?"

"Erich Wolff, Eberhard's son," said the teacher. "He was a lawyer. But he'd wanted to be a musician. He played the piano, and I played the violin, and in my first two years in Kronenberg, before I joined the Party, we played duets together sometimes. He was married to—my cousin."

"Of course," I said, "Sibylle, the beautiful name."

I didn't need the light; I could feel the heat.

"What became of Erich?" I asked.

"He went to Italy, in '39, and died there. Of a heart attack. Or suicide. We don't know which."

"And his wife, Sibylle?"

This was it.

"She stayed here."

"Did you see her, after you stopped seeing the Wolffs?"

"Yes."

"How did she feel about your being in the Party?"

"She—she advised me to join. Not exactly *advised*, but accepted my reasons. She saw the necessity. She agreed with me that I might be able to help the Wolffs that way. I was to keep them advised—through her—of all developments and of any dangers and do what I could. She thought that might be helpful. And it was, up to a point."

"Up to a point?"

"Yes."

"She went on seeing her father- and mother-in-law, of course?"

"Oh, yes. We would be talking and she would say, 'You must excuse me now, I am going up to the Schlossweg, to the Wolffs', to *gaukeln*.' *Gaukeln* means 'juggle,' but it also means 'talk without saying anything,' 'beat around the bush.' It meant she was going to the Wolffs' and pretend, as one always did there now, that everything was the same as always."

"Do you know if she talked to the Wolffs about you?"

"She—tried."

"But you yourself never saw them again, after you joined the Party or after you arranged the 'sale' of their house?"

"No. Well—once. It was they that I saw in the café, in Baden-Baden that time, when I told you that it was friends of theirs that I saw. It was they I did not want to see me."

"When was that?"

"In '39, just before the war. I knew they were there, because my wife and Sibylle and I had driven down together, and, after we'd got rooms and gone out again in Sibylle's car, she stopped in front of another hotel and said to me, 'You'd better get out now.' It meant that the Wolffs were there, and she didn't want them to have to meet me."

"Or, maybe, you to have to meet them."

"Yes."

"Do you think that Sibylle would rather you hadn't joined the Party, even to help protect the family?"

"I think so, yes. . . . Yes."

"Do you think she was right, Herr Hildebrandt?"

"I—. I don't know, Herr Professor." (I noticed the lapse back to "Herr Professor.")

"I'd like to meet her," I said.

"She's dead," said Herr Hildebrandt.

It was dark in the room now, but I still tried to take notes, just a few words (the way a reporter does) to remind me, so that I could fill them out afterward. In the dark my writing ran all over the paper.

"Dead?"

"Yes. She worked in the 'underground,' Herr Mayer, to help people escape from Germany. That's why she stayed. Her husband was more than half Jewish; he couldn't help her. In '42, before the Sterns were deported, sent to the concentration camp at Theresienstadt and then to the 'East,' she was trying to arrange their escape into Italy. She must have been somewhere on the Swiss-Italian border. The Gestapo got her."

"And—?"

"Her family was told that she had been arrested and hanged herself in the jail at Constance."

"Had she?"

"No." This came like a shot. "No. She would not have hanged herself. Unless—unless things had reached the point where she knew she might talk without knowing it and endanger others."

I could not see Herr Hildebrandt now.

"Did she—did they—have any children?"

"A son."

"What happened to him?"

"I—." He stopped, and then resumed. "I—arranged it so that I was appointed his guardian. He's in the university now."

My wife rapped at the door to say it was time for dinner and to ask Herr Hildebrandt if he'd stay. He said "No," and I went to the front door with him without turning on the lights.

## CHAPTER 16

## The Furies: Johann Kessler

"I still say," said Herr Kessler, "that National Socialism was good for Germany."

"Was it good for you?" I said, on an off chance.

There was a pause. Then: "No."

"Why not?" I said, "if it was good for Germany?"

"Perhaps we will talk about that, one day, Herr Professor."

We did, one day, months later. It burst out. "Through National Socialism I lost my soul. I blasphemed. Every night, through all those years, I blasphemed; I said my children's prayers with them; I took the name of the Lord in vain. I wanted them to be Christians, and I myself had denied Jesus Christ."

Johann Kessler had been born and brought up a Catholic, in a Catholic village in Württemberg, in southern Germany. He was the second son in a large family; his older brother would inherit the Kesslerhof. He himself wanted to learn. At nine he had gone to the village priest and asked to be taught Latin. At ten he wanted to be a monk, and he was so insistent that his mother (his father was dead now) sent him with the priest to a Benedictine monastery nearby. The monks were kind to him, but there were no other children and he had to get up at midnight and dawn for Mass; at the end of a week he wanted to go home. The monks told him that he might come back, if he wanted to, at eighteen.

At eighteen he was a soldier. At seventeen he had been a bank clerk, leading a glorious life in town. The day the first World War began he enlisted and served as an Army regular through the war. He participated in the suppression of the Communist rebellion in Munich after the Armistice. Then he was demobilized, got a job again as a bank clerk after a year unemployed, wound up in Frankfurt, jobless again, in the depression of 1931, and moved to a village just outside Kronenberg, where he worked for a year as manager of an estate and was unemployed again.

He was very happily married to a fine, large woman, a good "free-thinking" Protestant. She had never been converted to Catholicism, but he had gone on being a Catholic, less ardently than he had been as a child, of course, and the Kesslers' two children, a boy and a girl, were being brought up in the Catholic faith. Like a good woman, Frau Kessler respected her husband and his wishes; like a good man, he was warmly devoted to his children, much more so than any of my North German friends.

Herr Kessler was an engaging personality, a semilearned man among unlearned men, and a popular public speaker, in the rolling, sententious Fourth-of-July vein, a favorite at weddings and birthdays, at veterans' meetings, and at assemblies of the nationalist Kyffhäuserbund. Politically he was a good Catholic centrist of the conservative, clerical-agricultural wing of the Center rather than its Christian Socialist–trade-union wing. But he had no compunction, in 1933, against joining the National Socialist Party in the hope of getting a job. He was placed in personnel work—where he belonged—in the Kronenberg Labor Front office and was appointed one of several "Party Orators" for the county, one of the little men with big voices who addressed small-town meetings.

He was allowed to speak on the Party's history and on German history and culture but never received (or asked for) the special permission required to speak for the Party on "the Jewish question." Every Sunday morning at ten the Party had a two-hour service at the local theater. It was not exactly a religious service, although the speakers, and especially Party Orator Kessler, often took religious or, more properly, spiritual themes.

Those who came to the Sunday-morning services, like those who spoke at them, knew that they should have been in church; at least the hours conflicted. After the Church-Party split began to develop, in 1936, the Party services became more ritualistic, more specifically a substitute for church. When, a year or two later, Church-Party relations had become bitter, it was not uncommon at the close of the Party service for the SA and the Hitler Jugend to march noisily (even singing) past the churches, whose services, beginning at eleven, were in progress. Kessler became the most popular speaker in the vicinity at the Sunday-morning meetings of the Party.

One day in 1938 Kessler was asked to perform a German Faith Movement funeral service, for a Nazi who had died in the new racist-naturalist Nordicism of Alfred Rosenberg, the official Nazi philosopher. No pastor in Kronenberg, not even Weber, who was a Nazi, would conduct such a service; Rosenberg's Faith Movement was the purest paganism, with the orb of the sun as the center of its symbolism. It was radical even for Nazism.

The man who had once been the boy who wanted to be a monk, whose dying mother had placed her missal in his hands and said, "Whatever happens to you, never

stop praying," had a hard time deciding. The County Leader of the Party, who himself had not left the Protestant
Church, did not order or ask him to perform the service.
It was the Party red-hots who put pressure on him, men
above whom, in natural gifts and feeling, Kessler stood
high. But it was a chance for the man who had once wanted to be a monk to be a cleric, of some sort, and, besides,
"There was no one else to conduct the service. That part
of my impulse was Christian. But the service—the service was not."

That evening, when Kessler came home, he told his
wife that he had left the Catholic Church and asked her
to say the children's prayers with them. She looked at him
and said nothing. She finished the dishes and then started
to the children's room, when the two children's voices
were heard in a jingle they always sang when they were
ready for their father to come in for prayers: "The children will not go to sleep, 'til Daddy's asked God their
souls to keep." Kessler pushed past his wife, went in himself, and said the prayers, ending with the usual words, "*In
Christus Namen, In Jesus' name.*"

That night, having said nothing more to his wife, he
went to the parish priest and told him he was no longer
a Christian. "I was going to tell him about the funeral,
but he knelt and prayed—"

"Did you?"

"Kneel?"

"Yes."

"No."

"Did you pray?"

"No. No, I didn't. I waited until he stood up, and then
I left."

"Were you going to tell him about the children's prayers?"

"Was I?"

"Yes."

"No."

"I went home," Herr Kessler continued. "I told my wife, and talked to her almost all that night. It wasn't so serious for her, because she was not church-connected. And she wasn't interested in politics or in history. I had read Rosenberg's *Myth of the Twentieth Century*, the 'bible' of the Faith Movement. It was on the Papal Index, and, although I could have got permission from my priest to read it, I hadn't bothered to or hadn't wanted to. Inside I had been turning against the Church ever since I'd become a Nazi, against the political Church, the Papacy as a government. Canossa, the struggle of the German kings against the popes, the right of Germany and Germans to be free from an outside government—this was the way I had been thinking. It is the way I still think, too.

"All this I told my wife. She didn't say much, almost nothing. Only at the end she said, 'And the children?' And then she added, from the Bible, 'The father's blessing builds the children's house.'

"What would happen to my children, my children?" he went on, one moment impassioned, the next didactic. "They could not go to church any more or to Sunday school. And the teaching in the public schools is not adequate for the moral development of children. Many times afterward I talked with teachers about it. I never got a satisfactory answer. *Blut und Boden*, blood and soil, the eternal life of the plants, of the animals, of nature—that's only a part of the religious story; it isn't religion.

"I told my wife: 'When they're twelve or thirteen, they

shall decide for themselves.' I knew when I said it that that was a lie, the same lie, at bottom, that dominated the Hitler Youth, the lie that children can educate themselves. Children who grow up without religion cannot decide about religion for themselves; that's a fallacy, that people can choose intelligently between what they know and what they don't know. What it was, was an excuse for me, a shimmer of hope to excuse me, hope that they would find what I had lost, that they, my little children, would absolve me!

"At the end, when I had finished talking that night, I was more tired than I have ever been before or since. I told myself—not my wife—that I could remain a Christian in soul. It wasn't true. It wasn't true. The next day I declared my intention to leave the Church before the county court. It was done. After that, I never had a quiet hour—"

"Until after the war?"

"What has the war to do with it?"

"I mean, until now, when things are changed again."

"Do you mean that because the Nazis are gone, and the outside has changed, that the inside has changed? There are things that don't change so easily, Herr Professor. When I say, 'After that I never had a quiet hour,' I mean every hour after that, this hour included."

During the next six years Herr Kessler was called upon more and more often to perform German Faith Movement funerals, baptisms, even weddings. There was no church service, of course, for the funerals, only a cemetery service, and no sermon but, rather, a speech, "no Bible, never a word about God or the soul, the whole personal afterlife denied by the clearest implication." The baptism celebrated nature as the source of life and the child's father as the "life-giver," and the wedding joined the couple as "Germans."

"But," said Herr Kessler, "man is still man, he must be comforted in the presence of death and sobered in the presence of life. Those who had left the Church—Evangelical or Catholic—had no place to go. And no—pastor."

"But the municipal marriage office performed weddings, didn't they?"

"Yes, but Germans are religious, including those who believe they are not. Especially as regards death. During the war, it was hard in the hospitals. If a wounded soldier died confessed in the Church, or even if he died unconscious and his religion was unknown, the Church would bury him. But when they died having said they had left the Church, and their identity was unknown or their relatives couldn't be found, the hospital called the Party office, and they asked me to officiate."

"Even if they were not known to be members of the Faith Movement?"

"Even then. Even if they were not known to be members of the Party. Very few, that we knew of, were members of the Faith Movement. But, if men died who had left the Church, what was there to be done? We were glad to do it. I was glad myself, although I knew it was blasphemy; so far had I fallen that I was glad to be of 'service.'

"Millions had left the Church—the Protestant much more than the Catholic—before 1933. Not just Social Democrats and, of course, Communists, but people in general. That had been going on since 1918, more and more all the time. Protestants, especially, didn't believe in the Church any more, because the Protestant Church was the official Church, the State Church, and its head was the King of Prussia, who happened to be the Kaiser, the Emperor of Germany. With the Kaiser gone, the Church didn't know where it stood; it was as if God had run away to the Netherlands. Only when the Nazi flag flew over it again did it know (or think it knew) where it stood.

"The Catholic Church was different; the head and center of the Catholic Church were outside Germany. The German Catholic—and, if you include Austria, Germany is half Catholic—had an allegiance which, while it was not temporal, had a temporal capital, Rome. This 'divided allegiance' the Nazis hated, and I hated it with them. But it was just this 'foreign loyalty' that provided a greater possibility of Catholic resistance to Nazism."

"Which, however," I said, "did not materialize."

"That's so," said Herr Kessler, "not in the masses or the priests, but for another reason. But, for one Protestant *prelate* who resisted, you found two or three or four Catholic prelates.

"Outside Catholicism only women, and especially old women, were very religious any more, except in the villages; and to some extent this was true even there. The Protestant cathedal churches stood almost empty, sometimes with more tourists than communicants. The women tried to make their husbands go to services with them for the children's sake, but they were not always successful. The sermons had always been dull, and now they had lost any great meaning, any comfort, any relevance to people's lives.

"The trouble was that the Church—Catholic as well as Protestant—was supported by taxes. Thus it did not have to consider the people's wants in order itself to survive, or minister to their needs. When their wants and needs changed, the Church, especially the Protestant Church, didn't know it. Only in the villages (those that could still support a resident pastor) were the people and the Church in real contact. Otherwise, only a few young and enthusiastic pastors ever called on their parishioners, except in great sickness. If you were ever to see your pastor, you had to call on him in his visiting hours, which were during workingmen's working hours, and then you had to sit and wait for him, as you would at the dentist's, and he would look at his watch while you talked; or perhaps you would be told to come back at the same time next week. There were exceptions, many exceptions, the whole Christian Socialist movement, for example; but, in general, the Protestant clergy acted like high civil servants, which, after all, is what they were.

"I do not mean to say that the Catholics were better, and there certainly was no more Catholic resistance to Nazism than there was Protestant. But there was a reason for this. The reason—it had both the best and the worst consequences—was that the priest was close to the people. After all, he had no more status in the German State than they had. In the Catholic villages, in the years after the first war, you would not find a Communist; everyone belonged to the Catholic Center Party; the priests had real power because they were close to the people. In the Evangelical towns it was different, especially where the industrial workers lived. In Westphalia, for instance, you would find the workers on one side, the pastor on the other. The pastor did not belong to the people; the priest did.

"But why, then, you ask, did the Catholics go Nazi? Why didn't the priests hold them, as they had held them from Communism? The answer is twofold. First, Communism was atheist and Nazism was its enemy, supposedly the defender of religion. But there was another reason, and

217

I'm told that you see this today in Italy and France, where one hears that there are actually Communist priests. And that is that the masses of the people could not be held back from Nazism, so powerful was its appeal, and this same priest, who would not leave his people, went with them to Nazism, too."

I knew something about all this. My authority was Policeman Willy Hofmeister. In 1936 or 1937 each of the Kronenberg detectives was openly assigned to a local church as observer, to report on the "loyalty" of the sermons. In addition—this the detectives were not supposed to know, but they did—there was a Gestapo agent assigned to report on the fidelity of the detective's report. One day, at the height of the Church-Party struggle, Hofmeister was ordered to inform Pastor Faber, whose sermons he reported, that he must not read the pastoral letter sent out by the Protestant bishops to be read from the pulpits on the following Sunday.

To Policeman Hofmeister's horror, Pastor Faber coldly told him that the Church, not the State, would decide what was to be read from the pulpit. Hofmeister tried to "reason" (he puts it this way, fifteen years later) with the clergyman and told him that there would be a Gestapo agent present and that they would both, Faber and Hofmeister, get into trouble if the pastoral letter were read. Faber said that Hofmeister would have to look out for himself, and rose, ending the interview.

To my amazement, Hofmeister, who had by no means been an ardent Nazi, still, fifteen years later, resented the pastor's defiance of the "law," that is, of the authorities. He no more admired Faber's heroism—the letter *was* read from the pulpit—now than then. He himself, Hofmeister, had violated the "law," that is, what his superiors told him to do, by revealing to the pastor that there would be a Gestapo man present, and the pastor was willing to jeopardize an innocent man along with himself. "It was like a slap in the face," said Hofmeister, and I saw that even the policeman might have a hard time of it in the police state.

I could not, at first, understand Hofmeister's persistent failure to admire the pastor's great courage. I pressed the matter and learned that the policeman had always disliked the great pastor. "He was too high and mighty for us, a great theologian, you know, above the people. I was a member of his church, you understand. He had been my pastor for years. That did not mean a thing to him. When I went to him—this was years earlier—to ask him to come to the house to christen my daughter, he said, 'There will be a charge, of course, for coming to the house.' Like a doctor; worse than a decent doctor.

"After the ceremony, my wife offered Faber and his assistant wine and *Torte*. The assistant accepted gladly, but the pastor said "No," he would not have any. As soon as the assistant finished his wine, Faber said they would have to leave, but I said that the custom was that the guests at a christening must not leave *schief*, that is, 'out of balance,' with an odd number of glasses of wine. The assistant held his glass out, but Faber would not have any. When they were leaving, I asked the pastor how much it was customary to pay for a christening. He said three Marks, so I laid a three-Mark piece in front of him and a five-Mark note in front of his assistant. That's how *I* felt, and that's what kind of Christian the great Faber is."

"Were they all like that, the pastors in Kronenberg?"

"More or less. Not all. There was Weber, the one that become a Nazi. He was a friendly man, really beloved, even by those who disagreed with him. Ask anyone. And the

Catholic priest, Father Pausch, *there* was a man you could talk to. You would visit him, and he'd show you into the parlor, and you'd sit down next to a table on which there was an open box of cigars. The housekeeper would bring wine and glasses, and the priest would hand you the cigars, and you'd sit and talk with him, about conditions, yes, even about your problems, although you were not of his faith. And he would speak of his troubles. When the government forbade the continuation of religious services in the Church schools, Father Pausch accepted it (what else could he do?) and said to me, 'This is the saddest day of my life.' There was a man you could sympathize with, a man like yourself."

So I knew something about the Protestant and the Catholic clergy, at least about one Protestant clergyman and one Catholic, the heroic Pastor Faber and the unheroic Father Pausch, as they appeared to my Protestant friend Hofmeister. What Herr Kessler, the Catholic, or former Catholic, was telling me did not sound at all incredible.

"At the beginning of National Socialism," said Herr Kessler, "there was no effort to draw people away from the Church. Just the opposite. The Weimar Republic had separated Church and State, just as it is in America, you know, and the pastors, most of them, supported the Nazis in the hope of reuniting the two and rebuilding the Church. Certainly the Party call for 'positive Christianity' was clear, so much so that, in the first days of the regime, many liberals and radicals who had left the Church hurried to join it again as a means of 'covering up,' of proving that they were not leftists.

"But by and by the Party's own spirit began by itself to fill up the emptiness of spirit in people's lives. This was where the Church had failed. And people began to turn from the Church, which in spirit they had already left, to the Party. The Church blamed the Party for this, but in the beginning it was not the Party's fault at all. The Church created this vacuum, and the Party, in the end, took advantage of it.

"On the surface there were other things, but that was what lay underneath. On the surface the Church-State fight began on the 'Jewish question,' but it is important to remember that the fight did not begin for two or three years. The Party had not expected the Church to take a stand against anti-Semitism as such, and, with some individual exceptions, it didn't. Then the Party made the claim that baptized Jews, converts to Christianity, were Jews still and had to be dismissed from the clergy and, presumably, thrown out of the Church. Of course, that was a mistake, but the Party had to make it to be consistent. And the Church had to resist if it were even to maintain the pretense of being Christian; Christianity is evangelical; its business is to win *all* souls to Christ.

"Once the fight had begun, the Church leaders blamed the Party for luring the people away. Finally that was actually the case, but that was after the trouble began. And, when a man died who had left the Church, the Church people would say it was the Party's fault that there was no one to bury him. It would look bad for the Party, you can see that, and I was a Party man."

"A Party man first, or a Christian first?"

"A Party man, then."

"And now?"

"Now?—Nothing. But," Herr Kessler went on after a pause, "it was not just a matter of how it would look for the Party. There was something else. You ask why the hospitals would call the Party office when a soldier died who had left the Church. It was because people called the Party in all difficulties arising from the reconstruction of the country, and the Party always helped. This pattern was established from the first, long before the war. It was what made the Party so strong—it would always help. In religious matters, in domestic problems, in everything. It really watched over the lives of the people, not spying on them, but caring about them.

"You know, Herr Professor, we are told that not a sparrow falls without God's care; I am not being light when I say this—that not a person 'fell,' fell ill or in need, lost his job or his house, without the Party's caring. No organization had ever done this before in Germany, maybe nowhere else. Believe me, such an organization is irresistible to men. No one in Germany was alone in his troubles—"

"Except," I said, " 'inferior races' and opponents of the regime."

"Of course," he said, "that is understood, but they were few, they were outside society, 'over the fence,' and nobody thought about them."

"But these, too, were 'sparrows.' "

"Yes," he said.

"Could these," I said, "have been 'the least of them,' of whom Jesus spoke?"

"Herr Professor, we didn't see it that way. We were wrong, sinful, but we didn't see it that way. We saw 'the least of them' among our own people, everywhere, among ordinary people who obeyed the laws and were not Jews, or gypsies, and so on. Among ordinary people, 'Aryans,' there were 'the least of them,' too. Millions; six million unemployed at the beginning. These 'least,' not all who were 'least' but most of them, had somewhere to turn, at last.

"You say, 'Totalitarianism.' Yes, totalitarianism; but perhaps you have never been alone, unemployed, sick, or penniless, or, if you have, perhaps never for long, for so long that you have given up hope; and so (you'll pardon me, Herr Professor) it is easy for you to say, 'Totalitarianism—no.' But the other side, the side I speak of, was the side that the people outside Germany never saw, or perhaps never cared to see. And today nobody in Germany will say it. But, believe me, nobody in Germany has forgotten it, either.

"In the Labor Front every person we placed in a job remained our responsibility, our care. The owner of a café tried to mistreat a girl I had placed there. She came to me. I warned him. He did it again, and his business was closed. Totalitarian?—Yes, of course. He was an *alter Kämpfer*, an Old Party Fighter, this man, and at the hearing he said to me, 'You treat me as if I were a Jew. You will lose your job for this.' He took it up with the district office of the Party, without any success. And that was not an exceptional case. Totalitarianism?—Yes. But I am proud of it."

The Party Orator was getting oratorical. "Yes," I said, "I can understand that. But—what about your children?" I had yielded to the temptation to deflate him; I was sorry, but it was too late. The Party Orator shriveled, and there was Johann Kessler.

"The children," he said, "yes, the children."

"Excuse me, Herr Kessler," I said.

"That's all right," he said, "nothing to excuse. The children."

"Did your wife say their prayers with them after their first night?"

"No. I did. I had to, Herr Professor, I had to. They were too young to understand, don't you see?"

"To understand what?"

"To understand what—what their father was. I had to say their prayers with them, and I could not talk to anyone, not anyone, about it. Not because of the danger, this was not the kind of thing that would ever mean danger, but because of the shame. It was a lonely road; it still is—lonelier, I think, than never to have believed at all."

"Did you ever pray otherwise?"

"Yes. At Faith Movement funerals. At the end of my—my talk—you know, about what a good comrade the man had been, what a good husband and father, how true to our cause and our country, at the end I would say the Lord's Prayer."

"Aloud?"

"Oh, no. But that was different, you know."

"How?"

"Well, what you do to yourself and to God, God can carry, and you yourself don't matter. But what you do to your children—."

He broke off, and I said nothing, and then he went on. "Every night, all those years, even the last night, before I left home. We were all told to go north, to fight to the end, even the old men. So I started north, on my bicycle, and surrendered like everyone else. That night, too, when I thought I might not see my children again, I said their prayers with them, after I had kissed my wife."

"What did your wife say?"

"My wife never said anything about it, ever, after that first night. We didn't talk any more about it, in all those years. But she knew."

"And you, you knew all the time that you blasphemed?"

"All the time, I knew all the time that I was damned, damned worse every day. But I wanted my children to be Christians."

"Why, Herr Kessler?"

"Why does a man want his children to be better than himself?"

A month after the night her husband left home and was captured, Frau Kessler went to the parish priest and asked for Communion for the older child, the girl Maria. She had not been able to locate her husband, and she thought that, even if he were still alive, she might not see him again; she had heard that anybody who had been a Party Orator would certainly be classified as a war criminal. Three days later she got word that he was held in the compound at Darmstadt, and she went to see him. She told him what she had done. He wept. "Why?" I asked.

"Because God had had mercy on me, a sinner. I was damned. Whatever I did, whatever they did with me, I was damned. And God had had mercy, even on the damned."

"Can't a man always be saved, Herr Kessler?"

"I didn't believe that any more. I didn't even believe that. The Faith Movement denied the Redeemer."

Every Sunday, now, Herr Kessler's grown daughter and his almost-grown son worship with the congregation in the parish church. Maria (like so many girls in Europe, and unlike most girls here) plays the violin. Hans, the boy, sings in the choir with a rich voice like his father's, the Party Orator. The Party Orator, who now works in the shipping-room of the village feed store, goes to the church alone and sits at the back, outside the congregation. He has not asked to be readmitted to the faith, and the priest (who himself was a Nazi) shakes hands with him but has never spoken. "God can wait. He waited for me," the priest told Maria, who told me. In the biographical record which Johann Kessler wrote down for the United States military authorities on July 3, 1945, he gives his religion as *Gottgläubig*—non–church-connected believer in God.

## CHAPTER 17

# The Furies: Furor Teutonicus

Who, asks Tacitus rhetorically, would trade Asia or Africa for Germany, "a region hideous and rude, under a rigorous climate, dismal to behold or cultivate?" The German answer is obvious: the Germans. It's the wrong answer, of course; other people live in still ruder regions without getting into trouble. But for purposes of nationalist romanticism the German answer will serve.

Romanticism is the stuff of which men's dreams are made. National Socialism was a piece of this stuff, cut not from immanent villainy, "congenital criminality," but from the dream of freedom from unbearable conditions which have got to be borne. Since these conditions were more unbearable in Germany than anywhere else, who but the Germans should undertake, self-sacrificially, to free the human race from the human condition?

In their dream my friends turned, regretfully, all the way from the Christian obligation to one's fellow-men, with whom, through God, one identifies one's self, real men in a real world, feeble, fitful men, to the altogether transcendent obligation (much heavier than that which the Cross imposes) to produce Man the Imagined, Man like God, Man Who Once Was, German Man. We must remember that racial perfection was only the means—*the* means, to be sure —to moral perfection. Moral perfection was possible. And moral perfection, in Germany, would alleviate the human condition everywhere, even among those who, incapable of perfection because of their lower nature, would have to have alleviation forced upon them.

Seven of my ten Nazi friends had heard the joke—it originated in Germany during Nazism—and enjoyed it: "What is an Aryan?" "An Aryan is a man who is tall like Hitler, blond like Goebbels, and lithe like Göring." They, too, had smiled at the mass Aryanization, first of the Italians and then of the Japanese. They all knew "Aryans" who were indistinguishable from Jews and Jews who were indistinguishable from Nazis. Six of my ten friends were well below middle height, seven of them brunet, and at least seven of them brachycephalic, of the category of head breadth furthest removed from "Nordic longheadedness." None of this mattered; all this was only reality, a parliamentary quibble.

The German, said the German philosopher, has a yesterday and a tomorrow, but no today. Out of my ten Nazi friends, the "German spirit," manifest in the whole unbroken history of suffering and sacrifice of the whole German people, would, tomorrow at the latest, breed yesterday's German, "blond, blue-eyed, huge," as he appeared to the Divine Julius, who happened to be dark and squat. Men too heavy-laden can—and not only can but must—dream such dreams.

Wagnerian men like gods and Faustian men like angels people these dreamy lives—raise the tailor from his steaming bench, release the farm boy from his blistering plow handles, fit the burning feet of the shop clerk with winged sandals, transport them to dark forests (darker in Germany than anywhere else), whence, stripped to sword and shield and helmet, they hew their way to the top of the mountain.

There, in a combination Walpurgis-Wartburg, they hurl Teutonic-Christian fire at the lightning, driving it and its demons away.

The incubation of Germany was terrified by *das Wütende Heer, die Wilde Jagd,* the Huntsman's Wild Horde riding the night, and in the sacred groves the protective fire has never been allowed to die. In 1951 a German mayor burns the de-Nazification records in the town square. In 1952 the Berlin police stage the greatest torchlight display since Nazism. In 1953 a German pacifist—a *pacifist,* mind you—burns the "contractual agreement" with the Allies in public in Hamburg. And all over Germany, at the fall farm festivals, at the spring school festivals, the climax of the celebration is a fire of orgiastic proportions. In 1933 the anti-Christians burned a bonfire of books in Prussia to liberate Germany from the radical Jews; in 1817 the Christians burned a bonfire of books in Saxe-Weimar to liberate Germany from the reactionary Prussians.

On the night of June 29, 1934, Adolf Hitler burned his bridges behind him. The decision was made on the terrace of a hotel at Godesberg on the Rhine. Sitting there alone in the night, the Leader stared at a thousand men on the lawn in front of him; each of the thousand men held a torch; all of the thousand torches together formed a fiery Swastika, in his honor. The Leader, staring into that fire, made the decision to decimate the Party leadership. He left the terrace, commandeered his plane, and flew to Munich at midnight. The next morning was June 30, 1934, "the day of blood," the nation-wide purge of National Socialism.

The world once purged by flood ends always again in the surer purgative of fire. Deviltry runs deep in the "Teutonic Spirit." Those two little devils, "Max und Moritz," the German counterpart of our comic-strip mischief-makers, specialize in enormities undreamed of and undreamable by Peck's Bad Boy, Kayo Mullins, and Dennis the Menace. And, while it is a long way back from "Max und Moritz" to Martin Luther, who invited the Wittenberg students to the burning of the Papal bull which split the Church, the way is not trackless. The Lutheran Reformation, libertarian in its genesis, drove out of the religious life of the German people such sunshine as there was in Roman universalism; replaced it with a gloom which still defies theological permeation; subordinated the Church Militant to the Church Military; and re-established the sect of the patriot tribe.

It was dreadfully heroic, and dreadfully dramatic, when the Augustinian monk said, "*Hier stehe ich, ich kann nicht anders,*" and defied the greatest power on earth. It was less heroic and much less dramatic but no less prophetic of the Germany to come, when he decided that to "give to him that asketh of thee" did not mean to give him what he asks but, rather, what is good for him. It had taken a century to convert the English to Christianity, seven to convert the Germans; and in some sections of the land the new faith had died out altogether as late as the end of the eleventh century.

My friend Kessler was right; the resistance of Catholics, not to dictatorship, but to nationalist dictatorship and to racism and idolatry, was stronger, if not significantly so, than Protestantism's. The strength of the Catholic Church was the strength of the Catholic Church; the strength of the Protestant Church was the strength of the German State, whose Church dominated an almost half-Catholic country. In the Protestant north one says, "*Guten Tag*"; in the Catholic south, "*Grüss' Gott*, God be with you." It is a little harder (not much, but a little) to change to *"Heil Hitler"* from *"Grüss' Gott"* than from *"Guten Tag."*

The Catholic Church is, willy-nilly, protestant in a country whose State Church is Protestant. Bismarck's campaign against it, and later Rosenberg's and Goebbels' ("We will deal with this crew," wrote Goebbels of the Catholicism into which he was born, "when the war is over"), taught Catholics a little about living dangerously and cleaving joyously to a faith under fire. The common estimate that only 10 per cent of the nominal Protestants of Germany were (and are) free adherents to the State Church is, at least in Kronenberg, not low. Kronenberg had been 100 per cent Catholic until the Prince of Hesse, embracing Protestantism in 1521, suppressed the Catholic worship; from which instant on, Kronenberg had been 100 per cent Protestant. Under the American Occupation, after 1945, the Nazis' Sunday-morning paganism was replaced, in the same theater, by popular movies during church hours, and without any Protestant protest.

This dark Church of Luther, born not of bread and wine but of blood and iron, so remote from the universal surrender and the universal embrace in which the parent Church was born (if not bred), even in Luther's lifetime lost its libertarian impulses and has never been able to release the "little people" of Germany from the demonological terrors of the dark. They cannot resist the torchbearer who, with his torch, turns the black into day. I had several talks with a country pastor, an anti-Nazi, who, without challenging the *one* Scripture that "we ought to obey God rather than men," shook his head doggedly and reverted, again and again, to the *other* Scripture that "the powers that be are ordained of God." His three oldest sons had been killed in the German Army invasion of Russia; he will never, he said in tears, let "them" take his last son, Kurt; but I'm afraid he will.

So the Tree of Christ, freely planted in the fulfilment of perfect freedom, grows weak and dry beside the Oak of Odin. But it grows; believers and unbelievers and agnostics, big men and little, weak men and strong, good men and bad, left with me the conviction that there was one thing that would have made Nazism even worse than it was: the nonexistence of the Christian Church.

Tailor Schwenke may not have known what Christianity was; he may not have been a Christian; he may not have wanted to be; but he could not bear to look in the mirror and say, "I am not a Christian." As long as he could not, there was one way left to his heart, however hard or near-hopeless, that would have been closed had there been no Christian Church to claim him. He was, he assured me, "very religious, always," adding, as he always did when he spoke of any of the virtues, "Our whole family, always." As evidence of his religiosity, he taught me the hymns his confirmation class had sung sixty years before, *Ich will dich lieben, meine Stärke* ("I Will Love Thee, My Almighty") at the beginning of the confirmation, and *So nimm denn meine Hände* ("Take Thou My Hands") at the end. For a seventy-one-year-old man, who was almost fatally wounded in one war and served three years in prison after another, his baritone was remarkably beautiful.

"It was like this," he said. "The new National Socialist faith believed in God but not in the divinity of Christ. That's the simplest way to put it."

I thanked him for putting it simply, and he went on. "We little people didn't know whether or not to believe it. 'Is it right, or isn't it?' we asked ourselves" (after a thousand years of "very religious" Christianity). "One believed one way, one another. It wasn't ever decided. Perhaps, if the war had been won, it would have been decided finally."

"By whom?"

"By the men on top. But they didn't seem to have decided yet themselves. A man didn't know what to think."

This "very religious" old brute was the only one of my nine Protestant friends who left the Church. But he did not turn to the pagan Faith Movement, nor did he apostasize for religious reasons at all. It seems that in 1934 a fine young SA man wanted to be married ("He had to be," the tailor's wife interrupted) and told the pastor that he wanted to be married in his fine SA uniform. The pastor refused. So Tailor Schwenke, now Sturmführer Schwenke, wrote to the pastor that the young man did not have enough money to buy a suit. "Did he?" I said. "No," said Schwenke. "Maybe not," said Mother Schwenke. The pastor then agreed to the uniform.

After the regular service, on the appointed Sunday, Schwenke led his Storm Troop, all of them in uniform, into the gallery of the church. When the pastor, who had gone into the sacristy, came out and saw the Storm Troopers, he stood in front of the altar and the waiting couple and said to the congregation, "What kind of business is this?" Then he performed the ceremony, in brief and unfriendly fashion, and, when it was over and Schwenke tried to speak to him, he turned away.

The district Party office, having heard of the incident, suggested that the tailor apologize to the pastor, but he refused. Then the case reached the district Church Council, and the chief pastor summoned the tailor and suggested that he apologize. "He didn't say I had to, so I didn't. But I was disgusted by the whole thing and resigned my church membership. That's the way I am; our whole family's that way. I started a petition to get that pastor out of his church —his daughter was married to a half-Jew—and a year later he was pensioned. That's all they want anyway. They just work for a salary and a pension, like everyone else. If they weren't paid, they wouldn't work."

A few days after this conversation, a local pastor of my acquaintance, who knew I had been talking with the tailor, called on me and asked me if I thought that Herr Schwenke was a Christian, "a real Christian. I know that that is a peculiar question, but his application to re-enter the Church is before the Council."

"I should guess," I said, "that he's as real a Christian now as he ever was, but it would only be a guess."

"That isn't real enough," said the pastor.

"Why should he want to re-enter the Church if he isn't a Christian?" I said.

"Most probably," said the pastor, a bright young man, "to have the Church carry his *Überfracht*, his excess baggage, for him."

"Isn't that what the Church is for?" I said, just as brightly.

"Ah, yes," said the bright young pastor, who had recently been to America, "but there's so much *Überfracht* in Germany. We Germans seem to be born with it," and he handed me an American cigar.

# PART II

## The Germans

# Heat Wave

*Intervening events have driven from all but the hardiest memories the disaster of June 14, 1907, the day that the entire Temperate Zone was hit head on by the worst heat wave in history. Although the suffering of streetcar passengers generally was noted in the chronicles of the disaster, one of the most singular incidents (or congeries of incidents) of that singular day was, so far as I know, never reported. The press had, understandably, overlooked the fact that in those days, and on that day, June 14, the streetcars everywhere in the world carried placards which read: "Windows Are NOT To Be Opened before June 15."*

*In downtown Milan, where the cars round the Duomo, an Italian threw a rock through a streetcar window and ran.*

*In Barcelona a Spaniard fell asleep and rode to the end of the line.*

*In Leeds an English rider called the attention of the Yorkshire Post to the situation, in a strong letter, and, after the letter was picked up in the Times, a Parliamentary debate ensued and the Liberal Government fell—ostensibly on the issue of window regulation.*

*In Graz the streetcar windows were in such bad condition that, although they were closed, the breeze came through and no Austrian suffocated.*

*The Bucharest Surface Lines were sold to a Turkish syn-*

dicate reliably reported to represent the interests of the Government of ———.

In Lyon a tram passenger cried "Liberté!" and drove his fist through the window. At the sight of his bleeding hand, the Lyonnaise in the dreamy, picturesque Place de Ville rioted.

The Swiss Cabinet, in an emergency session, ordered fans installed at once on all the municipal railways.

In the Scandinavian capitals it was cool, even muggy.

In Omaha an American opened the streetcar window.

In Hannover a German, having read the placard and consulted his mechanical pocket calendar, sat back comfortably in his seat, kept his coat on, and read his paper; but that evening he beat his small son, who, twenty years later, joined the NSDAP, or National Socialist German Workers' Party.

## CHAPTER 18

# There Is No Such Thing

It is an article of the modern faith—an article all the more hotly held for its dubiety—that there is no such thing as national character. Nothing may be said about a whole people, e.g., in America about Negroes, Jews, or Catholics. This article, like others of older faiths, may, of course, be (and everywhere is) suspended for the duration of war. George Washington said that the New Englanders were "an exceedingly dirty and nasty people"; Alexander I of Russia said that the French were "the common enemy of Humanity"; and Dr. Joseph Goebbels said that the English "are a race of people with whom you can talk only after you have first knocked out their teeth." That such things are said not merely by civilized people in uncivilized times or by uncivilized people in civilized times may be seen in the observation of General Nathan DeWitt, the West Coast Area Commander of the United States Army, in 1942: "A Jap is a Jap. It makes no difference whether he is an American citizen or not. You can't change him by giving him a piece of paper. The Japanese race is an enemy race."

Between 1933 and 1945 the most curious things—some of them wrong, as things said in partisan passion sometimes are—were said of the whole German people. While the political consequences of some of the things that were said were unfortunate, I think it was right to generalize about

239

the Germans. There is such a thing as national character, even though the Nazis said there is.

This is not to say that the character is bounded by national, racial, or religious boundaries or that every member of the nation, race, or religion involved displays the character in the same degree or even in any degree. It is only to say that a sufficiently pronounced outlook—and inlook—is to be found in a sufficiently large proportion of Slobovians everywhere to manifest itself decisively in the behavior of Slobovians generally and of Slobovia as a nation; and this in spite of the radical differences among the Slobovian tribes themselves. It is only to say that we are justified in at least looking for something common, and even peculiarly common, in, say, the Germans.

What we find, in the way of national character, certainly does not entitle any whole people to do anything to any other whole people, no whole people having shown any moral superiority over any other during the whole of their collective existence. The woman who made a lampshade of the skin of innocent Jews was a German, but the man who made a blanket of the scalps of innocent Indians was an American. If every American did not so distinguish himself, neither did every German. And, if there were only one innocent German or one innocent American, the greatest wrong would inhere in associating the fact of national character with the right or, worse yet, the duty to do something to all of the nationals. Burke did not say, in behalf of the American colonists, that he could not bring himself to characterize a whole people; he said that he could not bring himself to indict them.

Nor does it follow from the fact of national character that the characteristics are either innate or indelible. The Roman character certainly changed between Romulus and

Romulus Augustus. The Spaniards were the terror of the world, a few centuries back; and so, a little later, were the Swedes. And the Americans were once sober, devout, and penurious. "Much learned trifling," says Gibbon in one of his savage little footnotes, "might be spared, if our antiquarians would condescend to reflect that similar manners will naturally be produced by similar conditions."

The distinguished Englishman who not so long since accused the German people of *congenital* criminality overlooked the view of respectable English historians that the main stream of the English character is not Celtic at all but Germanic, not to mention the London *Times* of November 11, 1870, which carried the following Letter to the Editor:

"That noble, patient, deep, pious and solid Germany should be at length welded into a Nation, and become Queen of the Continent, instead of vapouring, vainglorious, gesticulating, quarrelsome, restless, and over-sensitive France, seems to me the hopefulest public fact that has occurred in my time.—I remain, Sir, Yours truly, T. Carlyle."

It is not necessarily mischievous to speculate about the cause and the cure of the Germans, nor need such speculation involve either Germanophilia or Germanophobia. As the dust unsettles in Europe, Germany and the Germans have again emerged as the first order of unfinished, and probably unfinishable, business. If, in the present division of the world, Germany were united, for despotism or for constitutional government, there would be a substantial basis for predicting the near future of Europe and perhaps of the world. But Germany is divided, the Germans are divided, and the German is divided. Sixty million Germans are the bloodless battleground of prewar peace. The battlers have no time to inquire into the character of the prize they pursue, even though such inquiry might facilitate their pursuit. To them, in their respective hurries, Germany is so many bases, so much production or production potential, and so many units of so many men. But Germany, like Russia, America, or Slobovia, is something special. Germany is the Germans.

The national behavior of Germany between 1933 and 1945—and, it would seem, of most Germans—indicates a character that is just about as unattractive as a character can be. Among the million or so who ran, or tried to run, away from National Socialism, there were many who opposed it on principle. Maybe a million more fought it, or tried to fight it, from within. A few million more didn't like it. But so many Germans liked it (and not just some of it, but all of it) that it may justly be said to have represented the predominant national character of the time. And National Socialism, made in Germany, out of the German character, is the worst thing that modern man has made.

Worse, certainly, than Communism; for it is not the performance of political systems which justifies or condemns them, but their principles. Communism, in principle, supposes itself to represent the wretched of the earth and bars no man by nature from Communist redemption; the Nazis, in categorical contrast, took themselves to be the elite of the earth and consigned whole categories of men to perdition by their nature. The distinctions between these two totalitarianisms may not command much interest in the present temper of the Western Christian; they are still distinctions.

National Socialism could have happened elsewhere in the modern world, but it hasn't yet. Up to now it is unique to Germany. And the deception and self-deception it required were required of a people whose civilization, by common measurement, was very highly advanced. German

242

music and art, German belles-lettres and philosophy, German science and technology, German theology and education (especially at the highest levels) were part and parcel of Western achievement. German honesty, industry, family virtue, and civil government were the pride of other Western countries where Germans settled. "I think," says Professor Carl Hermann, who never left his homeland, "that even now the outside world does not realize how surprised we non-Nazis were in 1933. When mass dictatorship occurred in Russia, and then in Italy, we said to one another, 'That is what happens in backward countries. We are fortunate, for all our troubles, that it cannot happen here.' But it did, worse even than elsewhere, and I think that all the explanations leave some mystery. When I think of it all, I still say, with unbelief, 'Germany—no, not Germany.'"

The Germans resist all ready-to-hand analysis of social behavior. Every important factor in their development has been present in the development of other peoples who have not, at least recently, behaved themselves as badly as the Germans. To say that they were Christianized late is too easy; so were the Scandinavians. To say that the notion of equality, connected or unconnected with Christianity, is new to Germany will not do, either; the Peasant Wars of the sixteenth century were certainly egalitarian. The Germans were nationalized late, it is true, but so were the Swiss, comparatively, and the Italians were just as late. Industrialism was a century late coming to Germany, but it was later still coming to Czechoslovakia and Finland, and it hasn't reached India yet.

All these tardinesses are, applied to the Germans, marginal or, at best, inconclusive. There is only one easy inference left—that there is something not just different, but uniquely different, about the Germans. The minor consequence of this easy inference is the proliferation of theories about the Germans, and of studies to bolster or undo them. This proliferation has reached the point where being studied is the most crowded single profession in Germany. The foreigner (except the Frenchman, who is immune to the Germans) cannot spend a week in the country without coming down with a pernicious case of theory.

But the major consequence of this inference is something much more dreadful—namely, its acceptance by the Germans themselves. And the Germans do not, as we know, go half-hog about anything. The theory—passion, rather; for that is what theory becomes when it falls into German hands—that there is something different about the Germans was the wellspring of National Socialism. But it pervades German culture, Nazi, non-Nazi, anti-Nazi, and pre-Nazi. It posits the existence of a "German spirit" as something apart and, above all, very interesting. Croce, a "confessed Germanophile," observing everywhere in Germany the inscriptions *deutsche Treue, deutsche Tapferkeit, deutsche Grossmut,* German fidelity, German valor, German generosity, wryly decided that the Germans had "confiscated for themselves all the common human virtues."

And, as Germans ascribed a spirit to themselves, so they infused other peoples with other, non-German and (on the basis of local pride) inferior spirits. The behavior of Jews was not to be understood in mundane terms or differentiated as between Jew and Jew; the "Jewish spirit," a notion nebulously supported by misreading the ancients from Moses to Esdras, was adequate to explain the behavior of Jews. And when the behavior of a Jew—or of an Englishman or of a crocodile—was good, as it once in a great while was, and could not be explained by the spirit peculiar to the species involved, it was dismissed as aberration. The rest of the world, falling victim to the "German spirit" fantasy, finally, in an equal and opposite reaction, accepted it as something existent, apart, very interesting, and, on the whole, objectionable.

This "German spirit," taken to the German heart as innate and indelible, created, as any such concept must, a world independent of common sense and of common experience. This "German spirit" created German philosophic idealism uninhibited by history as surely as it created German racism uninhibited by biology. But what created the "German spirit"?

## CHAPTER 19

## The Pressure Cooker

I have a friend, in America, with whom I once discussed the question of the indeterminate prison sentence for felonies. Himself an opponent of prison sentences of all kinds, he was by way of being a firsthand authority in the field of penology; in his time he had left a half-dozen jails and penitentiaries without, as he put it, permission. When I met him, he was on his way to the Institution for the Criminally Insane at Menard, Illinois. Nobody could break out of Menard. My friend did, a few months later, and when I last heard of him he was at Alcatraz.

"I'll tell you," said Basil Banghart, for that was his name, "what's wrong with the indeterminate sentence. If you tell me to pick up a big rock and carry it, and I say, 'Where to?' and you say, 'To that pile over there,' and the pile is a mile, or two miles, or five miles away, and I say, 'And then can I put it down? and you say, 'Yes,' I can pick it up and carry it. But if I say, 'Where to?' and you say, 'Until I tell you you can put it down,' why, I can't budge it. My condition then is that of a native I met in the United States Penitentiary on Marietta Avenue in Atlanta, Georgia; I am just too po' to tote it."

Every one of my ten National Socialist friends, and a great majority of all the Germans I met, no matter what their political history, their wealth, their status, or their cultivation, all seemed to me to be somehow overloaded with *Überfracht*, excess baggage, which, in the words of Basil Banghart's native, they were too po' to tote. There seems to be something heavy about the Germans—not, to be sure, about all of them, and not in the same degree or in the same form in those who are. How many of them are heavy? How heavy are they? I don't know. I can't imagine. All I know is (as every tourist has observed who has ever got out of the bus) that there seems to be something heavy about the Germans.

Their dumplings, their liturgy, their Blitzkrieg are heavy. So is their humor; they even have a word for the enjoyment of another's misfortune. Their bowing and scraping are heavy, and their operas (and especially their light operas). Their poetry, too, Goethe almost alone excepted (and not always he; read his *Erlkönig*). Fantasists have even said that their women's legs—Marlene Dietrich being the exception here, as Goethe is in poetry—are heavy.

We are in an uproar; our German friends pound the table (we make a note of the fact that they pound the table) and ask if we are to understand that Mozart is heavy? No, we are not; we are to understand that he came from Vienna. Are we to understand that Stefan Georg is heavy? No, we are not; we are to understand that he was exiled to Switzerland. What do we mean by talking about "the Germans"? How would we like it if somebody said that "the Americans" are money-mad? (A cry of, "They are," is heard above the uproar.) How would we like it?— Not at all, but how are we to judge our own madness?

Why is the Germans' politics so desperately heavy; their scholarship so marvelously heavy; their philosophy, with Will, Duty, and Destiny its central terms, even heavier than their public law and their public fountains? Their

247

language—what is there left to say after Mark Twain's *The Awful German Language?*—is so deadly heavy that it cannot be got under way without being pushed from behind. *Strč prst skrz krk*, which is Czech for, "Put your finger through your throat," is a bit heavy, to be sure, but *Die, die die, die die Äpfel gestohlen haben, anzeigen*, is a no less impossible way of saying, in German, "Whoever reports the apple thieves."

You may not say of the Germans (as you do of the Swedes) that you find them dull, for the Germans are capable of the wildest excursions; or (as you do of the Swiss) that you find them smug, for the Germans are most uneasy; or (as you do of the English) that the Germans are pompously reserved, for German pomposity is always assertive (for centuries the high bust has been known to Paris dressmakers as à la prussienne); or (as you do of the Russians) that they are stolid (or, when they're on our side, stoical), for the Germans complain continuously. There is supposed to be something fascinating about the moodiness of the Hungarians; in the Germans this moodiness is manic-depressive, and depressing. What there is about the Germans, let them march or dance, let them roar or sing, is something heavy.

The German's hand is heavy, on his wife and children, on his dog, on himself, on his enemies. His heel is heavy, as we know, and his tread, even when he is mushroom-picking-bent in the woods, is heavy. His woods and his winters, his whole world, are heavy. The German—with, naturally, some several millions of exceptions, including whole provinces—seems to be a heavy, heavy man. How do a people live with the Danes on one side, the French on another, the Poles on another, and the Austrians and Italians on another, and develop a state of being at such extraordinary variance with their neighbors? Only the North Swiss and the Rhenish Dutch, both of whom love nothing less than being taken for Germans, are much like them.

This catalogue of German characteristics is, of course, a moderately mad exaggeration. The whole gamut of variations in persons and places is ignored. German *Moselwein* is as light as French *Moselle* across the river; and Goethe and Dietrich are Germans and, had they lived in the same time and town, might have been very good friends. Who has not seen a Scotsman or a Bengal with a single plane from his clavicle to his occiput—or a German likewise constructed without saying, "Look at that German's neck?" Let us say, then, that there seems to be something heavy about the Germans.

This heaviness has a character of its own. It is not solidity, for the Germans are the most volatile of human compounds; nor is it rest, for the Germans are the eagerest of beavers. It is not a dead weight which has gone just about as far as it can go and has made its peace with gravity. It has, rather, a living character, exerting a perpetual push and implying a perpetual restraint, like a buttressed wall. It betrays pressure and consequent counterpressure, which between them seem to me to account (better, at least, than any other crude notion) for German autocracy within and German aggression without.

We are speaking, of course, of living substances, persons; and the analogy of the "German spirit" with centripetal and centrifugal interaction is (besides being obvious) bound to be imperfect. Any explanation of human behavior in terms of a single condition, or set of conditions, is oversimplified anyway, and probably unsound. But no durable harm should issue from the pursuit of the analogy if, while we pursue it, we remember that analogy and will-o'-the-wisp are cousins.

To try to account for human behavior on the basis of pressure and counterpressure requires the antecedent recognition that psychological pressure is just as real as "real" pressure. The Germans have, to begin with, more than their share of "real" pressure. I am sorry to have to say that Hitler said that Germany was encircled, because I am sorry to have to say that Hitler was right. Germany has more frontiers—and they are "soft" frontiers—and more historically dissimilar neighbors than any other nation on earth. Its people first knew and became known to the world through the hostile invasion of their land.

It has, by being prepared to invade, and by invading, been defending itself against this invasion, unconsciously since the Spanish succession to the Holy Roman Empire, consciously since the destruction of the Empire by Napoleon. At the Peace of Pressburg, in 1805, the full focus of European pressure finally fell upon the future German nation, and there it remains. From Richelieu to Barthou the first principle of French policy was the encirclement of Germany; the mortality of "Schuman Plan" ministries in France since the first fine flush of post-1945 *rapprochement* suggests that the principle is still operative.

The North Sea, far from being an open coast, has been the "northern front" against Germany since the seventeenth century. A hostile Denmark and an unfriendly (and often hostile) Netherlands pressed in upon that one German outlet, with England and Sweden behind them. The French seized it in the eighteenth century, and the English sealed it in the nineteenth. The first World War ended with the "central powers," that is, Germany, more central than ever—doubly encircled, geographically by the partition of Austria-Hungary and the erection of Czechoslovakia and the Corridor, politically by the world alliance which excluded Germany and Russia. It was not anti-Semitism or socialism or the New Order that first animated the Nazis; their first slogan was, "Break the chains of Versailles." *Der alte Fritz* had broken the circle, by making peace with Russia in 1756, before it was quite completed; *der kleine Adolf* had to begin with the circle closed.

In 1888 Wilhelm II, then Crown Prince, wrote to Bismarck that Russia was "merely waiting for the favorable moment to attack us in alliance with the [French] Republic." Bismarck disagreed, but the year before, as insurance against a two-front war, he had made his secret treaty with the Tsar, agreeing to support the latter's occupation of the entrance to the Black Sea. "I wake up screaming," he wrote later, when Wilhelm accused him of being pro-Russian, "when I dream of our Russian alliance failing." He had reason to; his dismissal, and Wilhelm's abandonment of his policy, brought the French-Russian entente into being and the destruction of Imperial Germany.

What the rest of the world knows as German aggression the Germans know as their struggle for liberation. And this liberation has no more to do with individual liberty than it has in Poland or Abyssinia or South Korea—nothing whatever. "I don't want what belongs to nobody else," says the peasant in the story, "I only want what j'ines mine." Every aggression is a defense—at worst, a premature defense—including that of September 1, 1939. Were not the French and the English, in July and August, making frantic overtures to Moscow, to tighten the circle of Europe? Were they letting their ideological differences with the Communists embarrass them? Why should the Germans? Who (except, of course, the innocents who read and write the newspapers) could suppose that ideology had anything to do with it? Twelve hard years later Herr Schumacher, the Social Democratic leader, arose in the German Bundestag to say, "The German military contribution makes sense if the world democracies will defend Germany offensively to the east."

"Defend Germany offensively." Wilhelm's plea for "a place in the sun" is identical with Hitler's for "living space." In 1914 the great German economy bestrode the Continent; in 1939 Germany's population density was lower than England's. The problem had something, but only something, to do with population density and economics, still less with colonies. Germany's need was *every* place in the sun, *all* the living space. The man who dreams that he can't breathe in a telephone booth can't breathe in a circus tent. Bismarck's nightmare is the perpetual nightmare of Germany.

Proponents of the theory of aggression as a conscious, purposive pattern of German history—still more, those who propound it as German nature—have always had a hard time explaining Bismarck's indifference to both colonial expansion and Pan-Germanism. He armed Germany to the steepletops, created a naked power state faster than any man in history except Friedrich Wilhelm I and Adolf Hitler, and what was his purpose? His purpose never wavered; with power and even with war as his means, it was the perpetuation of the German Reich which he saw himself as having completed.

External pressure—real or imaginary, it doesn't matter which—produced the counterpressures of German rigidity and German outbreak, the ordered, explosive propensity of the pressure cooker. How rigid will the rigidity be, how big the outbreak? The answer is: How great is the pressure?

Ask the carrot in the cooker how far out it wants to go, or the German dictator to set a limit to his requirements. The transition from the Lincolnian sentiment of *Deutschland über Alles*, "The Union above the States," to its latter-day implication of world domination was inevitable; there is no basis for supposing that the Germany we have known recently would stop short of world domination, or stop there. How much air does the man in the nightmare need when he cries out, "I can't breathe"?

What do we find inside the pressure cooker, among the carrots? We find the perfect pattern of organization, be it in the street-cleaning department, the Church, or the concentration camp, in the Hegelian order of the morally absolute State or the Kantian order of the morally absolute universe. Who has ever reached for the stars like the Germans, breaking asunder the bindings of reality that constrict the human heart and restrain that teetering creature, the reasonable man? Reality's ambivalence makes Hamlets—cowards, say Hamlet and Hitler, who burned *Hamlet*—of us all. Hitler cut all the knots that freemen fumble with. He did not resolve the problems that immobilized his people; he smashed them. He was the grand romantic. I asked my friend Simon, the "democratic" bill-collector, what he liked best about Hitler. "Ah," he said at once, "his 'So—oder so,' his 'Whatever I have to do to have my way, I will have my way.' "

## CHAPTER 20

## "Peoria über Alles"

Take Germany as a city cut off from the outside world by flood or fire advancing from every direction. The mayor proclaims martial law, suspending council debate. He mobilizes the populace, assigning each section its tasks. Half the citizens are at once engaged directly in the public business. Every private act—a telephone call, the use of an electric light, the service of a physician—becomes a public act. Every private right—to take a walk, to attend a meeting, to operate a printing press—becomes a public right. Every private institution—the hospital, the church, the club—becomes a public institution. Here, although we never think to call it by any name but pressure of necessity, we have the whole formula of totalitarianism.

The individual surrenders his individuality without a murmur, without, indeed, a second thought—and not just his individual hobbies and tastes, but his individual occupation, his individual family concerns, his individual needs. The primordial community, the tribe, re-emerges, its preservation the first function of all its members. Every normal personality of the day before becomes an "authoritarian personality." A few recalcitrants have to be disciplined (vigorously, under the circumstances) for neglect or betrayal of their duty. A few groups have to be watched or, if necessary, taken in hand—the antisocial elements, the liberty-howlers, the agitators among the poor, and the known criminal gangs. For the rest of the citizens—95 per cent or so of the population—duty is now the central fact of life. They obey, at first awkwardly but, surprisingly soon, spontaneously.

The community is suddenly an organism, a single body and a single soul, consuming its members for its own purposes. For the duration of the emergency the city does not exist for the citizen but the citizen for the city. The harder the city is pressed, the harder its citizens work for it and the more productive and efficient they become in its interest. Civic pride becomes the highest pride, for the end purpose of all one's enormous efforts is the preservation of the city. Conscientiousness is the highest virtue now, the common good the highest good. (Is it any wonder that the German people, whose nation disorders the world, have established the world's best-ordered cities, the Milwaukees of America as well as of Germany?)

What if the emergency persists, not for weeks, months, or even years, but for generations and for centuries? Unrelieved sacrifice requires compensation in the only specie available. Peoria—let Peoria be our beleaguered city—is seen, little by little, to be different from Quincy, Springfield, Decatur. It is something special to be a Peorian, something, if say so we must, heroic. Tales of the founding of Peoria, once taken lightly, reveal that our city was no ordinary city to begin with. Legends turn out to be true. No wonder Peoria sticks it out, sees it through; see the stuff Peorians are made of, always were. Peorians are superior people, superior blood and superior bone; their survival proves it.

Their ancestors, they recall, established the city against the most fearful odds; their descendants will deliver it against odds more fearful still. There will be a New Peoria, a Greater Peoria, a Thousand-Year Peoria. The world will ring with its timeless fame, kneel at its topless towers. And Peoria will be a model to mankind; Peorian courage, Peorian endurance, Peorian patriotism—these will be a model to a world that, because it has never been tried like Peoria, has grown soft, decadent, plutocratic, has fallen prey to rot and to the parasites that rot carries with it.

And whom, meanwhile, among Peorians, have we called to the helm in our hour, our aeon, of struggle, in our place of danger?—Peorians who are tried and true, men who have served their city and never disserved it, men who have represented the best of Peoria to the world, who have always known its glories and extolled them. We want the Old Guard, not the *avant-garde*; the doers, not the do-nothings; the clear thinkers, not the skeptics; the believers in Peoria, not the complainers and the cranks. We don't want the men who always wanted to make Peoria over and who see our trial as their opportunity; this, of all times, is no time for divisiveness.

The things that a country honors will be cultivated there. What shall we teach the young Peorians, who will follow us? What life shall we hold out to them as the highest life? —Why, the life they will have to live to deliver their city, in a Peoria oppressed and encircled. The flabby and effete must go, and with it the dabbling, the faddism, the free thinking that squander our people's time and their energies, divert them from the overriding need of their city, and debase their tastes and their morals. Peorianism is, as Daniel Webster would have said, foursquare, rock-ribbed, copper-sheathed; red-blooded; undoubting and undivided; staunch, stern, rugged, simple, brave, clean, and true. Every influence on our people (above all, on our young people) will be Peorian.

We Peorians cannot live as others. We would not if we could. See them—Quincy, Springfield, Decatur—hopelessly unprepared for a struggle such as ours, with their niggling parliamentarism (the Lend-Lease debate; the Army-McCarthy hearings), their democratic corruptionism (Teapot Dome; the five-per-centers), their corrosive individualism (Tommy Manville; H. D. Thoreau). See them fattening while Peoria hungers. See them exploiting Peoria's prostration. Quincy, Springfield, Decatur, have always hated Peoria. Why? The answer is suddenly obvious: because we are better than they are.

Why do the Poles, egged on by the English, or the Serbs, egged on by the Russians, begin these world wars against Germany? The chauvinist braggadocio of my ten Nazi friends—excluding the teacher and, to a lesser degree, the cabinetmaker and the bank clerk—was of an order, I thought at first, that I had never before encountered. And then I remembered: the "new boy" in the neighborhood at home, on the Calumet Avenue of my childhood, ringed round by the neighborhood gang and trying to brazen it out alive. "Betcha my father can beat your father." Betcha my fatherland can beat yours.

"The whole world has always been jealous of Germany," said my friend the bill-collector, "and why not?—We Germans are the leaders in everything."

"We Germans," said my friend the tailor, the only one of the ten who deserved to be called an ignoramus, and a lazy ignoramus to boot, "are the most intelligent people in the world, and the hardest working. Is it any wonder that they hate us? Have you ever seen a Jew or an Englishman work when he didn't have to?"

"Twice we have had to fight the whole world, all alone," said the baker. "What good are the Italians or the Japanese?"

But I could always count on the tailor to go the whole hog: "We won *both* wars, and *both* times we were betrayed."

## CHAPTER 21

## New Boy in the Neighborhood

Germany is the "new boy" in the neighborhood of the
Western world. The one durable consequence of the first
World War was the unification of a Germany some of
whose states, up until then, had their own kings and courts,
their own armies, ambassadors, and postal systems. And
even the war did not complete the unification; Bavaria and
Prussia, which hated one another, both defied the Weimar
Republic with impunity, the one from the right, the other
from the left.

Nationhood was nominally forced upon the dozens of
"Sovereign German States" in 1871 by Prussia, of which
the King of Württemberg had said, a half-century earlier,
"Prussia belongs as little to Germany as does Alsace." The
nonexistent Germany of 1870 was composed *entirely* of
foreigners, ethnically and historically so hodgepodged that
an East Prussian or a Bavarian was just as likely to be
taken for a Pole or an Austrian as for a German. Only
by his language could a German be distinguished, and not
always then; Low and High German are as mutually unintelligible as German and Dutch.

The language itself—a *Mischmasch*, Leibniz called it—
reflected the German miscegenation, the "disgrace" which
the elite passed on to the populace. "I have never read a
German book," the greatest of all German heroes boasted

at the end of the eighteenth century; and his friend Voltaire wrote home from the Prussian court, "We all talk French. German is left for soldiers and horses." Pre-Nazi nationalism tried to drive "loan" words out of the language—even universal European terms like *Telefon*—and Nazi nationalism intensified the campaign. But in vain; German remained a *Mischmasch*.

German nationalism was, and still is, the effort to create a German nation. The independence of the old German States had its merits, in spite of the ridiculous fragmentation it perpetuated and the dozens of ossified nobilities and their clumsy Ruritania courts in imitation of a Versailles long gone. Culture flourished (to be sure, at the whim of whimsical princes), but it was under such princes, and with their self-serving patronage, that German culture was great. It would be very nice, said Goethe to Eckerman, to cross the thirty-six States without having one's trunk examined thirty-six times, "but if one imagines the unity of Germany with a single large capital for the whole nation, and that this great capital would encourage the development of genius or contribute to the welfare of the people, he is wrong."

The nationalization of Germany, although it came too late to perform the historic function it performed everywhere else, was not to be stopped. When the liberal philosopher Feuerbach wrote his friend Friedrich Kapp, "I would not give a row of pins for unity unless it rests on liberty," Kapp, a "Forty-eighter," who had left his Fatherland to find liberty, wrote back from America: "To be sure, it is disagreeable that Bismarck, and not the democrats, achieved this magnificent consolidation, that the reactionary Junkers and bureaucrats of old Prussia rule. But are not the results achieved, and does it matter *who* is responsible for such a great achievement?"

Germany was a nation, but in 1871 it was prematurely a nation; in 1914 and in 1918 still prematurely. Like all parvenus, the German nation had, and still has, a compulsion to display its wealth, its nationhood, and a desperate terror of losing it, not of being broken apart from without, but, more terribly, of falling apart within. Englishmen and Frenchmen know that they are Englishmen and Frenchmen; when I asked a Danish Communist whether, in his heart, he was a Dane or a Communist, he said, "What a silly question; every Dane is a Dane." But the German has to be reassured that he is a German. The German pressure cooker required, and still requires, the fierce, fusing fire of fanaticism under it.

Russia and the United States of America have both, until recently, at least, been spared this peculiar experience of German nationalism, partly because of their longer national history, partly because of their isolation. Like the other two "Pans," Pan-Slavism and Pan-Americanism, expansionist Pan-Germanism is the none-too-paradoxical consequence of the dread of decomposition. As long as the self-consciously fragile German nation is threatened, internally no less than externally, it will threaten the world, and foreign statesmen who divide the Germans into our friends and *their* friends would do well to be mindful that those Germans who are neither, or who are one today and the other tomorrow, are thinking of Germany, not of Democracy or Communism.

Just as German nationalism was the effort to create a nation, so German racism was the effort to create a race out of a geographical group none of whose stocks, according to all the available pre-Nazi measurements, was Nordic.

261

Ethnical heterogeneity is greater among the Germans (taking the Austrians as Germans) than it is among any other of the world's peoples except the Russians and the Americans.

True, my ten friends, not one of whom met or even approached the Nordic standard, rejected their own "Aryanism." But they did accept a kind of racist "Germanism," a biologized mystique which, I was surprised to discover, they were not alone in accepting. A university graduate of the pre-Nazi era, an anti-Nazi intellectual, when I asked her how many Jews there were still in Kronenberg, said, "Almost none—but, then, you would have to take biological as well as historical and religious data to find out exactly."

My friend Simon, he of the secret Talmud, when he told me that, yes, the Jew Springer was a decent man, and I asked him how there could be a decent Jew when the "Jewish spirit" was a matter of blood, replied: "Of course it's a matter of blood. It might skip a generation"—he had certainly not read Mendel—"but it would show up in the next. Only when the proportion of Jewish blood is small enough will it no longer be a danger to Deutschtum." "How small," I said, "would it have to be?" "The scientists have that worked out," he said.

Herr Simon was not alone in his preoccupation with "pollution." The tailor's son, Schwenke, spoke frequently of the "race injury," the relations between "Aryans" and "non-Aryans" of opposite sexes, the special province of the Nazi SS. He and Simon both told me, in some genuine terror, mixed, I felt, with some of the titillation always involved in discussing sexual relations, that Jewish householders invariably hired "German" housemaids (this much was true, since housemaids came largely from the peasant or unskilled working classes), for the express purpose of "ruining" them. Neither Schwenke nor Simon, of course, had any evidence.

Once—as far as I could learn, only once—a Jew was seen walking through the streets of Kronenberg wearing a sandwich-board sign reading, *Ich habe ein aryanisches Mädchen beschändet*, "I have ruined an Aryan maiden."

"No one looked at him," said Policeman Hofmeister.

"Why?"

"Everyone felt sorry for him."

"Why?"

"Because it was such—such nonsense."

"Nonsense?"

"Yes. Here's a Jewish boy. He has a German"—non-Jewish, the policeman meant—"girl friend. They quarrel. That can happen. They call each other names, then threaten each other. Now they hate each other, although maybe they are still in love; you know, that can happen, Herr Professor. She threatens to denounce him. He dares her to, and she does. And then this—this nonsense."

Policeman Hofmeister was less remorseful about the gypsies, whose treatment was, if anything, more horrible than that of the Jews and who had no voice anywhere in all the world to cry out for them. The gypsies, said Policeman Hofmeister, who would not have said this about the Jews, were *Menschen zweiten Grades*, second-class humans, submen. "The idea," he said, "was to preserve the pure gypsies," the biologically pure, that is, "to preserve them intact, if possible, although, of course, outside the framework of German rights. But the gypsy *Mischlinge*, the mongrels, the half-breeds, were a great danger to the race, through intermingling. Gypsy blood"—I thought of the waltz—"was bad. Still"—here was a good man speaking, who *thought* he believed in "blood" and not in social determinants—"one felt sorry for them, for the conditions in which they had to live, without homes or towns or decent provisions for their children. How could they help themselves?"

"You will have to admit, Herr Professor," said Baker Wedekind, "that Hitler got rid of the beggars and the gypsies. That was a good thing. The gypsies had lots of children, charming children, too, whom they taught to cheat and steal. In the village, in my childhood, we locked our doors when gypsies were there; otherwise, never. They were an alien race, alien blood." He, too, would not have said that I should have to admit that Hitler had done a good thing in getting rid of the Jews.

I think that what worried Policeman Hofmeister and Baker Wedekind was their own common knowledge. The achievements of Jews in every field in which the "Germans" excelled gave rise to an essentially schizoid condition in my friends. The inferior race, the Jews, was also, like the Germans themselves, superior. The gypsies would have made a better Devil for German racism, if only the Devil were not, by definition, superhuman as well as inferior. The gypsies were adequately inferior, but they were not, in German terms, superhuman. They were, quite literally, such *poor* Devils. The Jew would have to do—if he could be distinguished from the German.

## CHAPTER 22

## Two New Boys in the Neighborhood

In other countries governments have been willing to foment and exploit—but always deplore—anti-Semitism. In Germany, and in Germany alone, was it made the cornerstone of public policy. Why? The peculiar ferocity of civil war, the war of brother against brother, comes to mind as hypothesis. The hypothesis is not original; Rauschning says that Hitler once told him that the Germans and the Jews could not live together because they were too much alike.

The Germans and the Jews are wonderfully alike. There are, of course, great and obvious differences between them, because the Jews are few, scattered, anciently civilized, and southern in origin, while the Germans are many, concentrated, primitive, and northern. That the Jew is tasteful and epicurean, more so than the German, is the mere consequence of his geographical origin and his cultural age. That he is subtle, much more so than the German, is the mere consequence in part of his geographical origin, in part of his defenselessness. That his passion for individual independence is exalted, as the German's is not, is the mere consequence of the world's pariahism; and his interest in righteousness, which is not nearly so prominent among the Germans, the mere consequence of the unrighteousness of that pariahism.

There is (or, until very recently, was) no Jewish nation

to suffer pressure and put consequent pressure on both its members and the outside world. It is the *individual* Jew who is both object and subject of the pressures which, in Germany's case, are sustained and exerted by the nation. Germany's internal Diaspora, the first Thirty Years' War, set the stage for German romanticism and German aggressiveness. The history of the combative, incurably restless German nation begins with the reduction of Germany to the depths. The history of the individual Jew is parallel. But what the German nation could seek by weight—its restoration, its "place"—the Jewish individual had to seek by speed.

The dispersed and scattered Jews—who were once much more fiercely tribal than the Germans—were compelled by their situation to become cosmopolitans. This forced cosmopolitanism of the isolated Jew has two polar consequences. Oppressed by each nation, the Jew must be the reformer of the nation, as Germany, isolated and oppressed by the world, must be the reformer of the world. At the same time the Jew must be the most adjustable of men. Except for his religion—which, in the modern West, is weak—he has no continuing mold to contain and shape him. He has nothing to hold to, to fall back upon, to hide behind when war, revolution, famine, tyranny, and persecution sweep over him. He has nothing to turn to but God.

The German has Germany. The German individual, living his changeless generations in his own land, among his own people, and on his own soil, has had no need for adjustability and has never developed it. What for the Jew is the central problem of life does not—I must say *did* not, for times are changing—exist for the German.

From the Castle hill in Kronenberg one can still see the country German in the second half of the twentieth century—the thousand-skirted costumes (the Protestant and Catholic aprons tied differently), the oxen (and often the women and the children) pulling a perforated cheese cask on wheels through the fields for irrigation. The first World War shook the little valleys; on the walls of a village church one counts a hundred memorial wreaths from the first World War, in a village of a thousand population. The peasant youth began to move to the towns. The second World War blew the town and city people out of their houses and packed the railroad trains and the roads.

After 1918 the immobile German, incapable of adjusting to the new conditions inflicted upon him, turning romantically and meaninglessly toward the hope of restoring the old, found himself bewildered and increasingly helpless, while the Jew was in the element in which, through no fault (or virtue) of his own, he thrives best: changing conditions, requiring rapid and radical adjustment. Instead of saying that the Jews were the "decomposing element" in Imperial Rome—a favorite citation of the Nazis— Mommsen should have said that the Jew was able, because he had to be, to adjust himself to a decomposing, as to any other kind, of Rome.

Between 1918 and 1933 this marginal man, the Jew, this *Luftmensch*, this man in the air, in a situation which put a premium on speed and a penalty on weight, rose to such power in a decomposing Germany that his achievement looked dangerously like that of a superman. But wasn't the German to be the superman?—Very well, then. The order in which the Jew was usurping this role would have to be reversed, the standards of supermanliness redefined to fit the German. Superman, the German, would not adjust to this world; he would adjust it. *So—oder so.*

The pliant German, beaten into shape by centuries of

nonresistance, could not compete with the subtle Jew. Germany, the marginal nation, had always had to struggle to survive—but not the German. The German had only to do as he was told, while to do as he was told would have been fatal to the Jew. The Jew had to take chances, and so did the German nation. But the German individual, unless he was crazy drunk, could not take chances. The Jew did not drink; he had to be light to live. The German nation had to drink to lighten itself, and what do nations drink but blood?

In Germany or in England or in Russia, everywhere, indeed, except in the lost Homeland, the Jew had to be light as a feather and fast as the wind. Like Germany—but not like the German—he was hemmed in by hostile neighbors. He had to fight—honorably, if possible, dishonorably, if necessary, like the German nation. He was driven, like the German nation, to every extreme and every excess of good and evil, and his situation evoked in him whatever geniuses survival required of him. Moses Mendelssohn and the Jewish pander were both Jews, just as the Germany of Schiller and that of Streicher were both Germany. Germany is the Jew among nations.

"They are always *insisting* on something," the hostess of one of the presently decrepit but eternally fashionable resort hotels on Lago Maggiore said. She was speaking of the Germans collectively. "One can't say just what it is that they seem to be insisting on. But they are uncomfortable, and they *must* make the management and the rest of the guests uncomfortable. Just like the Jews." "*What?*" I said, collectively insulted. She laughed. "Not every Jew," she said, "and, of course, not every German; only enough of them to make one think, always, 'the Germans.' Perhaps I am prejudiced. I am half-German myself."

Being beset, in fancy and in reality, has produced in the Jews and in the German nation the compensatory assertion of superiority and messianism. Each of them must save the world; so only, saving the world, are Germany and the Jew to be saved. But neither is evangelistic. Conversion (which implies humility) and love (which implies submission) have no place in either's mission. The remaining alternative is mastery; mastery, of course, for the sake of the mastered. In the Germans the necessary means of mastery, imposed upon the benefactors by the intransigence of the prospective beneficiaries, were lately seen to be genocide. But genocide was not unknown, once, to the Jews, and, if survival requires excessive measures, the salvation of the whole world ennobles their use.

To other, less hard-pressed, peoples, the prejudice of the Jew against intermarriage is unintelligible. Among Westerners, only the Nazis share this prejudice. Doctrinal restrictions are not involved, as they are among Christians, where the prohibition against marriage is dissolved by conversion. To the Nazi the Jew is forever a Jew; to the Jew the non-Jew is always a non-Jew. In both cases the inference of taint is inescapable. And in neither the Nazi (who is nothing but the German stripped of religion) nor the Jew is there any confidence that the threatened taint might be diluted or dissipated; in both, the overriding concern is purity. That this arrogation of purity is an impudence other peoples than the Germans and the Jew will agree. But other peoples live in a different world from the Jew and the Germans. These two live in a world of their own.

The German Jew was the perfect German. The *Jewish Encyclopaedia* has, I suppose, fifty times as many citations of German specialists as of all the Jews all over the rest of the world together. Was there ever a "better" German than Bismarck's adviser, the Jew Bleichröder, or than Wilhelm II's, the Jew Ballin? And who but the Jew Stahl laid the constitutional foundations for what we call "Prussianism" in Germany? It is the German Jew who, in a minority, will soon or late dominate Israel; already we hear, in Israel, of what we think of as peculiarly German forms of extremist tendency, the same tendency toward "Nazi" behavior observed among the Jewish prisoners in Buchenwald by Professor Bruno Bettelheim.

And how this German Jew loved his Germany, for which he was willing to give up his Judaism! How German he seemed to be abroad, so much so that everywhere in the Allied countries in the first World War the Jew was suspected of being pro-German! What happened to him from 1933 on he could not believe; he stayed on, until 1936, until 1938, until 1942, until—. "It won't last," he told himself. What made him think it wouldn't? Why, this was Germany, his Germany. And now, in England and America, in France and Brazil and Mexico, there is a new kind of Jew, the Jew who has learned, when he speaks of those who a few years ago were his countrymen in his beloved country, to say "the Germans," to distinguish them, just as Hitler did, from the Jews.

The "Lorelei," the song of the witch of the Rhine who dazzles and wrecks the boatman, is the German people's most popular song, not today, or yesterday, but always; so popular that the Nazis did not dare eliminate it from the songbooks. Instead, they included it with the wonderful line, *Dichter unbekannt*, "Author unknown." Every German knew that the author of the most German of all German folksongs was Heinrich Heine. It took Heine, the German Jew, to write in exile:

*Ich hatte einst ein schönes Vaterland.*
*Der Eichenbaum wuchs dort so hoch, die Veilchen*
  *nickten sanft.*
*Es war ein Traum*
*Das küsste mich auf deutsch und sprach auf deutsch*
*(Man glaubt es kaum,*
*Wie gut es klang) das Wort, "Ich liebe dich!"*
*Es war ein Traum.*

It is untranslatably beautiful:

Once I had a Fatherland.
The oak grew there so great, the violet so small and
  sweet.
It was a dream
That kissed me in German and in German spoke
(If only you knew how good it sounded in German!)
The words, "I love you."
It was a dream.

It took Heinrich Heine, the Jewish German, to write:
"Better to die than to live, best of all never to have lived."
With the world—and themselves?—against them both,
both Germany and the Jew appear to be indestructible.
The Nazis' "final solution" of "the Jewish question" was
the destruction of the Jews, as the world's "final solution"
of "the German question," advanced by the Morgenthau-
ites, was the destruction of Germany. We may assume that
the Morgenthauite program to reduce Germany to a primitive peasant nation was no more final than the Nazis' program to reduce the Jews of Germany to primitive peasant
persons, "working on the land." What the world was too
civilized to do (or to attempt to do), the Nazis were not.
But the Nazis no more succeeded in reducing the status of
the Jews than the world succeeded in reducing the status

of Germany. German recovery, a few years after the lost war in 1945, was the wonder of the world. And the twenty thousand Jews left in Germany were on their way to greater distinction, in both the highest and lowest endeavors, than ever before.

The survival of Germany is much more easily explained, historically and anthropologically, than the survival of the Jew, two thousand years from his Fatherland and scattered into dozens of hostile environments. He has survived. Perhaps he has survived so that the survival of Germany, and of the Germany we have lately known, might bear witness to the world that there is more in the world than meets the eye. It may be that the explanation of survival is not exhausted by historical and anthropological analysis or by social-psychological curve-making; it may be that Cain's answer to the Lord is relevant, too.

As the fate of the Jews—and of Germany—approached its climax in the last months of the second World War, the *Jüdisches Nachrichtenblatt*, published weekly by the German Jews at the order of the Nazi Government, to communicate "directives" to those of Nazism's victims who were left alive, shrank in size and content and, finally, in frequency of publication. It shrank, too, in the quality of paper allotted to it, and it is for that reason that I wish to publish, in its original form, on paper which will outlast the March 5, 1943, issue of the *Nachrichtenblatt*, a story which appeared in the lower right-hand corner, on the reverse side of the single sheet, manuscript-paper size, which constituted the publication:

### Alles zum Guten

*Immer gewöhne sich der Mensch zu denken: "Was Gott schickt ist gut; es dünke mir gut oder böse."*

*Ein frommer Weiser kam vor eine Stadt, deren Tore geschlossen waren. Niemand wollte sie ihm öffnen; hungrig und durstig musste er unterm freiem Himmel übernachten. Er sprach: "Was Gott schickt, ist gut," und legte sich nieder.*

*Neben ihm stand ein Esel, zu seiner Seite eine brennende Laterne um der Unsicherheit willen in derselben Gegend. Aber ein Sturm entstand und löschte sein Licht aus, ein Löwe kam und zerriss seinen Esel. Er erwachte, fand sich allein und sprach: "Was Gott schickt ist gut." Er erwartete ruhig die Morgenröte.*

*Als er ans Tor kam, fand er die Tore offen, die Stadt verwüstet, beraupt und geplündert. Ein Schar Räuber war eingefallen und hatte eben in dieser Nacht die Einwohner gefangen weggeführt oder getötet. Er war verschont. "Sagte ich nicht," sprach er, "dass alles, was Gott schickt, gut sei? Nur sehen wir meistens am Morgen erst, warum er uns etwas des Abends versagte."*

*(Aus dem Talmud).*

In English:

### EVERYTHING HAPPENS FOR THE BEST

We know that whatever God sends us, however good or bad it may seem to us, is good.

A pious man came to a city whose gates were closed. No one would open them to let him in. Hungry and thirsty, he had to spend the night outside the gates. Still he said, "Whatever God sends us is good," and he lay down to sleep.

Beside him stood his ass, and his lantern burned to ward off the dangers of the dark. But a storm came up and extinguished the lantern. Then a lion came up and, as the pious man slept, tore the ass to pieces. Awakening, and seeing his plight, the pious man said, "Whatever God sends us is good," and serenely awaited the sunrise.

Day broke. The pious man found the gates open, the city laid waste and plundered. A band of robbers had fallen upon the city during the night and had murdered some of the citizens and enslaved the rest. The pious man had been saved. "Didn't I say," he said to himself, "that whatever God sends us is good? We must wait until morning, and then we will understand the meaning of the night."

(From the Talmud).

## CHAPTER 23

## "Like God in France"

Substances move, under pressure, to extreme positions and, when they shift positions, shift from one extreme to the other. Men under pressure are drained of their shadings of spirit, of their sympathy (which they can no more give than get), of their serenity, their sweetness, their simplicity, and their subtlety. Their reactions are structuralized; like rubber balls (which we say have "life" in them because they react in such lively fashion to the living impulse outside them), the harder they are bounced, the higher they go. Such men, when they are told not to cut down a tree, won't cut down a tree, but when they are not told not to cut down a man, they may cut down a man.

The German who is dedicated to instant self-immolation for the sake of Germany is the same German whose day-to-day egotism amazes the world. This egotism, always "idealized" (that is, romanticized), is, as has often been observed, the very heart of German philosophy; but it is also the basis of the habitual callousness of ordinary life. It is as if there were, in the human heart, only so much selflessness; pressure requires so much of it of the Germans that they are left with almost none for volition.

I know that the unconcern for others displayed, say, by the American who plays a hotel-room radio late at night, is everywhere common in an individualistic civilization except, perhaps, among the English; but nowhere, not even among the English, are "manners" as rigidly emphasized as they are among the Germans, and nowhere as among these people who swarm to tribal sacrifice have I seen men so invariably fail to offer old women their seats in busses, streetcars, or trains. Nowhere have I seen so many old men and women staggering through train sheds with heavy suitcases and never an offer of assistance from the empty-handed, nowhere such uniform disinclination to assist on the scene of an accident or to intervene between children fighting on the street. But the service in German hotels, restaurants, and stores is superb. One "minds one's own business" in the small affairs of the street, in the larger affairs of the job or the family, in the great affairs of the State.

Grimly preoccupied with themselves; deadly serious and deadly dull (only the Germans could have been unbored by Hitler); tense, hurried, unrelaxed; purpose-bedeviled, always driven somewhere to do something; taking the siesta like Communion, with determined, urgent intent; sneering, and not always genteelly, at the Frenchman sitting "doing nothing" at his café (wie Gott in Frankreich, "like God in France," is the German expression for "carefree"), at the Italian talking his head off over his endless dinner; incapable of quiet without melancholy or frustrated fury; insatiably hungry for the heights or the depths, stone sober or roaring drunk; forever insisting that man is born to suffer —and then begrudging the suffering; unresponsive and over-reactive; stodgy and unstable; uncalm, the inventors and prime practitioners of "stomach trouble"; tormented, exhausted, unable to remain fully awake unless they are angry or hilarious—these, with more than a little hyperbole, with millions of exceptions and contradictions and still more millions of variations, are the ways and the woes of men under pressure.

Men under pressure are first dehumanized and only then demoralized, not the other way around. Organization and specialization, system, subsystem, and supersystem are the consequence, not the cause, of the totalitarian spirit. National Socialism did not make men unfree; unfreedom made men National Socialists.

Freedom is nothing but the habit of choice. Now choice is remarkably wide in this life. Each day begins with the choice of tying one's left or right shoelace first, and ends with the choice of observing or ignoring the providence of God. Pressure narrows choice forcibly. Under light pressure men sacrifice small choices lightly. But it is only under the greatest pressure that they sacrifice the greatest choices, because choice, and choice alone, informs them that they are men and not machines.

The ultimate factor in choosing is common sense, and it is common sense that men under pressure lose fastest, cut off as they are (in besieged "Peoria") from the common condition. The harder they are pressed, the harder they reason; the harder they *must* reason. But they tend to become unreasonable men; for reasonableness is reason in the world, and "Peoria" is out of this world.

The besieged intellect operates furiously; the general intelligence atrophies. Theories are evolved of the grandest order and the greatest complexity, requiring only the acceptance of the nonworlds, the Ideas, in which they arise. The two extremist doctrines that have seized hold of our time—Marx's, denying that there is anything in man, and Freud's, denying that there is anything outside—are Made in Germany. If you will only accept Marx's "human nature has no reality" or Freud's "conscience is nothing but the dread of the community," you will find them both irresistibly scientific.

277

In such exquisitely fabricated towers a man may live (or even a whole society), but he must not look over the edge or he will see that there is no foundation. The fabrication is magnificent; the German is matchless in little things, reckless only in big ones, in the fundamental, fateful matters which, in his preoccupation, he has overlooked. That a Wagner should be a vulgar anti-Semite (or stand on his head, or wear a ring in his nose, or whatever) is one thing; he was "only a genius." But that one of Germany's two greatest historians, Treitschke, should be a ravening chauvinist, that the other, Mommsen, should find in Julius Caesar "the complete and perfect man"—these are something else. Max Weber could be "the father of sociology," but he could not see what was sociologically unhealthy in the institution of student dueling.

Who is this Einstein, who was "only a scientist" when he conceived the atomic bomb and now, in his old age, sees what he has done and weeps? He is the German specialist, who had always "minded his"—high—"business" and was no more proof against romanticism than his tailor, who had always minded his low business. He is the finished product of pressure, the uneducated expert, like the postal clerk in Kronenberg whose method of moistening stamps on the back of his hand is infallible. The German mind, encircled and, under pressure of encirclement, stratified, devours itself in the production of lifeless theories of man and society, deathless methods of licking postage stamps, and murderous machinery. For the rest—which is living—the German has to depend upon his ideals.

## CHAPTER 24

## But a Man Must Believe in Something

It is the Germans' ideals which are dangerous; their practices, when their ideals do not have hold of them, are not a bit better or worse than other men's. Where do they get their ideals? "The 'passions,'" says Santayana, "is the old and fit name for what the Germans call ideals." This idealist slave of his own or another man's passions was twice sundered from Rome, in A.D. 9 and in A.D. 1555. In the year 9 the Germans expelled the founders of secular Europe; in 1555 they cut themselves loose from the *Weltanschauung* which the age of the Mediterranean fused in Italy from the Greco-Hebraic break with Syria and Egypt. This bright *Weltanschauung* rests upon the dogma of personal responsibility. This dogma is the first fact of our civilization. Its repulse left Germany peculiarly rootless.

Thought, like feeling, took root in irresponsibility, with subjectivism, relativism, "intelligent skepticism" its flower. It was not only in physics or in government that the Germans excelled in producing Frankenstein's monsters but in epistemology itself. Thought is all, but there are a thousand ways of thinking. The thinker can attach no worth to his thinking as against another man's because there is no reality to measure them both, only internal consistency, "system." At the same time no other man's system is, by definition, better than his. The superiority of the thinking lies—somewhere—in the thinker.

"A trite, nauseatingly repulsive, ignorant charlatan without *esprit*, who with unexampled impertinence scribbled
together twaddle and nonsense, which his venal adherents
trumpeted forth . . . the hollowest farrago of words devoid
of sense that ever satisfied dunderheads . . . repulsive . . .
recalls the ravings of madmen." This is a philosophical cri-
tique by one of Germany's greatest philosophers, Schopenhauer, of another of Germany's greatest philosophers, Hegel.
The "pedantic arrogance" of which Goethe complained in
the Germans was the self-assuredness not of common,
Western dogma but of the antidogmatic who, needing, like
all men, dogma to live by, had none to fall back on but
his own. Each man was his own "school"; you did not go to
Germany to get an education but to get a man or, more
exactly, a mind. The characteristic German professor did
not know the students or meet them (and there were no
student deans or advisers). He was a thinker, and a teacher
of thinking.

Cut from its moorings in Western dogma, German thinking shot up unencumbered to the clouds. Balloons ascended
everywhere. Which basket the fortunate few boarded was
a matter of fancy and favoritism; once they were off the
ground, they were all equally impervious to puncture by
reality down below. "He stands up there," said Willy Hofmeister, the old policeman; "I stand down here. I can't
argue with him. I'm not stupid, but he's spent his whole
life studying. He knows. I don't." He was contrasting *wir
Einfachen*, we simple people, with *die Gebildeten*, the cultivated.

Down below were *wir Einfachen*, the millions who were
some day to be Nazis, the "little men" who, as Balzac put it,
seemed to have been sent into the world to swell the crowd.
When I was first in Germany I asked a German theologian

to help me find one such "little man," one whom National Socialism had confronted with *innerlicher Konflikt*, moral struggle. The theologian replied: "Moral struggle?—They had none. They are all little sausages, *Würstchen*." German thought soared away from the *Würstchen*, carrying with it the elect, for whom the educational system above the eighth grade existed, and the stage and the philharmonic and the bookstores. For the rest—let the greatest of the great German masters say it:

> He who has Science has Art,
>   Religion, too, has he;
> Who has not Science, has not Art,
>   Let him religious be.

For the rest, there were the churches and the songs of Heaven and Home. At the Kronenberg Singfest, held in the auditorium of Kronenberg University at Easter, I saw not one of my academic colleagues. But eight of my ten "little men" were there.

To the extent that the big men influenced the little men, it was to convince them that thought, of which they themselves were incapable, was everything. There is, besides intelligent skepticism, unintelligent skepticism, and it was a long time ago that Nietzsche asserted that Germans *as a whole* were skeptics. The ground fell away from under the churches even while, in the gradually emptying sanctuary, those who were still credulous were promised the invincibility of German arms. When German arms proved vincible, the churches lost still more of the credulous.

But people who do not have a good religion will have a bad one. They will have a religion; they will have something to believe in. Men—not just Germans—cannot bear the pressure of life, however light it may be elsewhere compared with the pressure upon the Germans. Hitlerism was a mass flight to dogma, to the barbaric dogma that had not been expelled with the Romans, the dogma of the tribe, the dogma that gave every man importance only in so far as the tribe was important and he was a member of the tribe. My ten Nazi friends—and a great majority of the rest of the seventy million Germans—swarmed to it. German thought had not bothered to take them along on its flight. It had left them on the ground. Now they are back on the ground again, rooting around the husks of old ideals for a kernel.

The Germans were, when Hitler found them, emotionally undernourished. Life in a besieged city, even relaxation, is unrelievedly rigid. Happiness is dismissed as unattainable —the German word for it is derived from *Glück*, luck—and its pursuit then disdained as decadent. But it is duty-bearers, not pleasure-seekers, who go berserk. The ordinary hours of the German person, day by day, do not feed his hunger for expression. The decline of conversation is a very modern phenomenon, and a world phenomenon wherever the most modern means of mass communication have replaced it; but the malady of repression is something else. Repression is not the same thing as reserve, any more than denial (the Germans are peerless here) is the same as self-denial.

In a stifled, lid-on atmosphere, the "German" way of thinking flourished, exoteric, meticulous, and introverted; flourished in the starved soil of German emotion. National Socialism fructified that soil, and it bloomed suddenly red with fire and blood.

## CHAPTER 25

## Push-Button Panic

One Saturday afternoon in Kronenberg three house-paint-ers, who were off at noon, got hold of some Weinbrand at our house, and, when we returned from a visit, we found the house torn up and the painters howling drunk. Tante Käthe, our five-foot-tall housekeeper, was with us. She handed them mops and brooms and said, "Clean up and get out." In instant, silent sobriety they cleaned up and got out. They were back Monday morning for work, without a word of apology, a blush of shame, or a man-to-man wink.

The speed of the German is the initial speed of release under pressure, soon spent. Then the pressure reasserts itself, and the German re-emerges as he is: sober, a heavy, heavy man. His personality, under pressure, is just as exces-sively submissive as it is assertive. Its essence is excess. On November 9, 1938, word went through the country that the synagogues were to be burned. A million men, released like jack-in-the-boxes, sprang to action. Pushed back in the boxes, as they were by Göring's order the following morn-ing, a million men dropped their fagots; another sixty-nine million, who had not thought much about it the night be-fore, reproached the million in silence; and the work of arson, robbery, enslavement, torture, and murder proceeded in legalized form, in *Zucht und Ordnung*.

*Zucht und Ordnung*, discipline and order. My two friends Hofmeister and Schwenke, the policeman and the tailor, who hated one another and who represented two incompatible moralities, agreed that "it doesn't matter whether you call it a democracy or dictatorship or what, as long as you have discipline and order." The sensitive cabinetmaker, Klingelhöfer, and the insensitive bill-collector, Simon, said the same thing. Neither morality nor religion but legality is decisive in a state of perpetual siege. And the attest of legality is order; law and order are not two things but one.

The gas ovens of Belsen were peculiarly German; the improvised slaughter pits of the Ukraine were Nazi. The distinction is a large one. Nazism, like the Lutheran Reformation and all other German upheavals, contained revolutionary elements of improvisation. But Nazism was always at war with the Army. The Army was German. The remarkable fact of the *Putsch* against Hitler of July 20, 1944, is that a handful of Army officers could be found to undertake it; that it was planned so recklessly; that it happened at all, not that it failed or might have succeeded. It was treated as treason. What it was was un-German.

What was truly German was what has come to be called the cold pogrom, the systematic persecution, legal, methodical, and precisely co-ordinated, of the "national enemies." When you have combined "cold" with "pogrom"—they appear to be uncombinable—you have Nazi Germany, the organism *as a whole* gone wild, its organs admirably co-ordinated. The universal witness of the people invaded by the Germans is the nonhumanity of the conqueror, his push-button transition from fury to formality, from fire to ice and back again, depending on whether he is under orders or out from under orders. A Nazi might be moved by a prisoner's plea that he had a wife and children; but a German would say, "So have I."

The German's incapacity for calm, consistent insubordination—for being first and last a free man—is the key to his national history. Germany has often had a counterrevolution, but never a revolution. What the Germans would call a revolution the Americans would call a *Putsch*. "The German revolutionaries," said Lenin, "could not seize the railways because they did not have a *Bahnsteigkarte*"—the tenpfennig ticket admitting visitors to the train shed. The Reformation and the Counter Reformation were both counterreformations. (Luther's "peasant" uprising ended with Luther's tract *Against the Murderous and Rapacious Hordes of the Peasants.*) The German War of Liberation against Napoleon saddled Germany with peacetime conscription, and the revolutionary unification of the Reich in 1871 was achieved by the reactionary Junker of Prussia.

The German breakout—call it liberation, call it aggression, call it what you will—is a kind of periodic paranoid panic. In between times, the pressure from outside having supervened, and having been passed on from Germany to the Germans, the next panic cooks silently, symptomlessly, in *Zucht und Ordnung*. To blame Germany—still less the Germans—is to blame the thistle for its fruit. It is fantastic to suppose that, with the pressures of destruction, defeat, partition, foreign rule, and cold war superimposed upon those that already existed, "it" will not happen again. It not only will happen; it must, unless the life of seventy million Germans is altered at the very depth and they find a way to live *wie Gott in Frankreich*, "like God in France."

# PART III

*Their Cause and Cure*

# The Trial

## November 9, 1948:

### "HEAR, YE TOWNSFOLK, HONEST MEN"

*It is ten o'clock in the morning in Kronenberg, and, in the Courthouse just below the Castle, the three members of the ——th District Court of Hesse have ascended the bench to pronounce judgment. Except for the defendants and their counsel and a few close relatives of some of the defendants, the courtroom is almost empty, for the fact is that there is not much interest in the pending case in Kronenberg.*

*Kronenberg is a quiet town. It is one of the quiet old "picture-book towns," of which there are (or were) so very many in Germany. Most of them are partly destroyed now, some of them wholly. But old Kronenberg is (as it always has been in the wars) but lightly scarred. And, like all lightly scarred towns now, Kronenberg's prewar population is almost doubled, and around the railroad station and along the lowland of the Werne there are shacks and hovels which are not seen in picture-books.*

*Kronenberg must be excused for not keeping up its picture-book appearance. You see, there are no tourists now. (Who would come to Germany?) And the Kronenbergers— even those who had savings have just been wiped out by the currency stabilization—are preoccupied with staying alive. The town is shabby, very shabby, and the weeds are head-*

high in the lot where the synagogue stood, and the iron fence, which still surrounds the lot, is rusted.

But the ruins of the war are few in Kronenberg. Two or three times sorties of planes crisscrossed the town in the night and burned a dozen houses down and fired into the streets; that was all, in quiet little old nonindustrial Kronenberg, except for the day that the bombers, apparently aiming at the railroad station, set fire to the University Eye Clinic a mile away from the station and burned up fifty-three blindfolded patients.

Still, one doesn't measure the damage entirely in ruins; one measures it, too, in years of air-raid alarms, night after night; in the price of unpasteurized milk; in the bundle of kindling that costs a day's work to buy and is gone in an hour. The Kronenbergers are tired people, too tired to climb the Castle hill to the Courthouse to hear all about it all over again.

The three judges sit silent until the Katherine bell, the Parish bell, and the Town Hall rooster have given their dissynchronous notice that it is ten o'clock; then the senior judge, having first exchanged nods with his colleagues to his right and left, begins to read the decision:

"This is the first case arising from the synagogue arson of November 9, 1938, to be decided under the full jurisdiction of the German Courts. The previous cases were adjudicated in de-Nazification proceedings under the United States High Command for the Occupation of Germany. . . .

"Every defendant in this case, as in all preceding cases, has argued that he was acting under superior orders. The doctrine was asserted by the International Military Tribunal at Nuremberg that superior orders do not constitute a defense of a crime against humanity. This doctrine is not clear to this court. Citizens must obey the law and the officers of the law, or anarchy will rule. And yet, no man should commit an offense against humanity. Here we have an apparent contradiction.

"But in the instant case, the truth of the charges does not require clarification of this doctrine or resolution of the apparent contradiction. We may, therefore, proceed to a finding.

"In this case we do not know who gave the original orders or whether original orders were given. We know that in one night, November 9, 1938, five hundred and eighty-six synagogues were destroyed in Germany, and the Court takes judicial notice of this fact which led to the disgrace of the German nation and a tragic misunderstanding of the German character everywhere in the world.

"In the instant case, there is testimony, which the Court does not exclude, that the synagogue was on fire many minutes, or even hours, before any of the defendants in this or in previous cases approached the scene of the crime. It seems likely that this was true and unlikely now that any more of the offenders will ever be identified. Official and unofficial records of all kinds which might have been relevant appear for the most part to have been destroyed before, during, or at the end of the war.

"But the charges here, of breach of the peace by a public mob and of criminal arson, do not require us to answer the many questions which will probably remain unanswered to the end of time. Under the statutes, participation is culpable, and, if the Court may revert to the claim of superior orders, it may be said that evidence of willingness, or even of eagerness, to carry out such orders has been considered. Such willingness and eagerness have, in some instances, been found. . . .

"In the days preceding the crime, it had to be expected,

and was in general expected, that in case of the death of the wounded Diplomatic Counselor vom Rath in Paris, there would be violent measures taken against the Jews. The widely prevailing, artificially fostered tension pressed for release. Against the threatening danger stood such institutions for the usual preservation of public order as, for example, the police, who were themselves either anti-Semitically inclined or stood aside inactive.

"It has been established that there were no police at the scene of the crime; why, we do not know judicially. Under these circumstances it was to be expected that a group of persons, even of two men, would run into no resistance worth mentioning, especially when these persons were garbed in the SA uniform. The smallest group could pose a threat to public peace. They could reckon with the fact that their measures were approved in the highest official places, and the institutions responsible for the preservation of public order would not unsheathe their weapons.

"In assigning the punishment, the Court has considered, as favorable to leniency, the fact that the defendants have never been convicted of any crime except those arising from their political activity. They did not belong to the 'criminal class.' They had been good citizens and, as far as the record is before us, honorable men. Political passion made criminals of them. As members of the Party and of the SA they were overcome by year-in-year-out propaganda. Their educational level is not high, although all of them are fully literate and all of them had religious training in school in their childhood. This is said here because they seemed to take no responsible position as individuals toward the problem of respect for human beings who believed other than they did.

"The crime was committed at a time when the leadership of the State would not punish such assaults against unpopular persons or groups or their property and in this sense favored and even urged such assault. In addition, many of the highest officials of the State competed with one another, in the interest of their own political popularity, in the most violent denunciations of such persons or groups, thus arousing the passions of ordinary citizens who look to their public officials for counsel and direction.

"Certain facts, however, argue against leniency in the instant case. . . .

"Nearly all the defendants in all the cases arising from this criminal act have denounced one another (and accused one another of denouncing them in order to exculpate themselves or gain an advantage). This has not been a spectacle of which Germans may be proud. And it has had the effect on this Court and, apparently, on others, of destroying the weight of all denunciations and counterdenunciations.

"In addition, nearly all the defendants, caught in multifarious self-contradictions, have said that they cannot remember what they said in earlier proceedings, or that the events at issue occurred too long ago for them to be sure of anything, or that too many things more important in their lives have happened since. The witness Karl-Heinz Schwenke, former SA Sturmführer, brought here from prison, where he is serving a three-year sentence for his part in the arson, has made a particularly unhappy spectacle of himself in this respect. His claim that he is an old man and cannot remember clearly would, if it were taken seriously, invalidate his repeated assertion that he should be regarded as a man of honor because he is a Christian and has applied for readmission into the Evangelical Church, which he left during National Socialism. If, at sixty-eight and, apparently, in good health, he is too old to take responsibility for his past acts, he may be equally too old to know what a Christian is. . . .

"It is true that, in the fortunes of politics and war subsequent to November 9, 1938, all the defendants in this and the other cases arising from this criminal arson have suffered loss of property, liberty, or health, or all three. But so have those of their fellow-citizens who committed no crime, including those of Jewish ancestry or faith. If this Court could turn history back, it would, and so, undoubtedly, would the defendants; but it cannot and they cannot.

"Still, the punishment of these defendants will not restore the property rights that were lost, the human rights that were lost, the lives that were afterward lost, and the abandonment by many of our people, including the defendants, of their honor and humanity, which led to the loss of these other values and shamed our German nation and our German civilization. . . .

"Since the principal perpetrator (in so far as we have evidence), the former Sturmführer Schwenke, was sentenced to three years upon conviction of this crime, the present defendants, whose roles were subsidiary to his, should receive lesser sentences. The Court therefore. . . ."

## CHAPTER 26

# The Broken Stones

One sunny spring afternoon our seven-year-old, Dicken, was playing in the alley outside our house in Kronenberg when a flight of four American jet planes came screaming over the town, circled it, and went away. They were the first planes of any sort we had seen or heard over Kronenberg and the first jets we had seen or heard anywhere. Everyone ran to the window. Down below we saw Dicken's playmates, six-, seven-, eight-year-olds, transfixed, like him, with wonder. But there were bigger children, too, ten or eleven and older, playing in the alley, and they, the bigger ones, ran away howling with terror, their hands clasped on top of their heads. "Didja see the jets?" said Dicken, when he came in. We said "Yes," and Dicken said, "Why did the big boys and girls run away?"

War, between 1939 and 1945, had come at last to the country of the "war men," the Germans. And from 1943 on, after Hermann Göring (who had said in 1941, "If a single bomb drops on Germany, my name is Hermann Meyer") had become Hermann Meyer, war came into the "war men's" houses to live with them, to eat with them, to sleep in their beds, and to take over the teaching of their children, the care of their sick, and the burial of their living. On May 9, 1945, Germany was a world of broken stones.

On May 9, 1945, there were no more Nazis, non-Nazis,

anti-Nazis. There were only people, all of them certainly guilty of something, all of them certainly innocent of something, coming out from under the broken stones of the real Thousand-Year Reich—the Reich that had taken a thousand years, stone by stone, to build.

Those stones were the houses—not the munitions plants or the switchyards, but the houses. In the city of Worms, the railroad roundhouse stood miraculously untouched; and a half-mile away stood a whole row of walls that were once apartment houses; and so it was in Frankfurt, where the I.G. Hochhaus, the headquarters of the world dye trust, was undamaged; and in Berlin, where the Patent Office was intact. And so it was everywhere in Germany, for the war was a war against houses. One raid knocked one-third of Freiburg over; Dresden was destroyed in twenty-four hours. And Hamburg! And Munich! And Rotterdam! Warsaw! Coventry! Stalingrad! How could Americans understand? They couldn't.

Americans, one-fifth of whom change their abode every year; Americans, building a brand-new America every fifty years; Americans visiting Antietam *battlefield*, Gettysburg *battlefield*, Bull Run *battlefield*—how could they understand the world of broken stones that once were houses? Houses mean people. The war against houses was a war against people. "Strategic bombing" was one of war's little jokes; the strategy was to hit railroads and power plants and factories—*and houses*. Right up until the total collapse of steel fabrication at the end of 1944, the Germans had four rails in the yards for every rail in use; within two to six hours after a yard was hit, it was moving again. But sleepless workers weren't moving so fast, and terrified workers were moving still slower, and workers whose homes were gone (and maybe a wife or child) weren't moving fast at all.

Americans, visiting their Civil War battlefields, wouldn't know that it isn't a man's life and his work that yields the bomb its big dividend but his *accumulated reason* for living and working. In the first case, he's only a dead enemy. In the second, he's a live ally. In the war that came—for the first time—to the "war men" of Germany, the parlor was the prime military installation and the pictures on the parlor wall the prime military objective. If the bomb hits the factory worker's parlor, it can let the factory go. The way to win wars is to hit the pictures on the worker's, the miner's, the soldier's parlor wall. And a bombardier who lets go from a mile or two up, or even five, can hardly miss over Berlin—or Kronenberg.

Words are worthless, and pictures, each of them worth a thousand words, are worthless. Seeing is not believing. Only having been there, having been hit or not hit running to or from it, and being bedeviled forever by what might have been done a half-hour before or a half-minute after is worth anything. A book might have been saved, or a pair of shoes, or a mother or a child. Or a passport. Or a child might have been saved if a pair of shoes had been let go, or a mother if a child had been let go.

And words and phrases like "hit," "got it," "kaput," "knocked over," talk about prize fights or three-balls-for-a-dime at an amusement park. All that words can say is that Stuttgart was "hit" or Bremen "hit hard" (or Coventry or Stalingrad—or Seoul). It's like saying that Christ, in the course of his carpentering, got a nail through his hand. Better not say it at all.

Those houses against which the war was waged were built —even the tenement houses—of stone or Gargantuan timbers laced together and covered with a smooth, impermeable stucco. There were, in Germany, no rural slums, no bulging, leaning, or caving barns, no tar-paper or clapboard shanties, no abandoned homesites, rotten fences, great mountains of rusting automobiles, nothing left to oxidize and blow away. Everything had been built to endure to the last generation. Maybe this was the last generation.

## CHAPTER 27

## The Liberators

The defeat of Germany and the Germans in 1945 was not intended to relieve the pressures which had made them what they were. And it didn't. On the contrary, to all the old pressures which produced totalitarianism and aggression, it added, necessarily, new ones—the guilt-finding and punitive processes; the dismemberment first of the country itself and then of its business and industry; reparation costs, indemnification costs, occupation costs—and the Occupation.

If any occupation ever had a chance of succeeding, it should have been the American (sometimes called the Allied) Occupation of western Germany. As occupations went, it was probably the most benign in history, in part because the fortunes of their history have nourished benignity in the American people, in part because the Occupyees turned out to have the same kinds of tastes and talents, and even cousins, as the Occupiers. That the Occupation did fail—if its object was to do any better than Versailles—is now clear, I think, to anyone who does not define peace as order or democracy as balloting. It failed because it was an occupation, and no occupation has a chance of succeeding.

The day the American troops came to Kronenberg, a sergeant rode through the town in a jeep and designated homes which were strategically located for occupancy by the troops responsible for maintaining security. One of the homes belonged to a woman with two babies; within a few hours her furniture was out on the street, along with her and her children. She addressed the corporal in charge of the eviction, explaining to him, in English, that she was not a Nazi but an anti-Nazi. His reply was not unfriendly. He said, "Too bad, lady."

It was too bad, lady, but that's the way it was. It was an occupation; worse yet, a *civilized* occupation, which, as such, violated Machiavelli's inviolable injunction either to liberate or exterminate a conquered people but under no circumstances to irritate them by halfway measures. The halfway measures of the American Occupation were halfway just, but they were halfway unjust, too. How could they, being civilized, have been otherwise?

The American determination to do something about Nazism meant that something had to be done about each of some twenty-five million Germans. It required the employment of thousands of their countrymen, selected, necessarily, in great haste by Americans who were themselves selected in great haste; and this meant the wrong men all around. Long before the de-Nazification process came of its own weight to an ignominious halt, it had become a bottomless swamp. In the absence of records—anti-Nazi and Nazi files had both been destroyed as first the Nazis and then the anti-Nazis swept through Germany—the defendants invariably accused their accusers. It was a field day for paying off old scores. Oaths piled up on every side until they reached the heavens to which they were addressed. In Kronenberg University, eight years after the war, there were still pending one hundred and sixty libel suits filed by faculty members against one another.

Of course the American Military Occupation was Draconian; men cannot be taught to hate and kill on Wednesday and to love and cherish on Thursday. But by 1948 those Americans who *wanted* to participate in the punishment of the Germans had had enough blood to drink and had all gone home. With the substitution of civilian for military control of occupied Germany, things looked up. Unfortunately (and ironically), the advent of civilian control coincided with the outbreak of war—the cold war between the United States and the Soviet Union.

The civilian High Commission for the Occupation of Germany began its work in the shadow of that new situation. United States Commissioner McCloy commuted twenty-one of the twenty-eight remaining death sentences of Nazis and vigorously pushed the program of "reorientation and re-education" that had been laid out, in dreamy detail, in the post-1945 and pre-1948 world. But the brave new program was doomed from the start. Between 1950, when the Korean War began, and 1952, when the dreamers disappeared from the American government, the program limped along, ever more lamely.

In 1952 it ended, without notice. Local "Resident Offices" of the High Commission reverted to their prior status of United States Army subposts; the re-educators and reorienters, who had been coming and going at the Germans' expense, went. German-American Youth Centers and German-American Women's Clubs closed quietly; dedications of new hospitals and schools, with German "counterpart" funds and American oratory, stopped. The members of the "United States Occupation Forces in Germany" were informed by the United States that they were now members of the "United States Defense Forces in Germany." Only the State Department propaganda establishments—the United States Information Centers, or *Amerika-Häuser*—

remained to mark the spot where the German character was to have been transformed.

Between mid-1950 and mid-1954 the budget of the United States High Commission and related agencies was reduced 75 per cent, and personnel was cut from 2,264 Americans and 12,131 Germans to 780 Americans and 3,650 Germans. Even more spectacular was the reduction in the number of automobiles operated (usually with German chauffeurs) to serve the urgent needs of the re-educators, from 1,545 in mid-1952 to 251 in mid-1954. The decline in civilian activity was more than matched by the rapid-as-possible redevelopment of the American military establishment in Germany. In the fall of 1954, although the remilitarization of Germany was not yet legalized, Robert S. Allen reported in his Washington column that, in addition to all American forces and facilities in Germany, there were being built by the United States a $250,000,000 weapons stockpile and a $100,000,000 food stockpile for six German Army divisions.

The failure of the American Occupation had little or nothing to do with German resistance to it. Apart from their impotence and their hunger and the Occupation's absolute control, the Germans were *ausgespielt*, played out, for a while at least. Nine of my ten Nazi friends were positive that they would never again join a political party, any party. Always credulous and submissive, the Germans had just had twelve years' intensive training in total credulity and total submissiveness; the Occupiers found them marvelously docile, even unresentful, Germans to the manner born.

They were actually indifferent to the general civil corruption—something unknown even in the Third Reich—introduced by the American black market. It was not for them, good Germans, to complain of the morals of their new rulers. They might grumble, in their poverty, at having to pay fifty cents for a package of cigarettes while the rich who had come to democratize them paid a dime, but by and by American cigarettes so saturated the black market that the grumbling was inconsequential. The rich Americans got still richer, but the poor Germans got good coffee for half the legal German price; one way or another, every third German was a direct or indirect beneficiary of the black market. In a few years they were hardened—these once pretentiously honest Bürgers—to monstrous financial scandals. The State Department's construction of "Westchester-on-the-Rhine" for American officials—including five $100,000 homes and one at $240,000—did not, in 1953, excite even the Opposition in the Bundestag. Hadn't Germany's rulers always been kings?

The failure of the Occupation could not, perhaps, have been averted in the very nature of the case. But it might have been mitigated. Its mitigation would have required the conquerors to do something they had never had to do in their history. They would have had to stop doing what they were doing and ask themselves some questions, hard questions, like, What is the German character? How did it get that way? What is wrong with its being that way? What way would be better, and what, if anything, could anybody do about it?

## CHAPTER 28

## The Re-educators Re-educated

From the beginning, the American Occupation was an operating model of nondemocracy and a demonstration of high-pressure salesmanship. But where were the buyers? None of my ten friends had ever taken advantage of the resources of the Kronenberg *Amerika-Haus* except Herr Hildebrandt, the only one of the ten who didn't need to be won to democracy. Besides the children who attended the ever repeated free movies of the Grand Canyon and Niagara Falls, the *Amerika-Haus* patrons were, in the main, pro-Americans from 'way back and students writing papers on American subjects assigned them by their hurriedly Americanized instructors. Prior to the onslaught of McCarthyism in 1952, the *Amerika-Häuser* still stocked American books of all sorts, all of them, unfortunately, in English. They were no more read by my friends—or burned—than the anti-Nazi *New York Times* had been when it was available in the fashionable hotels of Nazi Berlin.

What the Germans needed was to see what democracy was, not to hear it touted. But in my year in Kronenberg there was not one controversial public discussion or debate under American sponsorship or control. In East Germany, a few miles away, the Communists were beating the drum for Communism; in Kronenberg the Americans were blowing the trumpet for Americanism; and in both places, not so long since, the Nazis had been burning the torch for Nazism. But the Germans had—in their own polite phrase— had a noseful of beating, blowing, and burning.

The Germans were, after 1945, in a position to begin to judge Nazism, whose blessings and curses they had now experienced, if only they could begin to have the experience of another way. But they would first have to see another way in operation before their eyes and be attracted to its practice. They would certainly fumble it at first—or second—but who hasn't? They might misunderstand it and even misuse it. But how else would they ever discover what it was? When my little boy cuts the tail off the cat and I say, "When will you learn how to be a good boy?" he replies, "I already know—you've told me a thousand million times."

Freedom is risky business; when I let my little boy cross the street alone for the first time, I am letting him risk his life, but unless I do he will grow up unable to cross the street alone. For the American Occupation to have chosen freedom for the post-Nazi Germans would have been dangerous; even my anti-Nazi friends, so thoroughly German were they, were opposed to freedom of speech, press, and assembly for the "neo-Nazis." But it was the fear of freedom, with all its dangers, that got the Germans into trouble in the first place. When the Americans decided that they could not "afford" freedom for the Germans, they were deciding that Hitler was right.

Free inquiry on a free platform is the only practice that distinguishes a free from a slave society; and, if the post-Nazi Germans needed force, they needed it for the one purpose it had never been used for in Germany, namely, to keep the platform free. What they needed was the town meeting, the cracker barrel—to see, to hear, and at last to join the war on the totalitarianism in their own hearts.

What they needed was not the Grand Canyon or Niagara Falls but the Sunday afternoon forum in Bughouse Square and the thunderous cry of American authority: "Let 'im talk, let 'im *talk*."

My friend Willy Hofmeister, the old policeman, was amazed, and kept adverting to his amazement, that *Mein Kampf* had not been banned in America during the war. What the Germans needed, so sorely that without it no effort, no expenditure, no army would ever help them, was to learn how to talk and talk back. In the *Amerika-Häuser* and on all the other American-controlled platforms they heard lectures on Goethe's Debt to Edgar A. Guest and learned the old, old German lesson of listening to their betters tell them what was good and what was great and what was good and great for them.

What they needed, and went on needing during the whole of the American Occupation, was the peculiarly American genius for contentious and continuous talk in a framework not of law but of spirit. Everything else they needed they had genius enough, and more, to produce for themselves.

Why should America have undertaken, in 1945, to export freedom, above all to a people who had habitually squandered their own and eaten up other people's? The question may or may not have had merit, but it was too late, in 1945, to ask it. The American Occupation had added something new to the history of occupations: idealism. It had undertaken to do something more than punish, collect, and control: it had undertaken to civilize the Germans.

The two tottering old civilizations of Europe, France and England, showed small appetite for what they may have thought an impossible ambition, and they dragged their heels at every turn. But there were two new civilizations on the German scene, the United States and the Soviet Union. They, with their conflicting views of civilization, were ardent with regard to their respective areas of control, and, if either of them had not wanted to be, the other's ardor would have forced it.

It was on the East-West border of divided Germany that these two new civilizations met, each of them committed to world revolution, both of them so long isolated that they were only now, in their confrontation, compelled to consider their commitments. The Declaration of Independence did not say that all Englishmen—or their overseas colonists —were created equal. It said that *all men* were created equal, and with certain inalienable rights. The *Communist Manifesto*, too, proclaimed the equal rights of all men but, denying creation, deprived the rights of their inalienability. Down the middle of Germany the quarrel, avoidable, perhaps, if the two revolutions had not found root in the two repositories of world power at the moment, was joined in 1945.

Now, what makes civilizing so hard is that, even if the primitives recognize their own condition as primitive (which I don't know that they do), they do not always recognize that of the civilized as superior. The Germans, for example, had thought themselves, and not other people, superior. And, in addition, the impeccability of the civilizing intention is always clouded by suspicion and the suspicion fortified by events of recent memory. Being beaten is not the best immediate preliminary to being civilized or re-educated or reoriented. The post-Nazi Germans were bound to have difficulty, for a while, in believing that those who had beaten them so bloody and burned their country down had done so for their own good or were interested in their own good now. The nature of the case was against us, even in genuine peacetime conditions, which, certainly after 1948, no longer obtained.

Still, as the American Occupation learned that what was done in ten centuries cannot be undone in ten days, some small progress might have been made in time. As the sting of punishment, collection, and control was relieved, receptivity to the American world revolutionary effort might grow in Germany, and the effort itself, if only it were not abandoned in a new isolationist temper in America, might become more imaginative. By 1948 there were signs of hope. No West German would have said, outside an official statement, that his government was free, much less democratic; but words like "freedom" and "democracy" were everywhere heard, especially among the rising generation.

The public schools were full of free books, free movies, and free lectures in praise of freedom and free enterprise, in praise, above all, of peace. And the pupils were memorizing the blessings of democracy as assiduously as their older brothers had memorized the blessings of National Socialism. More significantly, the private elementary and secondary schools, from which public school reform had always emerged, were alive again in the land.

Of the universities, "it is difficult to predict . . . but a start has been made," said James M. Read, very cautiously, when he resigned as education chief of the United States High Commission in 1951. The intellectual sheep and goats were still separated at the age of ten or eleven, but, if a higher education was still beyond the children of three-fourths of the people, the West German universities, most of whose students were working their way through, no longer had to plead guilty to the Communist charge that, where the East German universities put a premium on poverty as a condition for admission, those in the West excluded the work-

ingman's son altogether. A chair of political science or social research appeared here and there, and there were, in
five or six universities in the American and English (and
even, at Tübingen, in the French) zones of occupation,
government-supported or at least government-tolerated
efforts to introduce a program of general education on the
fringe of the specialized curriculum.

No American would have said in 1948, outside an official report, that a transformation had been wrought, or
even wedged, in the German national character except on
one point, and that was militarism. "The war-making power
of Germany should be eliminated," General Eisenhower of
SHEAF told Henry Morgenthau and Harry Dexter White
in 1944, and everybody present and absent agreed with him.
In 1945 the Americans interrogated some 13,000,000 individual Germans—and indicted some 3,500,000 of them—
under a statute "for the de-Nazification and demilitarization of Germany." In his 1946 speech in Stuttgart, United
States Secretary of State Byrnes reaffirmed the Potsdam
principle that Germany should be *permanently* demilitarized and added: "It is not in the interest of the German
people or in the interest of world peace that Germany
should become a pawn or partner in a military struggle for
power between the East and West"; and in 1949 the new
Bonn Government pledged "its earnest determination to
maintain the demilitarization of the Federal territory and
to endeavor by all means in its power to prevent the re-
creation of armed forces of any kind."

Everywhere the German turned, he was told that American idealism had come to liberate him forever from the
curse of militarism, from its money cost, its cost in life,
and its cost in reducing his character to barracks-room ser-

vility. And, with a readiness that should, perhaps, have been disturbing, he seemed to believe what he was told.

It is hard to exaggerate the impression which this American ideal made upon the Germans—an impression supported, of course, by their own experience of the second Thirty Years' War of 1914–45. "The German people display no eagerness for military service," High Commissioner McCloy was able to report. "The distaste for military service as such [is] something new in German life." Then, suddenly, in 1948, with the cold war warming up in Berlin, the American ideal was reversed.

## CHAPTER 29

# The Reluctant Phoenix

The first modest proposal, heard in late 1948, was to arm the West German police, on the ground that the Russians had already armed an East German police force. But this little tit-for-tat soon gave way to the call for twelve West German divisions. "The Germans are great fighters," said Senator Thomas of Oklahoma in late 1949. "If the United States gets into a war, we shall need fighters." "It should be enough," said General Collins of the United States Joint Chiefs of Staff in 1950, "if we send arms. Our sons must not shed their blood in Europe." Shortly thereafter, the New York Times put it in plain American: "America has the right to demand a dollar's worth of fight for every dollar it spends."

But the phoenix showed no disposition to rise from its ashes. The "war men" were tired, dead tired, of war, and General Eisenhower of NATO felt called upon to reassure them in 1950: "If the Allies were to rearm the Germans, they would be repudiating a whole series of agreements. It has been announced officially in Washington, London, and Paris that no such action is contemplated." And so it had been. But the Germans were so tired, and so vocally tired, that the General was moved, as late as 1951, to inform Washington, London, and Paris that he wanted "no reluctant divisions in an army under my command."

He was, however, going to get them. The West German Security Commissioner—there was, of course, no War Ministry—announced that Germany would conscript 300,000–400,000 men. (It was peacetime conscription which Woodrow Wilson called "the root evil of Prussianism.") There would be, when the Germans (not to say the French) could be brought to accept the American "contractual agreement," in addition to peacetime conscription, nine new *Panzer* divisions, and "the German contingent will dispose directly of its own air force" of 75,000 men and 1,500 fighters and fighter-bombers. This "German contingent" (the Security Commissioner did not need to add) would be as strong as the forces with which Hitler attacked the West in 1939, and (the Security Commissioner did not add, but the Pleven Plan did) the national units of the European Defense Community would be, "in the beginning," under national, not international, control.

A few months after the beginning of hostilities in Korea, the American, British, and French foreign ministers took note—without expressing their own views—of "the sentiments expressed in Germany and elsewhere in favor of German participation in an integrated force." The sentiments were not confined, either in Germany or elsewhere, to governmental or militarist circles; in America, Walter Lippmann, writing in the very conservative internationalist *New York Herald Tribune*, was convinced that "Germany as a nation can be brought willingly into a Western coalition only if we can prove to them that we have the military power and that it is our strategic purpose to carry the war immediately and swiftly beyond the Vistula River." (It would not be the first time that the war had been carried immediately and swiftly beyond the Vistula River; the last time, Hitler did it.) And in Germany the very conservative nationalist *Stuttgart Zeitung* thought that "it is very probable that Great Britain's value to America as an ally will soon sharply depreciate. This would be tremendously important for us Germans. . . . If Anglo-American friction increases and Britain's position becomes weaker, we may expect that America may assign an increasing importance to Germany's role on the Continent."

After the 1953 elections in Germany, the Adenauer Government had enough power in Parliament to override the German Supreme Court's unwillingness to find that German remilitarization was permitted by the Constitution forced upon Germany by the victorious Allies of 1945. (The same thing was happening in Japan, where the new Constitution forbidding militarization forever had actually to be amended.) German industry, said General Hays, the Deputy United States High Commissioner, would be able to start turning out armaments "within six to nine months of receiving orders," and in 1953 Krupp of Essen, the company that built the Nazi war machine, displayed its new line of vehicles, complete with turret emplacements. "Once the go-ahead is given," Foreign Aid Director Stassen told the United States House of Representatives Appropriations Committee in the fall of 1954, "you will see one of the fastest jobs of building an army in modern history. The necessary equipment, most of which will be furnished by the United States, is well on the way."

Meanwhile, everything had been changed in the "Coca-Cola Zone" of West Germany. What was left of the American engine for re-education and reorientation was thrown into reverse, to serve the campaign for a new German *Wehrmacht*. The still-wet picture of the Curse of Militarism was turned to every wall, and the not-yet-dusty old masterpiece of the Defense of the Fatherland was rehung. Much could still be said, and done, against Communism. But not much could be done any more about the re-education of the Germans. Their re-education had been based too heavily on the theme that militarism had been the cornerstone of German totalitarianism, German war, and German ruin.

There were hitches here and there. At a fracas in Frankfurt in 1952 the German police picked up a flying squad of the Bund Deutscher Jugend, whose specialty was breaking up Communist, Social Democratic, and neutralist meetings. A few weeks later Minister President Zinn of the State of Hesse announced that the BDJ had been "created and financed by the United States" and that, on United States orders, it had set up a "technical service" to go into action in case of Communist invasion. This "technical service" was composed of one to two thousand former German officers up to the rank of colonel, all of them over thirty-five years of age. (*Bund Deutscher Jugend* means "German Youth League"). Many of them were former Nazi SS men. (Mere membership in the black-uniformed Schutzstaffel had been condemned at Nuremberg as criminal.) The "technical service" was being trained, with all kinds of light weapons, in a disguised lumber camp maintained by the United States in the Odenwald. (The penalty, under the Allied Control Law, for arming Germans was death and was still in force.)

What most exercised President Zinn—a Social Democrat —was the "technical service's" list of West German "unreliables" to be "removed." The list included fifteen Communists—and eighty Social Democrats, including the entire national leadership of the latter party. It included, in addition, the only Jewish member of the German Parliament. The "technical service," said President Zinn, cost the United States taxpayers $11,000 a month. HICOG—

the United States High Commission for the Occupation of Germany—knew nothing about it. Neither did General Eisenhower of NATO or President Truman of the United States or, of course, Chancellor Adenauer of Germany.

But everybody else knew something about it. The "technical service" was maintained by the United States Central Intelligence Agency, created by the United States National Security Council with a rumored budget of $500,000,000 completely concealed in the departmental appropriations of the United States Congress. "One would like to assume," said the pro-West *Frankfurter Rundschau,* "that the secret American sponsors knew nothing of the assassination plans. However, their support of a Fascist underground movement is bound to produce distrust of American officials. We refuse to fight Stalinism with the help of Fascism."

It was only a hitch, of course. And the Germans had been taught to have short memories. Still—. Two years later, in the hullabaloo that attended the disappearance of Dr. Otto John, "West Germany's J. Edgar Hoover," it developed that John, who reappeared in East Germany, did not like Nazis and had been having trouble with the Süddeutsche Industrieverwertung, or South German Industrial Development Organization. The Development Organization was, as it developed, a barbed-wire-surrounded compound of 30 acres in the dreamy Bavarian village of Pullach, in the American Zone. The Development Organization was developing a spy network of 4,000 agents in the Soviet Union. The cost of the development, according to the moderate, right-of-center *Paris-Presse* of August 27, 1954, was six million American dollars a year. And the Director of the Development was former Brigadier-General Rheinhardt Gehlen, Nazi intelligence chief in the Soviet Union during the second World War. His new job, said the *Paris-Presse*, was "to carry on for the United States the work he had begun for Hitler."

It was only a hitch, of course, but such hitches are mortal to mewling idealism. The Germans had been taught to have short memories, but there were a few whose memories carried them all the way back to the former German captain who persuaded the Allies to let his "Freedom Movement" have a few rusty old guns to repulse the Communists in Bavaria after the first World War. The captain's name was Röhm, Ernst Röhm. Could it have been the same Captain Ernst Röhm who founded the National Socialist Party?

## CHAPTER 30

*Born Yesterday*

All the Germans were not born yesterday. But some of them were; and youth is the time of ideals. When the West German Security Commissioner announced the details of remilitarization—including peacetime conscription—the London *Observer's* correspondent reported, on the basis of public opinion polls, that "the percentage of support for a German defense contribution dropped below 15, and the percentage of outspoken opposition, about 40 to 50 for the population in general, reached nearly 75 for the age groups directly concerned"—that is, for the young people. Student polls taken in three universities in Germany—without official sanction or supervision—showed opposition so nearly unanimous that the scientific basis of the polling went unchallenged. Youth is the time of ideals, and in the German generation that had known only war's horrors and none of its glories the pre-1948 American Occupation had planted an ideal that was brand-new in Germany.

The American "exchange programs" for German students, professors, journalists, and public officials had been screened from the start, to bring only pro-American Germans to America. Now—after 1948—the candidates were asked what they thought of the remilitarization of their country. "I'm against it," one of the high-school seniors who was accepted for the program told me, "but I said I was for it. You know, 90 per cent of our graduating class at the *Realgymnasium* signed a petition against remilitarization a month before my examination for the program. My name was on the petition, but I assumed that the American officials in our town had not sent it to the American examiners in Frankfurt, and I was right."

"Why," I said, "did you guess that the petition had never been sent to Frankfurt?"

"Because everybody tells his superior what his superior wants to hear, and the superior in Frankfurt does not want to hear about opposition to remilitarization. Look, Professor, we are used to this in Germany."

The young people's resistance to remilitarization was led by German churchmen, Protestant and Catholic, especially in the anti-Nazi Confessional Church, the "church within the Church" which is the most vigorous and numerous branch of German Protestantism. In mid-1950, when Pastor Mochalski, Secretary of the Confessional Church Council, established the Darmstadt Action Groups against remilitarization, the movement spread from the Darmstadt Institute of Technology to the Universities of Frankfurt, Mainz, Heidelberg, Tübingen, and Freiburg. Americans who were "warned" by the United States Consul in Frankfurt to keep away from this "Communist-dominated outfit" and who asked to see the evidence were told, "That's impossible. The evidence is classified."

Notices of meetings of the Niemöller-Heinemann-Wessel group of Protestants and Catholics opposing militarization were torn down by culprits unknown. But in Kronenberg, late in 1952, huge posters appeared on the kiosks showing a hairy red hand, tattooed with the hammer and sickle, seizing the thin white arm of a woman, over the caption "*Deine Frau, Herr Ohne Mich!*" "Your Wife, Mr. 'I-Won't-Fight-in-the-Next-War'!" The source of the posters being unknown, they would ordinarily have been confiscated by the police. But they weren't. "We are used to this, too," said my friend, the exchange student. "It may be that this poster was left over in Dr. Goebbels' storeroom."

Cynicism, the deepest cynicism, in Germany, among a people who, rather than believe in nothing, will turn to the most fantastic of faiths; cynicism among the young people, and youth is the time for ideals. Not that their elders were any less cynical, but, then, age is the time for disenchantment. "I suppose," said my friend Klingelhöfer, the cabinetmaker, "that the Occupation law 'for the de-Nazification and demilitarization of Germany' is repealed, now that we are to be remilitarized. Are we to be re-Nazified, too?"

Were they? A transition had set in among the Germans, a transition from the view that the American Way was, perhaps, better than their own to the view that the American Way was very good, indeed, but no better than theirs. The German press, controlled as it was by the Occupation, expressed itself by the amount of space it gave news, and it gave an extraordinary amount of space to the development of "McCarthyism" in the United States and especially to the incursion of book-burning into the libraries of the *Amerika-Häuser*. The bolder newspapers expressed themselves editorially, the anti-Communist *Münchner Merkur* nominating Senator McCarthy for honorary membership in the Communist Party and the anti-Communist

Weser-Kurier saying that Goebbels would have appreciated the Wisconsin Senator. "We in Germany," said the anti-Communist *Mannheimer Morgen*, "are fed up with what we had last time, when a whole party of McCarthys tried to control our thinking."

Some Germans were born yesterday; not all of them.

## CHAPTER 31

## Tug of Peace

The new German joke was: "How do the Germans feel about the situation?"—"Well, how does a bone feel between two dogs?" Pressure, once more, new pressure on top of all the old pressures unrelieved by war, destruction, and defeat. The Nazi rallying cry had been, "Germany, awaken!" Now the Americans and the Russians were crying the same cry. In time the Germans would yield to the new pressures. It would certainly be easier to re-re-educate Germans to militarism than to re-educate them away from it. "I wish," said a German pastor, "that we Germans didn't believe so *easily*."

The consequences of the pressure, of being needed, wanted, for war again, of being wooed wherever they went, they who so recently had been the world's untouchables, can only be guessed at; but they can be guessed at. "The German tragedy," said Reinhold Schneider, one of Germany's great living men of letters, "is as deep as ever. It is that nothing can be regarded as having a life of its own. Everything—whether music, or art, or religion, or literature —is judged almost exclusively on its conceivable political bearing. The most tortured and far-fetched conclusions are drawn from productions that were only created out of the urge to create or, if they had a goal, to enhance the outreach of the human spirit. Of course I am aware of the social responsibility of the artist, but to go over to the Marxist thesis, as the West seems to be doing, that everything is only an incident to a great political, and ultimately economic, movement is to sell out something that will impoverish the world, certainly to sell out that early hope that something new in the human plastic might emerge out of Germany's pain."

That was one way of putting it, but there were not many putting it that way. There were more who saw remilitarization as the only way to sovereignty; these were the nationalists. There were more who saw it as the way to professional activity; these were the ex-officers. There were more who saw it as the way to a job; these were the unemployed. And there were some ten million "expellees" (nobody had ever bothered to count them) forced into post-Nazi Germany from the liberated countries by the victors who decided at Potsdam that Hitler was right, after all: there was such a thing as a "German race," and its members, classified at Potsdam as "German ethnics," would have to live in Germany. The "expellees" were an immense and ever growing force for war against Russia as their only hope of getting back home.

Growing, too, among the Germans, was the most intense pressure of all, the pressure to reunite their country, infinitely more intense than the pressure to regain the lost colonies in the twenties. West (and East) Germans had no relatives in German West Africa, but they all had relatives in East (and West) Germany. A new Hitlerism, if it arose in West Germany, would need only one plank in its platform: reunification. In 1953 the West Germans re-elected a Chancellor who told them, à l'Américaine, "We talk a lot about unification. Let us talk of liberation." But, when any speaker in Germany, West or East, used the word *Einheit*, unity, no matter how he used it, he was interrupted by wild, *Sports-Palast*–like cheering.

Unfortunately, *Einheit* was an old Nazi term, too. Still more unfortunately, *Einheit*, along with *Friede*, peace, was the slogan the hated Communists had painted on walls and billboards all over East Germany—on walls and billboards facing the West. The Germans, East and West, wanted the Americans out of Germany—five minutes after the Russians were out. But the Russians, who lost 17,000,000 people in the last war, would not get out, and neither would the Americans, who did not want to lose 17,000,000 people in the next one. The Occupation—West as well as East—was a matter of might. Might was something the Germans could understand without being re-educated or reoriented.

The Germans in the East did not appear to believe that they would get both *Einheit* and *Friede* from the Russians. The Americans did not speak of *Einheit* and *Friede* to the Germans in the West. They spoke of *Verteidigung*, defense, and offered it free. Well, the Germans wanted defense, too, above all against "Bolshevism." But defense was the offer made them by their own government in 1914 and in 1939, and in 1914 and in 1939 defense meant war. The Germans did not want war. They did not want peace at any price, but they did not want war at the price of death, and that was the price, when they were allowed to think about it, that they thought they would have to pay.

The German dilemma was, perhaps, most acute in Germany, but it wasn't really a German dilemma; it was the dilemma of Europe. If defense meant death, one had to consider defense very seriously. But the Germans could see the dilemma most acutely, because they could see that the Americans and the Russians were agreed that, if they had to fight each other, they would both prefer to do it in Germany. The Germans could see that, wherever the third World War ended, it would begin where they were, and their broken stones would be reduced to dust.

In the re-election of the conservative coalition of Adenauer in 1953, the central issue was the economy. Almost half the Bonn budget was going for social services; one-fifth of the population was directly supported by the State on pensions or doles. Still, the day after V-E Day, five-fifths were unsupported by anybody, and in 1953 the Germans were not in the mood to shoot even a thin Santa Claus. In the fall elections of 1954 the mood had changed—or, rather, the focus. Everywhere, even in Catholic Bavaria, Adenauer lost support and lost it radically. What had happened? What had happened was that the "European Defense Community," with its façade of an international army, had collapsed, and the Adenauer Government, under the most intense pressure from the United States, was trying to deliver a German Army, complete with a German General Staff, under the new "London Agreement."

The phoenix was dragging its talons. Professor Hans Morgenthau, of the University of Chicago, returned from a visit to his native land in the summer of 1954 and reported that he had raised the question of German rearmament "with scores of all kinds of people. I found only one man who came out in favor of it, and he is closely identified with the Adenauer Government." He added that "all four living ex-chancellors of Germany, representing the most diverse colors of the political spectrum from the extreme right of Papen to the extreme left of Wirth, have declared their opposition to the Western orientation of the Bonn regime." In the winter of 1954–55 the West German "Security Commissioner" was having the greatest difficulty in persuading young men to register voluntarily for the when-

and-if "defense force." At a mass meeting in Cologne, the magazine *U.S. News & World Report* said that the Security Commissioner "found more conscientious objectors than anything else. A check in key areas of West Germany indicates that the attitude of the young men at Cologne is typical of much of the country. Hardly anyone signs up. Antimilitarism suddenly has become one of the most popular political issues."

"Conscientious objectors" to volunteering are not, of course, conscientious objectors to conscription. "Actually," *U.S. News & World Report* concluded, "nobody in West Germany seriously doubts any more that the country will have an army by one means or another. But it is becoming apparent that the German soldiers of the future will be very different from the German troops who went to war in 1870, 1914, and 1939." "Fight?" said one of those anonymous officials with whom I spoke in Berlin. "Of course the Germans will fight. But they will fight a tired war, the way the French fought in 1940."

The Germans want, not at all oddly, to live. They would like to live well, but in any case they would like to live, well or badly. Their attitude may be unheroic; they ought, perhaps, to prefer dying on their feet to living on their knees. But they don't; and, unlike us, who have had neither experience, they have had both. What we, who have never been slaves, call slavery, they, who have always been what we call slaves, find less abhorrent than death. They hate Communism—under that name—but they do not love what we call liberty enough to die for it. If they did, they would have died for it against Hitler.

Americans who saw the love of liberty in the East-West refugee traffic and the East German riots needed to remind themselves that these same East Germans lived under totali-

## CHAPTER 32

# "Are We the Same as the Russians?"

The nineteenth century of Europe left untouched only three great bulwarks of autocracy—Russia, Prussia, and Austria. These were, in the phrase of the time, the three eastern great powers, in which the pattern of postfeudal absolutism, serving an agrarian and military nobility, with a subservient church appended, still survived in the West. German royalty's predilection for France and England—and its intermarriage with the latter's ruling house—gave the world an easy impression of Western orientation, which was fortified by the spectacular industrialization of the new Reich under Bismarck. But the perennial preoccupation of German scholarship with Russia (and vice versa) might have been a better clue to the future of Europe than the didoes of court society.

Russia (whose history has been epitomized as the search for a warm-water port) and Germany are the two have-nots, subjectively, with a long history of like, and co-operative, behavior, beginning with their postmedieval continental colonization (including a half-dozen amiable partitions of Poland) and their failure (or inability) to colonize abroad. Bismarck's support of Russia's Black Sea ambitions; the German General Staff's support of the October Revolution; Rapallo; the Molotov-Ribbentrop Pact—all these are seen, quite rightly, as German policy in a perpetual pincers situation. But German-Russian relations have always been happier than the relations of either one with the other European great powers. Behind the events of the immediate past are five centuries of remarkably peaceful penetration of the western Slav world by German traders and agriculturists and the concomitant Slavic influence on the East Prussian and Silesian temperaments.

We are late in discovering the essential resemblance of Communism and Nazism, diverted perhaps by the "advanced" condition of the Germans, perhaps by the confusion of Soviet Communism with democratic socialism; perhaps by both. But the circulatory course of anti-Semitism—from fourteenth century Germany to Russia (via the partitioning of Poland at the end of the eighteenth century), from Russia to Austria in the nineteenth, and from Austria back to Germany in the twentieth—should itself have been a sign of the singular congeniality of the Pan-German and Pan-Russian nationalisms. But it was not until the 1930's, when National Socialism overcame Germany, that we discovered, to our amazement, that the aboriginal "folk family," the herd sense of the tribe, was as deeply set in the Germans as it was in the Russians.

Some of the Germans have not discovered it yet. In Hamburg I was meeting with a group of students, and the discussion turned to Russia. "You don't know the Russians," said one of the students, addressing, apparently, not just me but the group generally. "I say that you do not know the Russians. I do. They have no idea of freedom. They would not know how to use it if they had it. They are a primitive, animal-like people. They simply have no conception of humanity or of human rights. I had a friend who was in a

Russian concentration camp. What they do there is hideous. You wouldn't believe it." Another student spoke up: "I had a friend who was in a German concentration camp. What they did there was hideous. You wouldn't believe it." The first student was enraged. "Are you saying," he shouted, "that we are the same as the Russians?"

## CHAPTER 33

# Marx Talks to Michel

"When two Russians fight," so the joke goes, "they tear each other's clothes off and then shake hands. When two Germans fight, they kill each other, but there won't be a button missing." The German's bourgeois development came late—the Russian's never—and his private property sense is as overdeveloped as a child's. But the Thirty Years' War of 1914–45 has proletarianized this man of private property, especially the bourgeoisie. In the inflation of 1945–48, as in 1919–23 (when, however, the retailers with stocks survived), the farmer not only held his own but traded food for whatever he wanted, and there were "Persian rugs in pigsties." Then the currency reform, on both occasions, hit the farmer, and his downward course began to follow that of the bourgeoisie.

The higher bourgeois were the first and the hardest and the most persistently proletarianized. They may not know it yet; Herr Doctor Schmidt or Herr Lawyer Schmidt or Herr Professor Schmidt or Herr Architect Schmidt or Herr Engineer Schmidt still has his professional title, and his title is property, as it is nowhere else in the Western world. But he has no real property, no tangible stake left in the social order. He has nothing to sell but his labor. Marx is talking to him.

A university department head in Kronenberg had no hot

water and no central heat in his four-room apartment, with a household of four adults and two children. Eight years and more after the war his family still gladly accepted gifts of used clothing, the crumbs of charity. I see him now, sifting his pipe dottle, looking for unburned flakes; I see his wife using tea leaves a second time, a third time, a fourth time. In a year in Kronenberg I encountered only one owner of a private automobile, and not one refrigerator. Eggs were sold by the unit; who had money to invest in a dozen at a time, or a place to keep them fresh?

In our older boy's class, the sixth grade, in a school in our bourgeois, nonindustrial, county-seat town in a fertile valley, 10 per cent of the children were, eight years after the war, going to school without breakfast; the next 10 per cent had unspread bread; the next 10 per cent, bread with a nonfat spread; and only the top 30 per cent had any kind of milk or milk-substitute drink under their belts. Our younger boy, in the first grade, brought his new friend Bienet home with him and gave him a banana. Bienet ate the banana—and the skin.

And all this was in "recovery" Germany, West Germany, where the living standard had always been higher than it was in the East and was now, of course, very much higher. And in a small town surrounded by woods, in this "recovery" Germany, only kitchens were heated in winter for want of a few cents for kindling. My Nazi friend, young Schwenke, recommended to me a cigarette-rolling machine with a cloth, rather than a plastic, roller; I asked him why he himself used the machine with the plastic roller; it was because it cost two and a half cents less than the other.

Of course there were mink coats in Düsseldorf, the *Rouge-et-Noir* (as the Germans call it) was packed day and night at Baden-Baden, and there were block-long Mercedes

331

limousines in Berlin. But, when the limousines had gone by, one might see the men, young men, middle-aged men, old men, going through the garbage cans (as if there were anything edible to be found in a German garbage can!). Nowhere was the assertion challenged that the spread between wealth and poverty in West Germany was much greater than it had been under the Nazis.

"Production is 150 per cent of prewar." But what is important is what is produced and where it goes. What was being produced in "recovery" Germany was not domestic consumer goods; machine tools are hard on the teeth. The soaring West German economy was an artifact, a political, cold-war, pump-priming operation like the soaring (if not so high) East German economy. To pile up the gold and dollar balance, tax concessions (paid ultimately by Michel, the standard chump of German comedy) were given exporters. Some of the units of the I.G. Farben chemical combine, broken up after the war, were bigger than ever; one typewriter manufacturer was exporting to one hundred and thirty-nine countries.

"Production is 150 per cent of prewar." But of Volkswagen's twenty thousand employees (including executives), only 2 per cent could afford to drive the cars they were making. In "150 per cent" 1953, the West German industrial wage was less than one-fourth of the American, the standard of living 15 per cent below that of armaments-saddled France, the per capita consumption of meat (which was unrationed) lower than austerity England's (which was rationed). The "150 per cent" was not going to the fifty million West Germans.

Since the end of the war, Germany, the only nation in Europe which did not enjoy the sovereign privilege of spending one-third to one-half its national budget on a military establishment, had constructed six times as many new housing units as "victorious" France; but it was still short four million units, and housing was still rationed to a maximum of one person per room. Unemployment figures, notoriously unreliable, ranged from a likely two million to an unlikely one million. There were no exact figures distinguishing part-time employment from employment and no exact figures on the ten million "expellees."

There were some simple distinctions which one might make—could not help making—by walking across the Potsdamer Platz in Berlin. In Communist East Berlin no worker was free—or unemployed; in Capitalist West Berlin one of every four workers was unemployed—but free. In Kronenberg, which had no heavy industry, unemployment of the normal working force (swelled by the "expellees") was 20 per cent in 1953, and an unemployed white-collar worker, with a family of four in one room, got a dole totaling $31.74 a month. He paid one-fourth our money price for rent, half our money price for food, and as much as we pay for all manufactured articles (including fuel and clothing). Our ten-cent bar of soap cost twenty-four cents in West Germany.

German men were coming down in money value as German materials went up; a shoemaker would work half an hour making repairs which did not require leather or rubber, and the bill would be twelve cents, but when he worked ten minutes putting on a pair of half-soles and heels, the bill was $2.50. The German people (not to be confused with German export and German industry) had not been rehabilitated. And they had not been rehabilitated by American aid. True, "they" had received three billion dollars in aid; true, too, they (without the quotation marks) had paid ten billion dollars in Occupation costs. And the aid, whatever forms it had taken and whichever persons it had reached, was, under the Marshall Plan and its successors, $28 per person in Germany, while it was $63 per person in England and $65 in France.

Whatever rehabilitation there was in Germany—the spectacular reconstruction not *of* the destroyed cities but *in* them—was the result of the back-breaking toil of seventy million German Michels. Tante Käthe, our housekeeper, was one of these Michels. "Work and save, Michel." Tante Käthe worked and saved. Twice she worked, and each time she saved close to $2,000, and each time, after 1918 and 1945, her $2,000 was inflated away. Tante Käthe, who reads and writes only the old German script, doesn't read or write much. She doesn't even know (any more than the shoemaker, whose materials are worth more than he is) that Marx is talking to her.

The German's acute property sense and his acute security sense have been at war within him during this whole second Thirty Years' War of 1914–45. The security sense is winning. The development of German anticapitalism was, at the turn of the century, phenomenal. In the first Reichstag, in 1871, the Social Democratic Party had two seats; in 1903, eighty-one; and before the first World War, with one hundred and ten seats, they were the strongest party in the country. In 1932 the anticapitalist forces held two-thirds of the Reichstag seats—the Left Center, the Social Democrats, the Communists, and the Nazis (the last receiving private support from German capital).

The dispossession of the German, especially of the middle class and most especially of the upper middle class, has been going on since the middle of the first World War, relentlessly, in "good" times and in "bad," moving toward completion. The propertyless Bürger does not cast his lot with the proletariat; but sooner or later his lot casts him. He lives (and, if he is old enough, dies) in his memories of *die goldene Zeit*, the golden time of the first Kaiserreich; but the grandchildren—it may be even the children—of this man have, without personal memory to sustain their illusions, lost them. When the situation has been bad enough long enough, there seems to be a neurotic incongruity, with only one entrance door for three families, in maintaining the hereditary doorplate with the family name engraved on it. So the grandson—or the son—takes it down. Marx is talking to him.

Marx doesn't care if, in this outbreak or that, or in this or that locality, he calls himself a Nazi, a Fascist, a Communist, a Nationalist, or an Odd Fellow. Marx is talking to the naked condition of his existence, not to the insignia in his lapel. "One hundred and fifty per cent of prewar" is the mumbo jumbo of dead financiers. Nothing costs money like war, whoever wins or loses. Nothing mass-produces proletarians like war, whoever wins or loses. Whoever wins or loses, Marx is talking to the man whose house and savings are gone, who has nothing to sell but his labor. Let the dead financiers talk of "150 per cent of prewar"; Marx knows that England and France, whose productive capacity, far from being destroyed, was scarcely touched, never recovered from the first World War. In the midst of the broken stones, the twisted steel, the burned-out shop, and the flooded mine stands the new proletarian: the German.

Remember—the Germans were rich once, by European standards, and now they are poor; so, subjectively, they are much worse off now than those who were always poor. They are approaching the point—no one knows where it is—where they will know that they are what they already are: proletarians. Between 1945 and 1955 it was costing Michel only

$155,000,000 a month to maintain the military forces that occupied his country; the minute he got his own military forces, that is, his "defense contribution" to "European defense," it would cost him $215,000,000 a month, just as a starter.

Michel hates Communism—*under that name*. But Hitler communized him, under National Socialism, and he never knew it. If this process of coming down in the world—not of *being* down but of *coming* down—continues, Michel will embrace some new, as yet unconceived "anti-Communism." But it will be Communism, just as National Socialism was, but more advanced in so far as materials, rising in value as men's value falls, are increasingly available only in collective form. And there is no reason, when the hatred of 1941–45 dies away, why this Communism (called, perhaps, "anti-Communism") should not be Russian, or Russian-German, a third Rapallo of the have-nots, who, like all have-nots, dream of being have-alls. There is, of course, the chance (on which Churchill bet and lost once) that the parties to the third Rapallo may destroy one another; but this chance is ever the rich man's dream.

Bourgeois pride, the title, the doorplate, the bow the higher *Beamte* receives from the lower, stand between Germany and Russia, but the pride, the title, the doorplate, and the bow are coming down. What the Germans did in Russia in the late war—and what the Russians did in Germany afterward—stands between them, too. The slogans of anti-Communism, pounded into the Germans by the Nazi Government and later by the American Occupation, these, too, will live for a while. But Frederick the Great and Bismarck, looking eastward, will outlive both the Nazis and the American Occupation. "Everyone knows," said the realistic Walter Lippmann late in 1954, "that the pull within Germany toward such a deal"—between West Germany and the Soviet Union—"is bound to be very strong, and to become all the stronger as Germany acquires great military power in her own right. The Russians," he went on, "hold big assets for a deal with the Germans: unification, withdrawal of the Army of Occupation, rectification of the frontiers, resettlement of the expelled refugees, trade, and great political influence in the destiny of Europe." The realist might have been even more realistic and added that Marx is talking to more Germans today than in 1914—or in 1939.

## CHAPTER 34

## The Uncalculated Risk

The way to relieve the pressure is to relieve the pressure. If, at whatever cost, the salvation of Germany, and therefore of Europe, and therefore of civilization, must be achieved, the test of every measure must be the test urged by the late Prime Minister of India: "Does it add to tension or not?" The Occidental who deplores the renunciation of both right *and* might implied here must narrow his eyes to an Oriental squint and keep them on the ball. If the Germans make the rest of the world suffer because they themselves suffer, and if they themselves suffer because they are under pressure, why, the first thing to do is to get the pressure off them. Niceties such as right and might must wait.

Take the pressure off them, and they might become insufferable. But they became insufferable with the pressure on them. Take the pressure off them, and they might claim that they won the last war. But that would be better than their claiming that they will win the next war. Take the pressure off them, and they might rearm. But they always have anyway. Take the pressure off them, and they might go Communist. But they did go Nazi.

The trouble is that the relief of the Germans would require something like the prior reconstruction of the world. To initiate—even to contemplate—a program of relief, there would have to be the kind of world that did not react to the proposal by asking, rhetorically, if the Germans are to be coddled for their crimes and paid off for losing the wars they started. It would have to be a world that could see beyond the end of its nose and turn that nose—together with the rest of its face—from the past to the future. It would have to be a world with—a *Weltanschauung*.

To say that this is not the kind of world we live in, or are soon likely to, would be to supererogate. A world that was disposed to relieve the Germans of pressure would have to be a world that itself was not under pressure, a world that breathed freely. So far are we from living in such a world that the two powers now dividing the world there is are both falling victim to the paranoid panic which brought Germany to its present pass, both of them sacrificing all other objectives to encircle their encirclers. In this one respect, at least, has Goebbels' perverse prediction been validated: "Even if we lose, we shall win, for our ideals will have penetrated the hearts of our enemies."

In such a world—the world we live in—such dreams as a United States of Europe are no further advanced in Europe than World Federalism is here. The Europa Union movement, in Germany as elsewhere, is widespread among, and only among, nongovernmental intellectuals, and especially among the young. At the University of Munich 88 per cent of the students, in a random sampling, favored "the unification of Europe" over "German sovereignty." But "the unification of Europe" means different things to different men —to some peace, to others war. And it is an ideal much more nebulous, and much more limited, than democracy. In the context of the world struggle, European Union means, first, military union of non-Communist Europe; second, economic union (presently supported by both the young idealists and the old cartelists); and last, if ever, political union. And any union that left Germany divided would take place only on paper, if there.

There may be a possibility that the relief of the Germans would interest the Russians, who, after all, invented Russian roulette. As the Germans now are, the Russians are afraid of them, and with good reason. "It is now clear," said the London *Times* in 1954, "that neither Russia nor the West can agree to German unification on terms compatible with their national interests. The linch-pin of Western defense—West German cooperation—remains the hard core of Russian fears. And the main Western anxiety—Russian armies in the heart of Europe—is, in the Russian view, the indispensable condition of Soviet security. In the state of the world today, neither fear can be discounted as mere propaganda."

In such a state of such a world, it might be that the United States of America, by seizing the initiative and proposing German reunification on other than nonnegotiable terms, would have to sacrifice its immediate national interest in order to satisfy the Russians that their own interests would be served (or at least not disserved) by agreement. If such a thing has never before been done—if a nation has never sacrificed its immediate national interest in order to advance that of another—it might be done for the first time in history on the utopian basis that the relief of the Germans, at whatever sacrifice of immediate national interest, would create the possibility of saving civilization.

The cure of the Germans will not be free in any case, nor is it guaranteed by any prescription. If Germany is thought of—as it seems to be now, and mistakenly—as somebody's satellite, nobody will bother to do anything about it except to prepare it for war, including civil war. And war is not good for the Germans. Only if the interested great powers decide that ultimate self-interest is more interesting than immediate self-interest will they be interested in relieving the Germans of pressure. But it would not do at all to have the great powers undertake the relief themselves; the quick switch from exploitation disguised (unsuccessfully) as benevolence to a program of genuine benevolence would only mystify the Germans.

After many, many years of thinking it over, and at very close range, Mr. McCloy, the retired United States High Commissioner for the Occupation of Germany, came to the conclusion that it might have been helpful to have had neutrals sit on the bench at Nuremberg in 1946. There were those who, in 1946, suggested a neutral tribunal at Nuremberg, but they were not listened to, and it is now too late to listen to them. But it is not too late to listen to those who now suggest that neutrals sit on the border in Berlin.

The disadvantages to the West—or to the United States—of finding a way to reunite Germany would be immense. A unified Germany, although it would be anti-Communist, would be Socialist, because four-fifths of the East Germans are Social Democrats; and there are some Americans who do not like Socialism. In addition, the "abandonment" of Germany would mean loss of face for the United States, a prospect most obnoxious to Occidentals. Worst of all, it would mean the surrender of the whole present policy of containment by force—at least in Europe—and the whole present ambition of liberation by subversion and insurrection. It would mean that wherever and however Communist expansion would be stopped—assuming that such things are stoppable by military means—it would not be stopped by war on the Vistula, the Oder, the Elbe, or the Rhine. It would mean that Europe could not be "held."

But the alternative prospect of having to depend upon

the Germans to "hold" it is not attractive, either. The Germans have not been—and are not going to be, in the next six months or six years—transformed from first-class totalitarians to first-class freemen. When we remember what most of them so recently and habitually were, or at least did, it seems hardly worth the trouble, if the Germans must save us, to be saved from Communism.

In this lugubrious circumstance, a circumstance in which any program of real relief is, perhaps, so unrealistic as to be unworthy of consideration, there are, nevertheless, a few things that the United States could at least avoid doing without being accused of utopianism. On the eve of the German election of 1953, a *New York Times* headline said, "U.S. Scans Food Aid for East Germans. Weighs Plan To Ship Surplus Stocks To Help Adenauer and Embarrass Russians." Two weeks later Dean Heinrich Grüber of the Berlin Protestant Cathedral told his congregation: "When a charitable project is undertaken without the true spirit of love, the blessing turns into a curse. We will gladly co-operate with those who work to relieve hardship, provided only that they do so without mental reservations and without devious intentions. But we refuse to co-operate with those persons or powers who use works of charity to disguise their political and propaganda warfare."

No nation gorged with unmarketable surpluses in a starving world will ever relieve another by exploiting the other's hunger for a couple of weeks to win an election. And a nation which, as a matter of public policy, attempts to do so attempts to do what it shouldn't. Neither the *New York Times* headline nor Dean Grüber's sermon was broadcast by the "Voice of America"; it is not nearly so hard to find ways to take the pressure off the Germans as it is to want to.

The story is told—apocryphal, we may hope—that a friend

of John Dewey's encountered him on the street one day long ago in wet windy weather, with his little boy. The boy was standing, rubberless, in a puddle of water, and Dewey was watching him from the shore. "You'd better get that child out of that puddle," said the friend, "or he'll catch pneumonia." "I know," said the philosopher. "I'm doing it as fast as I can. I'm trying to figure out a way to get him to want to get out." It does not seem likely that the United States Government will take a chance on the Germans' catching pneumonia. It has their health—not to say its own —to consider. If our government cannot, for reasons of State, demonstrate democracy to the Germans, in the hope that the Germans will take to it some day, private agencies may still try. There is no law, German or American, to prevent the construction of, say, a *Vereinigte-Staaten-Haus* across the street from every *Amerika-Haus* in Germany. There are plenty of vacant lots. *Amerika-Haus* would advertise, FREE LECTURE, and *Vereinigte-Staaten-Haus* would advertise, FREE DEBATE.

Children misbehave under pressure. The greater the pressure, the worse the misbehavior. The affected child may be the quiet type, but one day he burns the whole house down. If we are his parents, we may relieve him by ignoring his minor depredations; by setting him a good example; and, if possible, by loving him. In so far as he recognizes the parental authority—but only in so far as he does so—he may be gently controlled. The Germans do not recognize our parental authority, however well behaved they may be, and the danger of acting on false analogy is considerable. What is more, their depredations are rarely minor, and it is not always easy to love them. But the cure is probably somewhat the same. At least, beating the Germans has had the same consequences as beating the child.

America has a great name in Germany; it used lovingly to be called "Little Germany" among the Germans, and every one of my ten Nazi friends had one or more relatives, no further removed than second cousin or uncle, who had emigrated to the United States. It may not be arrogant to assume that the Germans look to us, even now, for light. If they do, it would be nice if we Americans could manifest some of the compassion that relieves the compulsive child. It appears that the big things that ought to be done cannot, for reasons of State, be done, even if the failure to do them means the ruin of the State. It may be all the more urgent, then, to do the little things; and St. Francis' words, "I come to you in little things," may still be the clue to the cure of the Germans.

But maybe nothing can be done for the Germans, in which case, whatever anyone else does, we should let them alone. The proposition that anybody can do anything about anybody else is absolutely indemonstrable. Doctors of the body abound, but there are no doctors of the soul, or psyche. A great psychoanalyst once pointed proudly to a former patient and said: "He used to be the unhappiest rotter in town. Now he's the happiest." It may very well be impossible for one whole people, except by their example, to help another whole people transform their character; and that may be why, until 1945, it was never attempted. But a one-tenth-of-one-per-cent chance is one-tenth of one per cent better than no chance at all. It is risky to let people alone. But it is riskier still to press my ten Nazi friends—and their seventy million countrymen—to re-embrace militarist anti-Communism as a way of national life.

## Acknowledgments

I am indebted to a very great many persons, none of whom may be charged with any responsibility for any of the things I have said in this book:

My friends who thought I might learn a little *something* in Germany, especially Robert M. Hutchins, then of the University of Chicago; Gilbert White and Douglas Steere, of Haverford College; A. J. Muste, of the Fellowship of Reconciliation; and Morris H. Rubin, editor of *The Progressive*.

My colleagues at the Institut für Sozialforschung, Frankfurt University, especially Professor Frederick Pollock, whose "baby" I was and who goaded and guided me, cried over me, prayed for me, and apologized for me from start to finish.

My two ardent assistants ("slaves" would be better) in Kronenberg, Frau Eva Hermann and Frau Martha Koch.

My three ardent friends in Kronenberg, Fräulein Dr. Gisela Prym, Dr. Leonora Balla Cayard, and Horstmar Stauber.

John K. Dickinson, of Cambridge, Massachusetts (and of Kronenberg), who, as I go through my notes, seems to have done all the research that went into this book; and the late Frederick Lewis Allen, of New York City, who, as I go through the manuscript, seems to have done all the writing in the course of preparing sections of the book for serialization in *Harper's Magazine* in 1954.

Professor Robert H. Lowie, of the University of California, whose remarkable study, *The German People: A Social Portrait to 1914* (New York: Rinehart & Co., 1945), was the richest of the many treasures of other writers that I plundered.

My friends in Carmel and Monterey, California, Isabel Devine, Louise van Peski, Janet Farr, Marion Chamberlain, Liesel Wurzmann, Fritz Wurzmann, Charles Mohler, Harlan Watkins, Ephraim Doner, Francis Palms, Dr. Bruno Adriani, and the late R. Ellis Roberts.

Robert C. McNamara, Jr., of Chicago.

My daughter Julie, who set my fractured German, especially in Heine and the Talmud.

My mother, who thought I might learn a little something somewhere.

Mutti, my wife.